North Sea Saga

North Sea Saga

Paul Jordan

PEARSON
Longman

Harlow, England • London • New York • Boston • San Francisco • Toronto
Sydney • Tokyo • Singapore • Hong Kong • Seoul • Taipei • New Delhi
Cape Town • Madrid • Mexico City • Amsterdam • Munich • Paris • Milan

PEARSON EDUCATION LIMITED

Edinburgh Gate
Harlow CM20 2JE
United Kingdom
Tel: +44 (0)1279 623623
Fax: +44 (0)1279 431059
Website: www.pearsoned.co.uk

First edition published in Great Britain in 2004

© Pearson Education Limited 2004

The right of Paul Jordan to be identified as author
of this work has been asserted by him in accordance
with the Copyright, Designs and Patents Act 1988.

ISBN 0 582 77257 5

British Library Cataloguing in Publication Data
A CIP catalogue record for this book can be obtained from the British Library

Library of Congress Cataloging in Publication Data
A CIP catalog record for this book can be obtained from the Library of Congress

10 9 8 7 6 5 4 3 2 1

Set by 3 in 10 pt Galliard
Printed in China
PPLC/01

The Publishers' policy is to use paper manufactured from sustainable forests.

Contents

List of maps, figures and plates

Maps

Figure

Plates

(In central plate section)

Acknowledgements

We are grateful to the following for permission to reproduce copyright material:

Charles Tait and Shetland Islands Tourism for Plate 55; David Collison for Plates 31, 33, 50 and 54; Diego Metozzi for Plate 53; Netherlands Tourist Board for Plate 35; Hans Hammarskiöld and the Vasa Museum for Plate 25; Hull Maritime Museum for Plate 27; Institute of Archaeology, Oxford for Plate 13; Jim Henderson AMPA ARPS for Plate 51; John Sayer for Plate 47; JTH Consulting for Plates 14, 15, 36, 37, 38, 39 and 40; National Museum, Denmark for Plates 1, 5, 7, 11 and 12; Norfolk Museums and Archaeology Service for Plates 3 and 45; PA Photos for Plate 30; Ray Sutcliffe for Plates 9, 17, 18, 19 and 20; St. Edmundsbury Borough Council/West Stow Anglo-Saxon Village Trust for Plate 16; Tyne & Wear District Museums for Plate 49.

Figure 1 from 'Doggerland: a speculative survey' in *Proceedings of the Prehistoric Society*, Vol. 64, reprinted by permission of the Prehistoric Society (Coles, B.J. 1998). Maps 4a, 4b, 4c and 4d adapted from 'Doggerland: a speculative survey' in *Proceedings of the Prehistoric Society*, Vol. 64, reprinted by permission of the Prehistoric Society (Coles, B.J. 1998).

In some instances we have been unable to trace the owners of copyright material, and we would appreciate any information that would enable us to do so.

Introduction

A s seas go, the North Sea it is not an ancient one. On the geological timescale, it is only a few thousand years old in its present form: even its parent body of water, as it were, the mighty Atlantic is young among the oceans of the world. As to the name by which most of us know it today, the fact is that our 'North Sea' has been called by several different names even in the recent past and only achieved its present title, by more-or-less common consent, in the early part of the last century.

The name of the sea

When the ice melted and the glaciers retreated and sea levels rose at the close of the ice age, it was then that people really came to occupy the quite rapidly changing world around – and, for a long time, across – what would become the North Sea of modern times. We don't know the languages that people were speaking from ten thousand years ago or by what names they knew the major rivers and all the creeks and ponds of their postglacial world, nor what they might have called the great sea in the north that gradually pushed them south-west and south-east over the postglacial millennia. It is from much later on that we first pick up on any name for the expanse of ocean we now (most of us) call the North Sea: and when we do, the name reflects the outlook of people not native to the North Sea region. The Greek geographer Strabo, who settled in Rome in 29 BC, regarded the North Sea as simply a manifestation of the great ocean that was supposed to circle the entire land mass of the known world. The Roman historian

Tacitus, who took an interest in the tribal world to the north of the Roman Empire, called it not unreasonably the Northern Ocean, but without knowing or probably bothering what the various northern peoples (sketched in his *Germania* of AD 98) might call it for themselves. This sea was north of the world to which Tacitus belonged and that was enough to identify it. With this title, Tacitus pioneered a long-lasting if intermittently employed naming of the North Sea that has triumphed in the end, with 'sea' preferred to 'ocean' as the true, huge oceans of the globe came into human ken.

The Roman writer Pliny of the first century AD and the Greek-Egyptian scholar Ptolemy of the second referred to the German Sea and German Ocean respectively, thus initiating the other persistent styling that only went out of fashion for good in the early part of the last century. Ptolemy's influence on medieval and early modern map-makers saw to it that the German association stuck, but the ambivalence about sea or ocean caused at least one map-maker to reserve *oceanus* for the North Sea and *mare* for the Baltic, whilst calling them both 'German'. Not unnaturally, Latin was soon translated into German and our North Sea appeared in the vernacular as 'Das Gros Teutsch Mer' on another German map. Mercator, on his famous maps of the late sixteenth century, used both German Sea and Ocean but always in Latin, for all his own German origins. The trading power of the German cities of the Hanseatic League, about which we shall hear much later in this book, did a great deal to help impose common usage of the German designation.

There were occasional efforts to get away from the German connection. The atlas of the Antwerp cartographer Abraham Ortelius, published at the end of the sixteenth century, claims Pliny as an authority for Northern Ocean and British Ocean, while a Danish scholar (Claudius Clavus) a century-and-a-half before floated 'Cimbric' on his map, taking his cue from the Roman version of an old tribal name for people living in Jutland. Sometimes Renaissance map-makers might call the waters close to Britain by the name of British, but the Britannic Sea almost always meant the English Channel.

The Normans and the Swedes of old used the adjective 'Western' to identify our North Sea and the Danes still do: because, of course, it is to the west of them. It makes the Danes the odd men out today when everyone else has settled for North Sea. The Dutch appear to have adopted this usage (after toying with 'Western' too) back in the early days of late medieval and

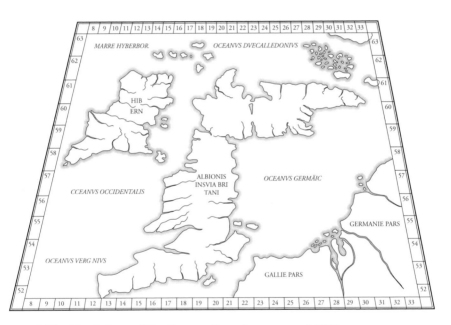

Map 1 The North Sea as 'The German Ocean' on a map of 1522

Renaissance map-making; they are, indeed, a people for whom the North Sea is decidedly to their north. And, just as the backing of the Hanseatic League favoured the German Ocean, so the naval eminence of the Dutch from the seventeenth century encouraged the widespread if gradual adoption of their name for the North Sea. (The French allowed 'Danish' as well as 'German' in the eighteenth and nineteenth centuries.)

A cartographic situation set in where both German and North were rather arbitrarily assigned to our sea: sometimes both together as, for example, *Mare Germanicum vulgo Noord Zee*, at the same time as the Baltic could become *Mare Balticum vulgo De Oost Zee*. (The Germans still call the Baltic the East Sea.) American maps were liable to use both North and German quite evenly, and British and German atlases of the nineteenth century did the same. It was the First World War that not surprisingly put an end to any British indulgence in the German option. More surprisingly, German cartography fell in line in the 1920s, leaving nowadays only the Danes to persevere with, from their point of view, their perfectly reasonable alternative.

At least the purely positional namings have the merit of giving the sea over to no one nationality and offering us a neutral and objective name for a body of water around which so many cultures, languages and ethnicities have come and gone over the eight thousand years or so since the North Sea was formed and people were able to come and live all around its shores – and for a long while, at the beginning, to live on what is now the bed of its southerly part.

The geological background

Structurally, the area of the North Sea is part of the lowland between the old, hard mountains of Scotland and Scandinavia and the not-so-old and softer hills of southern England, the Low Countries and northern Germany. The basic configuration of this lowland region has been in place since volcanic activity in Eocene times, some fifty million years ago, which resulted in the lava flows of western Scotland, the ash beds of northern Denmark and the zone of consolidated ash encountered in North Sea wells. (Our knowledge of North Sea geology has benefited greatly from drilling for oil and gas.) The Eocene volcano or volcanoes may have been in the Skagerrak or along the Norwegian coast, and the sea was evidently calm enough for wind-blown ash to settle pretty evenly on what is now the bed of the North Sea. A distant forerunner of today's North Sea was in place by Miocene times, twenty million or so years ago, with a channel connecting it to the Atlantic. That channel was not the English Channel of today, but an older geological formation of which the Severn Estuary is a modern manifestation. The Miocene was an epoch of real mountain building (which took in the Alps and Himalayas) but it was a more modest land rise that closed the channel between the old Atlantic and the old 'North Sea', ousting warm water life forms from the latter and replacing them with organisms favouring colder seas.

The raising of the land saw to it that in subsequent Pliocene times the old 'North Sea' retreated northwards and was replaced by a wide plain, with an old version of the Thames flowing north at this time as a tributary of an old Rhine to empty into the sea at a rather higher latitude than today, about 400 km north of where London is now located. Prototypes of others of the great rivers that run into the North Sea today – the Elbe, Weser, Ems, Scheldt and Humber rivers, among others – were also involved in this Pliocene network of outflows across what is today the very shallow southern half of our North Sea. The erosion of their beds, now submerged, accounts for some of the deeper trenches and holes in the otherwise never very deep North Sea, like the Silver Pit off the Wash – about 100 m – or the considerably deeper Devil's Hole off Edinburgh – 500 m or more. (The 300 m deep Outer Silver Pit, interestingly, has been tentatively attributed to a minor asteroid strike of sixty to sixty-five million years ago.)

During the glacially cold episodes of the Pleistocene Period, of the last million years or so, there was no North Sea at all. The glaciers spread south over all of north-west Europe and the precipitation thus removed from normal circulation in the world's weather systems – to be locked up in the glaciers' ice – no longer ran off into the oceans, which suffered a consequent loss of volume with falling sea levels everywhere. Even during the warm interglacial periods, which brought rising sea levels (until the glaciers grew again), it looks as though the land now under the North Sea sometimes remained substantially above sea level, connecting today's Britain and northern France to today's Netherlands, Germany, Denmark and Norway. During full interglacial periods, as warm as or warmer than today, Britain did experience insularity, as was the case in the Last Interglacial before the onset of the Last Glaciation.

At the time of the ice sheets' greatest advance, the ice lay over the whole area of the North Sea reaching down to a line across from the Thames Estuary to the coast of Holland. The advance and retreat of the glaciers deposited a thick bed of clay on the floor of the North Sea to be. The Dogger Bank off the east coast of England, where waters can be as shallow as 15 to 30 m (and where fishing remains so rewarding) is the remains of a glacial moraine, made up of earth and stones carried along by the ice sheets of the Pleistocene as they moved over dry ground.

The Pleistocene, with all its climatic variability, is the most recent geological epoch before wholly recent times (the Holocene). In very distant times, hundreds of millions of years before the Pleistocene, processes were already at work that would create geological features of the future North Sea, deep below any ice-age clays and moraines, of long-hidden but now very great importance: the petroleum and natural gas resources that have been exploited over the past half-century. The crude oil and the gas are the results of the accumulation of the remains of tiny marine organisms among sands and silts at the bottom of quiet sea basins, under intense pressure (with consequent heating) as the deposits piled up. Mud and sand hardened into shale and sandstone, shells and carbonate precipitates solidified into limestone, and the organic remains were turned into oil and gas.

Current geography

Any map that shows ocean depths reveals very clearly the general shallowness – particularly in its southern part – of the North Sea today, which it shares with the waters of the English Channel and, indeed, of the Atlantic Ocean to the south-west and the south of Ireland and down into the Bay of Biscay: all parts of the continental shelf on which the British Isles sit. But in the north-east sector of the North Sea there is a depression far more extensive and sometimes deeper than the pits and holes encountered here and there in the rest of this sea. The Norwegian Trench, which began to open up in very distant times but in its present form is probably the result of glacial action, keeps its course parallel with the coast of Norway from north of Bergen right around to Oslo through the Skagerrak arm of the North Sea that leads eventually into the Baltic. In the Skagerrak, the Trench achieves depths of some 700 m on the Norwegian side.

The deeps of the Norwegian Trench are matched by the rugged elevations of the mountains (glaciated to this day) of Norway north of Stavanger, broken by their numerous fjords. To the south-west across the northern half of the North Sea, Scotland shows a similarly upland character, though less broken than Norway's. The coasts of the lower half of the sea become less precipitous, both in the southern part of Norway and down the western side of Jutland and also along the north-east coast of England. With the fens of East Anglia and the delta region of the Netherlands, very low ground is reached, some of it in both areas recovered from the sea by human agency and much of it at threat from submergence in tempestuous times without the constant efforts of the people who live there to keep it dry.

It was the warming of the world at the final close of the last ice age, from some ten thousand years ago, that melted the encroaching glaciers, raised the levels of the oceans and eventually flooded the low ground that once joined Britain to the Continent. The final flooding perhaps occurred quite suddenly during exceptional winter storms, with the connection of the Atlantic and North Sea via the English Channel forced through perhaps as late as 6000 BC. After that, the basic configuration of North Sea coasts as we know them today was not fully achieved until about 1000 BC – and many quite significant changes have been effected since then, which go on to this day. The action of the sea is responsible in quite recent times for many features of the East Anglian coast of Britain, like the long shingle spit of Orford Ness, diverting the River Alde, or the much reduced coastline at Dunwich and Cromer where whole settlements have vanished during the last millennium. Across the sea in the Netherlands, the former Zuider Zee ('South Sea') was itself an accidental enlargement of the North Sea that repeated the process of flooding whereby its parent had come into being thousands of years before. And the Waddenzee, immediately behind the Frisian Islands, was once a marsh behind a natural dyke: the marshes have become a very shallow muddy sea and the dyke has become the chain of islands. In other places, like the fenland around the Wash in England and the Ijsselmeer in Holland (what is left, in fact, of the Zuider Zee), human beings have reclaimed great areas of land from the waters since the general dimensions of the North Sea as we know it today were fixed.

With the establishment in full postglacial times of its modern shape and connections with other waters (the Atlantic, the Norwegian Sea and the

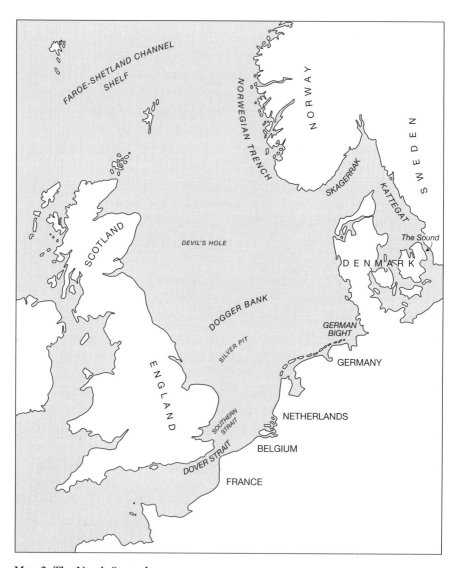

Map 2 The North Sea today

Baltic), the North Sea went on to achieve its present patterns of currents, temperatures, salinities and marine life. The North Atlantic current brings relatively warm waters into the North Sea via the English Channel and also, after passing up the western part of the British Isles, via the southernmost part of the Norwegian Sea round Orkney and the Shetlands, mingling with less warm waters from the north. Colder – and less salty waters – also come in from the Baltic through the Kattegat and Skagerrak. The circulation of waters in the North Sea that results from all these influences is counter-clockwise. A good deal of freshwater also finds its way in from the many rivers that flow into it.

Surface temperatures of the sea range in winter from 2 °C in the eastern parts to 8 °C between Norway and the Shetlands; in summer, the southern reaches can exceed 15 °C, while the northern area comes up to only about 12 °C. Air temperatures can run from 0–4 °C in winter to 13–18 °C in summer. Tides, generally rather irregular, average between 4 to 6 m along British coasts and less than 3 m on the north-eastern coasts of the Sea. In winter, the North Sea has always been known as a stormy place, and there can be rain and fog at all seasons. Sailing across it was never something that the seafarers of old chose to do lightly, and even coast-hugging could be hazardous among the shoals of some of its south-east coasts, especially those of Jutland.

The North Sea defined

Officially, the North Sea has been defined as the body of water that is con-tained south of latitude 62° N and east of longitude 5° W on its north-west side, north of latitude 58° 44.8′ N from the top of Denmark to the south coast of Sweden, and east of longitude 5° W and north of latitude 48° 30′ N at the south side. But this definition takes in the English Channel in the south and an area abutting the North Atlantic in the north-west that do not look on the map like natural parts of the North Sea, and it leaves out the Kattegat that rather does. In practice, we may take the North Sea to be that rhomboid of water, whose base line (with the bulge of Holland) runs from the Dover Strait and the Southern Bight north-east to the German Bight and the mouth of the Elbe, whose right side on the map goes up the west coast of Jutland with the eastward arm of the Skagerrak included to Oslo and Gothenburg (plus the Kattegat), then up the Norwegian coast to north of the opening of Sognefjord, whose top runs from there westwards across to the Shetlands along the shelf that borders the Faroe-Shetland Channel and whose left side drops from Orkney down the east coast of Britain back to Dover. That is an area of about 600,000 sq km, some 1000 km long and 640 km wide, involving, apart from open sea to the north, the southern coast of Norway, a short run of the south-east coast of Sweden, the northern and western coasts of Denmark, the north-western coast of Germany and the coasts that the Netherlands and Belgium possess, together with a minimal piece of French coast and all the eastern coastline of Britain with the Northern Isles. Our story of the human presence in the North Sea region won't often take us through the Dover Strait or into the Norwegian Sea, but it will take us through the Skagerrak into the Kattegat and the Sound on our way to and from the Baltic, whose history is at times very closely bound up with the North Sea's. It will also take us, of course, up some of the major rivers that flow into the North Sea, by which access can be gained deep inland (in the case of the Rhine, very deep – as far as Strasbourg).

The natural land habitats that border the North Sea, as well as the marine habitats of its different waters, show a great range of variation – as different as fjords and fens, with climates and associated flora and fauna that nowadays run from the subarctic to the warm temperate. Climate, weather, topography, vegetation, wildlife, life in the sea: all these natural features of the North Sea world come in very different guises in different places around it. They offer different possibilities of human exploitation and encourage different ways of life in different locations. Sheer physical separation of places imposes barriers and also invites communications: the North Sea is itself both a highway and an obstacle. And the whole scene is in flux, with changing people interacting in a changing world over the whole course of history and prehistory.

People first came to the general region of the North Sea in very distant times – if we contemplate the flint tools of Lower and Middle Palaeolithic epochs found south of latitude 55° (usually well south) in Britain and on the continent. These flints were knapped by the sort of evolving forms of humanity called *Homo heidelbergensis* and *H. sapiens neanderthalensis* (the latter better known as 'Neanderthal Man'). In their time, half-a-million to forty thousand years ago, there was often nothing that could be called a North Sea, as we have seen. When the first fully modern humans (*H. sapiens sapiens*), with their more sophisticated Upper Palaeolithic way of life, came to occupy caves in Britain and open sites in north-west Europe, the last ice age was still in full swing and the environs of the North Sea, together with the lands around it, were still either covered in ice or enjoying tundra conditions, with dry land across from southern Britain to France and the Low Countries. This is where the saga of human life in the region of the North Sea really begins.

Chapter 1

Rovers

U ntil the era of drilling for oil and gas in the second half of the last century, our knowledge of glacial and postglacial events within the confines of the North Sea itself was limited. The Dogger Bank was clearly of glacial origin, as were the mud deposits on the bed of the sea, but our picture of the advancing and retreating ice sheets was based on evidence like the moraines pushed along by glaciers on land on both sides of the North Sea, and we had no detailed idea of the situation in the area now under the water. In particular, we had only a very general idea of the evolving coastlines of the enlarging North Sea of postglacial times. It was clear, from occasional finds dredged up by fishing boats, that human beings were operating in areas now well and truly under water, between England and the European mainland, in remote stone age times. But where the precise coastal limits of those times at various points were – and so what territory was available for human exploitation in addition to the present dry land we can explore archaeologically – was very conjectural.

Thanks to the cores drilled out of the North Sea bed in the course of exploration for gas and oil, with their sequences of geological and biological change, we now know a lot more about the progress from dry land to freshwater or seawater shallows to full inundation as the North Sea grew during the worldwide rise of sea levels after the ice age. The array of evidence is very complicated, with the involvement alongside sea level rise of rising land levels in some places (e.g. in Scotland and around Oslo) where the weight of the glaciers was relieved in the postglacial meltdown. Longterm tilts of the North Sea region have raised East Anglia in the past and lowered southern England and the Low Countries (though with some reverses along the way). The North Sea bed has sunk under the sheer weight of melt water flowing into it and over it, quite apart from the sea level rise in itself, and there have been alterations to tides and currents as first the English Channel and later the Baltic came into play. Inevitably, it has required powerful computer modelling to arrive at the picture of events we now enjoy. As to the dating of all these events, we rely either directly or indirectly on the radiocarbon method for the most part, with its inherent margins of probability and its need for calibration to produce real calendar years. Real years are countable in the lake deposits on the margins of the Scandinavian glaciers but such absolute dating cannot be extended to events all over the North Sea area. The calibration of the radiocarbon dates is a subtle business, requiring different – and arguable – adjustments in differ-ent periods. In this book's early chapters we shall rather boldly round out figures derived by calibration in an effort to give some idea of real dates in real years, however rough and ready the approximations. That seems better in a popular work than quoting some dates as real BC or real years ago and others as radiocarbon bp (before the present).

The first people

Although our story of human life around the North Sea is to be concerned with the activities of fully modern human beings since the close of the last ice age, it is as well to remember that there was a succession of at least three glacial epochs before the latest one, with warm interglacial periods between them, and evolving humanity was present on the southern margin of where our North Sea would one day roll, at least during the interglacial episodes and into the last glaciation. Over a time-span of at least half-a-million years, earlier human types left behind them (in addition to the few-and-far-between fossils of themselves) their knapped stone implements, along the old banks of rivers like the Thames and Somme, or out on the North European Plain.

The Neanderthalers lasted into the latest ice age and were only replaced – in circumstances not yet fully understood – by fully modern human types at about 35,000 to 30,000 years ago. The changeover seems to have occurred during a milder interlude within the last glacial period, during which the moderns were able to expand into areas formerly occupied by the

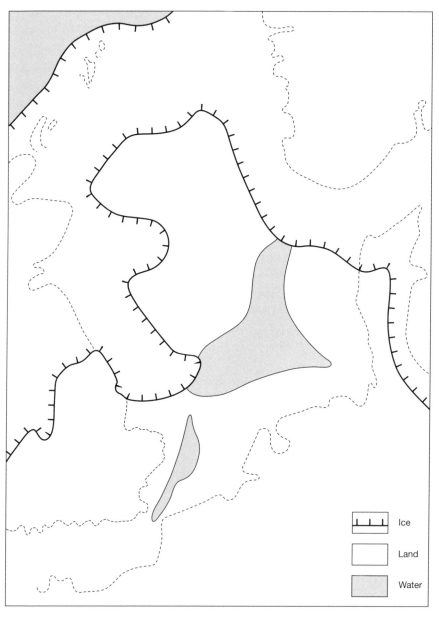

Maps 3 The maximum extent of glaciation during the last ice age, about 20,000 years ago

cold-adapted Neanderthalers. The moderns went on to exploit the advantages of their superior stone tool kits, and who knows what else in the way of better survival strategies, as the last ice age built to its very severe climax round about 20,000 years ago.

There was no hope of occupying the North Sea region in those days and what meagre population of moderns had managed to make a living in southern Britain before the full onset of the glaciation had long since been driven south across the land-bridge to France. The earliest piece of evidence for any reoccupation comes from Gough's Cave in Somerset, at about 14,000 years ago, when things got quite rapidly warmer and the writing was, so to speak, on the wall for the last ice age to date.

But there was still some way to go, with some oscillation of colder times to endure. There is a suggestion that between the Scottish and Scandinavian glaciers a large ice-dammed lake had formed, west of Denmark, which gradually shrank as the glaciers started their long retreat from about 17,000 years ago and dry, unglaciated land slowly emerged from Jutland to the east coast of Britain. There may have been another, smaller lake further south between East Anglia and Holland.

At about 14,000 years before the present, the glaciers were still in place in northern England and the Scottish Highlands, as well as along the coast of Norway, and from these glaciers their melt-water run-offs were cutting streams into the land between them. The shrinking of the lakes were probably still there in the otherwise dry land between today's southern Britain and mainland Europe. But there was open sea in the Norwegian Trench as well as to the north and west of the Shetlands and Orkney, which remained attached to Scotland. The North Sea as we know it was just beginning to appear.

People were beginning to live on the North European Plain again, in the area just south of the present southern shores of our North Sea, on a latitude with the parts of southern Britain where occupation was also reviving as we have seen. No doubt these people were starting to stray north into the lowland area still well above sea level between Britain and the mainland, freed of its icy burden. The remains they left behind them now lie on the North Sea's bed, but we can surmise their character from the archaeology of their relatives on both sides of the North Sea.

Reindeer hunters

During the oscillating colder and warmer times that comprise the declining last few millennia of the last ice age, the region around Hamburg and the base of Jutland was home to hunting bands who, during the colder phases, chased reindeer with harpoons carved from antlers or projectiles tipped with stone points. They also used antler picks and lived in tents of reindeer hide. In a warmer interlude, the projectile points gave way to curved flint knives with blunted backs, probably in the hands of a different set of people. The reindeer hunters had the benefit of bows and arrows (in pine) which the more famous hunter-artists of ice-age France had not enjoyed: they may not have painted any cave pictures, but they did set up a sort of totem-pole, 2 m long and pointed to help drive it into the ground, with an antlered reindeer skull on top, and in their latter years they evidently sacrificed animals in a lake at Stellmoor not far from Hamburg.

All over western Europe in the late stages of the retreating ice age, there was great variation among local groups as to the detail of their quite sophisticated hunting and food processing kits. Away to the west of Hamburg in what is now Britain, people were making the so-called Cheddar and Cresswell points that were in fact backed blades of flint. These hunters also employed reindeer and deer antlers, animal bones and teeth and occasionally mammoth ivory to manufacture both tools or weapons of practical use, and more imaginative items like beads made out of fox teeth or pierced batons of obscure but probably ceremonial import. Though nothing to compare with the spectacular cave art of ice-age France to the south has ever been found in Britain, there is some evidence of abstract doodling on pieces of bone, ivory and stone and an example of figurative art in the form of an engraved horse's head on a rib fragment from a cave in the Cresswell Crags, Derbyshire (where some rather crude engravings of birds and ibex have recently been reported).

The range of these 'Cresswellian' folk extended from the English West Country through South Wales to the Derbyshire Peak District, and close relatives were making very similar tools in East Anglia and the Low Countries. Their distinctive assemblage of tool types was succeeded by a variety of late glacial groups of products that were generally made out of smaller raw materials with less in the way of bone and antler use, and broadly similar tool types are known in northern France and the German

Rhineland, at about the same date of around 13,000 years before the present.

When conditions were relatively warm in these closing centuries of the ice age, there could be sea level rises that started to push open water into the low-lying area of the future North Sea. By some 11,000 years ago the coastline of the North Sea consisted of the Norwegian Trench all the way into the Skagerrak and a bay reaching south down the Scottish and north-east English coasts to the latitude of Flamborough Head. The Shetlands made a large island by now, with Orkney also larger than today but still connected to the mainland. There was another island, gone now altogether, midway between the Shetlands and the coast of Norway.

Over the next millennium, the bay to the east of the British coast reached further south and started to encroach eastwards below what is now the Dogger Bank, which was still connected to the European mainland across to Jutland, northern Germany and the Low Countries of today. Before the weight of water from melting glaciers and encroaching sea was imposed on this 'Doggerland', it was – in places at least – very likely more elevated in contour than it is now, presently under the sea. To the north-west, Orkney and Shetland were edging closer to their present configuration, and there was that large island between Shetland and the Norwegian coast, off Bergen. The river systems of the time probably included a northward flowing old Elbe and its tributaries, a similarly northward old Ouse and an old Rhine-Thames complex flowing into what would become the English Channel. Deposits in lakes that mark the annual meltings of the Scandinavian ice sheets, and can be accurately counted in years, establish the full retreat of the last glaciation at about 10,300 years ago, making a conventional end-date for the ice age.

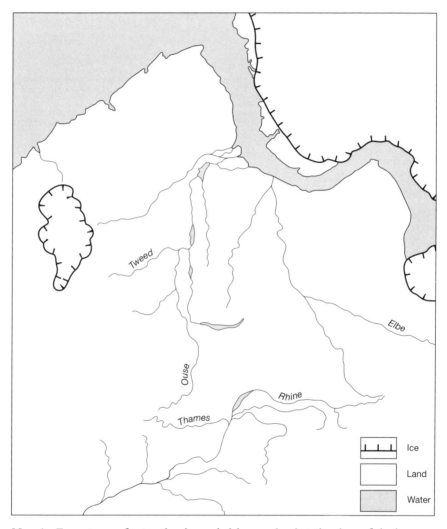

Map 4a Four stages of retreating ice and rising sea level at the close of the ice age: about 15,000 years ago

Source: Adapted from Coles, B.J. (1998) 'Doggerland: a speculative survey', *Proceedings of the Prehistoric Society*, Vol. 64, p. 59, Fig. 8, by permission of the Prehistoric Society.

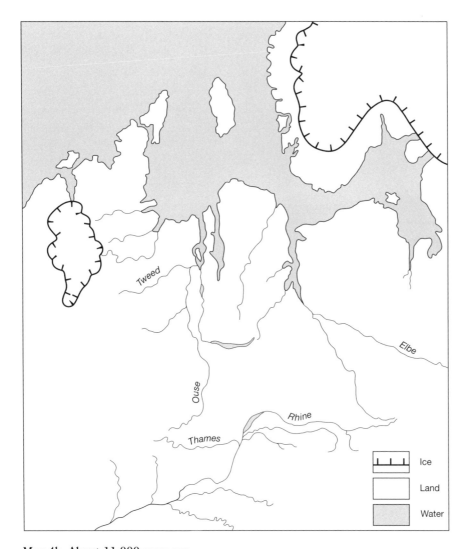

Map 4b About 11,000 years ago

Source: Adapted from Coles, B.J. (1998) 'Doggerland: a speculative survey', *Proceedings of the Prehistoric Society,* Vol. 64, p. 61, Fig. 9, by permission of the Prehistoric Society.

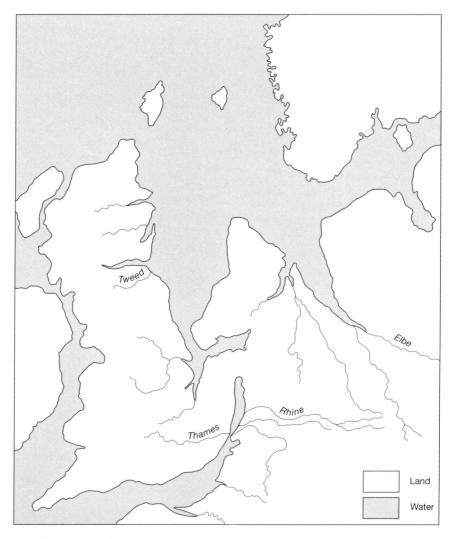

Map 4c About 10,000 years ago

Source: Adapted from Coles, B.J. (1998) 'Doggerland: a speculative survey', *Proceedings of the Prehistoric Society*, Vol. 64, p. 64, Fig. 10, by permission of the Prehistoric Society.

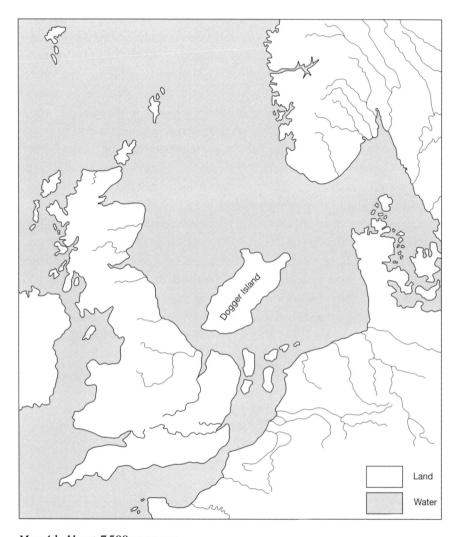

Legend:
- Land
- Water

Map 4d About 7,500 years ago

Source: Adapted from Coles, B.J. (1998) 'Doggerland: a speculative survey', *Proceedings of the Prehistoric Society*, Vol. 64, p. 68, Fig. 11, by permission of the Prehistoric Society.

Inundation

By 9000 years ago a narrow stretch of water running north up the east coast of Norfolk, probably incorporating what was left of the more southerly of the old ice-dammed lakes of fully glacial times, was threatening to bring the waters of the deepening English Channel into communication with the bay opening up south of Dogger, this bay being itself the site of the other and larger ice-dammed lake of earlier times. There must have been a time when high tides managed to flood over the nearly sea level ground that separated these stretches of water. As the sea continued to rise in the general melt-down, some more than usually savage winter storm might finally have breached the barrier and linked the Atlantic system coming through the English Channel with the developing North Sea, at some time around 6500 BC. Soon afterwards Dogger became, first at high tides and then in all seas, an island, now cut off from the lowlands west of Jutland. In this situation, a rapid development of new tidal channels would have ensued. The southern part of the North Sea has such a gentle gradient from deeper in the north to shallower in the south that from now on quite small rises in sea level could bring major changes to coastlines all around it. Even so, an archipelago of smaller islands may have lingered between East Anglia and the Netherlands, impeding the full development of modern marine con-ditions for a while. All these islands may have remained inhabitable, or at least reachable by boat, while they lasted: an antler artefact dredged up from the Dogger Bank of about 6000 BC suggests as much.

By shortly after 8000 years ago, Dogger may only have been exposed at low tide; a thousand years later, it and any other islands would have gone under altogether and, except along the Frisian coast between what are now the Frisian islands and the mainland and up the coast of Schleswig-Holstein and Jutland, the North Sea would have been looking very much as it does today. While there may also have been more land showing above the sea off the Norfolk coast, there were perhaps some places where the sea reached a little further than it does today. Maximum sea level relative to land was reached at about 7000–6500 years ago, when for example the coast north of the Tyne was a little more inundated than it has been since. At about this time the Baltic, hitherto for some long while a freshwater lake, was linked to the North Sea with the flooding of the Sound: the fairly shallow Baltic is the world's largest expanse of brackish (slightly salty) water.

More or less along with the close of the ice age, what archaeologists call the Old Stone Age (Palaeolithic Period) is reckoned to have ended in Europe. Of course, in some places at least, it simply shaded into the next conventional epoch of prehistory: the Middle Stone Age, better known among archaeologists as the Mesolithic. People were still roving hunters and gatherers but they were going about their business in a changed environment. It was a warmer and eventually more wooded world after the chill tundra and steppe of much of north-west Europe in ice-age times. The altered flora that went with this altered climate produced a new faunal situation: the mammoth, for instance, had probably disappeared from this region even before the end of the ice age, along with the woolly rhino; the reindeer in these parts was a rapid victim of postglacial changes, retreating north and east to newly available terrain more suited to nourish it. The herds of horses of former days also disappeared.

Some of the old hunters went with the reindeer, north into Norway and Sweden for example, reaching the northern tip by 8000 years ago, to continue as best they could their old way of life as the world around them changed. Others spread (and sometimes they needed boats to do it) into newly available living space in Scotland, northern Ireland and northern Denmark, not so much to continue as before but rather to find somewhere to occupy as land was being lost to the rising sea. Those who stayed at home, or did not chase the palaeolithic way of life in their new territories, adapted their subsistence strategies to the alteration of things and took up the mesolithic lifestyle.

A new world

The earlier part of the Mesolithic Period in north-west Europe was still relatively cool and dry, becoming milder and moister as time went on and the North Sea flooded over the lowland plain between southern Britain and the continental mainland. The almost treeless open country of the late glacial period gave way to birch and pine woods in the early Mesolithic and these in turn were replaced on heavier soils by a spread of denser mixed forest with a lot of hazel as times got warmer and humid. At Titchwell on the Norfolk coast of England, the remains of a forest which grew up on an old land surface come to light at low tide, and animal bones and flints of an early mesolithic character are found in it. This and other examples along the same coast bear vivid witness both to the submergence of the land between Britain and the continent and to the growth of woodlands on that land between the times of the glaciers' retreat and the flooding of the North Sea.

The early mesolithic finds made in Britain are very comparable in character and dating with the mesolithic material of Denmark: the general culture to which they all belong may well have originated, as one of the many late glacial variants, in the very area of the North Sea now submerged. As time went by, with the flooding of more and more land and the spread of the forests, the basic homogeneity of mesolithic material culture broke down. Movement and communication over long distances were plainly becoming more difficult, and local cultural variation was inevitable, with recourse to sometimes inferior raw materials of narrowly local availability.

To begin with, what would become the southern North Sea was an area of freshwater fen and lagoon, not perhaps too rich in aquatic life at the start as a result of the general killing of so many species, including freshwater fish, during the glaciated years. As fish populations recovered, this marshy lowland zone would become a rich source of freshwater fish before it was submerged. Fish-hooks, nets with bark floats and wicker fish traps have been found, especially in southern Scandinavia, that testify to the value of fishing in the north-west European mesolithic way of life. There was plentiful wildfowl and other game to be hunted too: in 1931 a Lowestoft trawler fishing about 40 km north-east of Cromer between the Leman and Ower banks, brought up from a depth of nearly 40 m a barbed point carved from red deer antler, buried in a lump of peaty 'moor log'. On typological grounds, this prong from a hunting spear is about ten thousand years old and belongs to the early phase of the Mesolithic Period. Points of this general type were common in north-west Europe in those times and other examples have come up from the seabed nearer the Low Countries. At about the same time, the human presence is known to have spread up into Jutland to the southern shore of the Norwegian Trench and the Skagerrak, and so we can conjecture that people were also living well to the north in the area now under the sea.

The rest of the contemporary tool kit, insofar as its items have come down to us (mostly, of course, in stone), was mainly based on the production of knapped flints so small in relation to those of earlier times as to be called 'microliths'. They were clearly made to be set in wooden or bone mountings, as saws and drills for example, with adhesive resin and fibre bindings. From

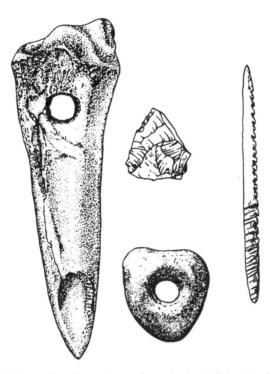

Figure 1 Mesolithic artefacts brought up from the bed of the North Sea

Source: Coles, B.J. (1998) 'Doggerland: a speculative survey', *Proceedings of the Prehistoric Society,* Vol. 64, p. 71, Fig. 12 (a) and (b). Reprinted by permission of the Prehistoric Society.

Sweden comes a pine arrowshaft with one microlith barb set in it, behind the point, in a way that suggests the delivery of poison. Some Danish mesolithic sites have yielded up the bows from which such arrows were launched.

As postglacial times progressed, there was more timber to deal with – both to clear out of the way on occasions and to use as raw material. Stone axes, small chisels, scraping and boring tools point to the development of carpentry – though the scrapers and borers were no doubt used on hides too, to make clothes and coverings for wooden shelters. There is evidence of structures with stake holes for poles at several mesolithic sites, with cobbled flooring at one of them in Yorkshire. At Star Carr in Yorkshire, there was a wooden platform without any covering structure. Some of these presumed shelters have hollowed-out floors and the antler mattocks employed to do such digging (as well as for roots to eat) have been found, worn down in evidence of their use. Off the northern coast of Norway, well beyond the northernmost limits of the North Sea, house foundations in stone have been discovered that date to more than 4000 BC, remarkable in themselves and testifying to the spread of the mesolithic way of life over the postglacial millennia.

Early boats

Carpentry and preparation of hides also made possible the construction of boats. Star Carr produced a possible paddle and sites in Scotland, Holland and Denmark have revealed the remains of dugout canoes, or log boats as maritime historians sometimes like to call them: the one from Perth was made from a log 4.5 m long by 1 m wide, hollowed out to 1.8 m in length at a depth of 60 cm. The Dutch example, from Pesse and around nine thousand years old, is very neatly carved out of a pine trunk, with square cut ends. The two from Tybrind Vig in Denmark, some six thousand years old, were found along with paddles, one of which carries dotted lines of decoration inlaid with some brown substance. The larger of the boats was 9.5 m long, carrying perhaps six to eight people and their fishing gear. Limited sea crossings may have been undertaken in such larger ones. There must have been skin boats, too, which not surprisingly have not so far turned up in the archaeological record, but quantities of rolled-up and unused birch bark, which might also have been used to clad a wooden framework boat, were found at Star Carr. At the time of Star Carr, early in the Mesolithic Period, its inhabitants might have trekked if they so wished, with perhaps a southerly detour round the encroaching North Sea Bay, to the Low Countries and Denmark of today. No boats were needed for that crossing, but canoes and coracles would have been very useful on the many creeks and ponds that broke up the lowland plain between the two areas. A boat of some sort, probably of the umiak skin-boat type of the Eskimos, would certainly have been required to fetch greenstone from a tiny island between Bergen and Stavanger in mesolithic times in Norway: it's 6 km out to sea.

Mesolithic subsistence was gained by foraging for plant food and, predominantly in all probability, by hunting. Coastal settlements of the time, where sea food might have made a significant contribution to diet, have mostly vanished under the North Sea. In the western Scottish islands and in south-west England, neither of which are in our North Sea zone, middens of shells have been found that have been interpreted as rather marginal and desperate measures to eke a living out of the collection of sea food –

similar sites are known in Denmark. The fact is that a single kill of an aurochs or red deer would have fed a lot more people for a lot longer than any amount of shellfish. But elsewhere in Scotland, fish from the sea were a more promising proposition, with the bones of cod, haddock, turbot, sturgeon and salmon turning up in mesolithic contexts. In western Sweden, bones of ling indicate that deep-sea fishing was practised, another sign that serviceable boats were being constructed. In Denmark, seals were sometimes taken and even whales occasionally attacked, perhaps after beaching. In Scotland an antler mattock was found in association with whale remains in a way that suggests its use to hack into blubber. It may well be that the ever changing northern coastline of the North Sea as it retreated south through postglacial times was often a rewarding place to live, even if the evidence of that life is now lost beneath the waves.

Hunting land animals was an important part of subsistence, too, and on the whole the Mesolithic was rich in game; though not as rich as some of the open hunting grounds of earlier, colder times. But the aurochs and the red deer, for a time the Irish elk, and the wild pig were available to hunt in a fauna whose only serious enemies to human beings were wolves and brown bears. At Vig in Denmark, an aurochs skeleton was found with a projectile point embedded in it. Pelts could be taken from pine martens, foxes and beavers, whose dams were also a focus for fishing. Bird bones are quite common on mesolithic sites, with migrating swans a target on one site in north Jutland. There is evidence for cooking pits in Dorset, and for potboilers heated in the campfire. From the late mesolithic tradition known as Ertebølle in Denmark and west Sweden, after 4500 BC, there come some examples of pottery, the production of which is normally associated in the archaeological record with sedentary, farming folk. Some contained the charred remnants of foodstuffs, which turned out to include grasses and fish. There was a similar manifestation of stable hunter-gatherer living in the Netherlands, with pottery, at about the same date: by this time, true farming people with a pottery-making tradition were living not so very far away in north-central Europe.

Improving on nature

There is some evidence that mesolithic people's dealings with animals went beyond just hunting them, however skilful a practice that may be. There are signs of deliberate forest clearance, with axe and fire, to promote the fresh growth of shoots and saplings so attractive to wildlife, especially deer. At a couple of sites in southern Britain, there is simply too much ivy pollen to be explained except as coming from winter fodder to attract deer or, even, to feed captured animals. At Star Carr, the age of deer bones reveals a culling process that points, at least, to purposeful interference with the herds that were hunted. All this looks like the beginnings of animal man-agement, of the same sort as was already under way in other parts of the world at the same time, at the start of the farming revolution. Canine bones from Star Carr, and Thatcham in Berkshire, show modifications consistent with the beginning of the domestication of the dog for hunting purposes, as do some from a site in the Rhineland called Bedburg.

Plant food was also collected but, of necessity, survives less obviously than animal bones as evidence of mesolithic subsistence. Among other things, there are water chestnuts and hazelnuts, the latter highly storable as winter provender. Whether the beginnings of any sort of horticulture were going on in the Mesolithic is hard to say – there are flints carrying the gloss that comes from harvesting grasses, but not set into any surviving sickle handles as is the case in the Near East with the beginnings of large-scale cereal gathering and planned cultivation, on the way to true agriculture.

Real farming brings long-term settled living in growing villages, with increasing populations. There was not much of that in the Mesolithic Period in north-west Europe. People liked to live by freshwater streams and lakes, or on the sea's margin, but their lives were conducted out of essentially tem-porary base camps, some of them long-lasting in favourable sites like caves, with a strong element of seasonal visitation about them. Their food resources were mobile and so were they, as and when required. They had no storable wealth or craft specialities, not even in the matter of their basic raw material, flint. They probably lacked fixed territorial limits, even when larger grouping began to emerge in the latter part of the Mesolithic Period. In general, it is a picture of small populations in small groups that interacted enough to share a common general technology and culture. These were bands, more or less egalitarian in their dealings, and not yet the tribes of later prehistoric times. Estimates have them running to a population den-sity of as little as one person per 10 sq km.

There was perhaps some social differentiation that went beyond age and gender. To be buried at all, for example, in those days might have meant you were a more than routinely important person. Not all skeletons from caves imply deliberate burial, but the site called Aveline's Hole in England's West Country appears to have had a line of fifty or so mesolithic burials, with very meagre grave goods in the form of animal tooth beads and bits of animal bone. The young male from Gough's Cave at Cheddar was of early mesolithic vintage, from about 8000 BC. But evidence from the British side of the North Sea is scant indeed, and not so much better from the continental side. The site of Vedbaek in Denmark has revealed a cemetery of seventeen or more graves, with twenty-two human individuals represented. Here an adult male was buried in clearly ceremonial circumstances, with deer antlers under his shoulders and hips, some flint tools about him and a deposit of red ochre around the head, in a manner reminiscent of some of the graves from ice-age western Europe. In one case at Vedbaek a bone point embedded between the ribs, in another a microlith in a long bone suggest at least the occurrence of hunting accidents – and maybe a fight or even warfare. At Skateholm in southern Sweden, bodies were buried in a variety of positions (outstretched, flexed, sitting up) and dogs were, in earlier times at least, accorded ceremonial burial.

The occupation levels at Vedbaek with which the cemetery is associated yielded up some evidently cannibalised human bones among the general refuse, which we are not forced to conclude to have been the remains of enemies of the Vedbaek people. Maybe the people in the cemetery were the top people of a society already showing some signs of social hierarchy (and indeed of semi-permanent settlement). There is a mesolithic cemetery in Latvia and isolated burials are known from Denmark and Poland, but the general paucity of human remains from these times suggests most people were, at best, left out to be exposed to nature by way of a funeral.

Art and craft

Like their late glacial predecessors in the North Sea region, the mesolithic people produced no startling works of art nor left behind them much to suggest the nature of their ideological interests (which is far from suggesting they had none). Mesolithic objects from the continent often show non-figurative designs, chevrons especially, which are matched on some bits of antler and bone from Britain. There is an engraved pebble from a mesolithic context in Wales, an aurochs' radius from the Thames with a related design.

The Danish Mesolithic features some little amber figurines and a nice line of schematised walking humans (one of them perhaps a shaman) scratched on a piece of bone. From another site in Wales comes a pebble some see as shaped like a phallus, but its mesolithic character is not certain. There are perforated cowrie shells from Oronsay. From the area around Mount Komsa in northern Norway, beyond the bounds of the North Sea, come remarkable life-size rock drawings of deer, bears, elk, whales and seals that seem to belong in spirit, if not in artistic merit, with the famous cave painting and engravings of ice-age France. Some drawings show people wearing skis. The tradition of rock drawing continued further south in Scandinavia into the Bronze Age.

But the most striking of mesolithic productions with intimations of the life of the imagination are the red deer skull and antler masks from Star Carr in Yorkshire and Bedburg in the Rhineland, the latter almost complete. A piece of skull attached to the antlers has been pierced in each case, inviting identification with similar mask-making among hunter-gatherer peoples of recent times. Speculation involves use of the masks as hunters' disguises to facilitate close approach to their prey, or – more intriguingly – as shamans' magic masks to be donned during totemic celebrations. Shamans might be called the first of the craft specialists in human history, and the mesolithic people weren't the first to harbour them.

The later and longer part of the Mesolithic Period in Britain sees the widespread adoption of a flint tool kit more microlithic and geometrical than before, usually without the large axes of the earlier phase. The North Sea had separated Britain from the continent, conditions were warmer and more humid, the oak-mixed-forests were spreading and the British Mesolithic was going its own way. Based on broad technological affinities, a geographical scheme of social territories has been suggested for the latter part of the Mesolithic, with a zone in eastern England, a Rhine-based zone from northern France to the northern part of the Netherlands, another from the northern Netherlands to the base of Jutland overlapping somewhat with an Elbe-centred zone, and a zone incorporating Denmark with the south Baltic coast and southern Sweden. The beginnings of a varied spectrum of human life around almost all the margins of the North Sea were now in place. It was going to make for some very dynamic interactions over the next seven millennia.

Chapter 2

Farmers and fighters

The full farming way of life came to Europe as an exotic practice, if not actually in the hands of immigrating outsiders. At all events, its ultimate inspiration lay in the Near Eastern Fertile Crescent, that arc of propitious environmental conditions stretching broadly from the Nile in the west up the eastern hinterland of the Mediterranean and down the streams of the Tigris and Euphrates to the Persian Gulf in the east – an arc in which the wild prototypes of both plants and animals useful to the first farmers thrived naturally at the end of the world's last glaciation. As we have seen, this period also saw steps towards the human management of animals and plants in north-western Europe, but real modification of wild species to turn them into deliberately cultivated and domesticated species began at an early date in the Near East, with rapid development of settled village life, from about 8000 BC onwards. The process by which the idea and practice of farming spread from south-east to north-west Europe covered a time-span from about 7000 to 4000 BC in all. The farming way of life reached the southern margin of the North European Plain between about 5500 and 5000 BC, which allows for the faint possibility, if no more, that its first appearance on the southern shores of the North Sea occurred at a time when the archipelago of islands (of which Dogger was the largest) was still in place, at least in part. At all events, boats capable of some degree of open-water crossing were needed to communicate the practice of farming to the British Isles, and likewise to the Danish islands, southern Sweden and Norway after the entry to the Baltic was opened by about 4500 BC. They were needed, too, to maintain the supplies of flint on which the first farmers depended for their tools. Skin boats, on light wooden frames, would have been well-suited to cold northern waters – as the Eskimos know – since they can be arranged to ship very little water: not surprisingly, no such boats of light wooden frames with flimsy skin or bark coverings have survived from the days of the first farmers, any more than from earlier times when as we saw they are likely to have already been devised.

The mostly wooded areas of the inhabited northern world were all in the capable hands of mesolithic hunter-gatherers when the idea of farming began to impinge on them. The mesolithic people had, in fact, taken the hunter-gatherer way of life about as far as it could go in a temperate environment, with great success, and their best haunts – like the coastal wetlands that fringed the North Sea – were scarcely ideal for the speedy adoption of agriculture and pastoralism, even with some experience of plant and animal management under their belts. In Scandinavia, the Ertebølle people at the close of the Mesolithic show signs of some influence from the farmers who were already making their presence felt from not so far away. The Ertebølle folk were still an overwhelmingly hunting and fishing people, but they were making rather crudely coiled pots (with pointed bases) in adoption of one of the characteristic technical innovations of neolithic times, and polishing their stone axes in the fashion that archaeologists have long used to distinguish the New Stone Age of the farmers from the preceding Middle and Old Stone Ages. Along with their piles of food debris (including a few sheep and cattle bones) called kitchen middens, at their often coastal sites, the Ertebølle people have left behind them some wooden implements like spades and some of their pots carry grain impressions that show their interest in cereal crops.

What was injected into the North Sea scene at the start of the Neolithic was not so much a new population of incomers as a new approach to earning a living, a new emphasis on cultivating crops and raising animals, together with the actual import of some new species of plant and animal, like wheat and barley and sheep and goats. Hunting and gathering did not disappear overnight and some people, for a long while, had no particular incentive to incorporate much if any of the package of farming innovations. But, nonetheless, the attractions of the farming way of life, along with its drawbacks, were steadily spread, for early farming practice was in itself rather predatory in its woodland clearance and advance. The mesolithic people were not entire strangers to the idea of interference with the natural order of the plant and animal kingdoms and they were already acquainted with the potentially domesticable cattle and pigs of their part of the world before ever sheep and goats were introduced to them. (It is worth noting that the sheep in question were not yet wool-bearing forms, but sources of meat.)

Immigrations

The fact that sheep and goats, along with wheat and barley, were introductions from fully-fledged farming communities who had spread into north-west Europe up the Danube from the south and east, suggests at the same time that some new people actually introduced themselves into the North Sea world, as neolithic immigrants into the mesolithic scene. These neolithic people can be identified as the spreading culture, from about 5500 BC, called – after its distinctively decorated pottery – the Linear Pottery Culture. From the Upper Danube, these people ranged to the Upper Rhine and the Neckar, then north to the area between Hanover and Magdeburg, down the Rhine into the southern Netherlands and to the southern part of Poland, finally to southern Belgium and northern France: clearing patches of forest to plant their fields and tend their herds of (mostly) cattle around their clusters of timber longhouses, up to 30 m in length.

Their spread made first for a situation in which pockets of farmers coexisted among the old hunter-gatherer inhabitants, and then for a fusion of neolithic and local mesolithic ways that saw the establishment of regional cultural groupings with distinctive characters in different areas, losing continuity with the original neolithic impetus from south-eastern Europe and the Near East. One such grouping was the cultural continuum up the Atlantic coasts from Brittany to the Isle of Man, Ireland and the Scottish islands, based on fishing as much as on farming. This culture went on to carry a tradition of megalithic tomb building, with some of the oldest tombs in Ireland dating back to about 4500 BC, at much the same time as the Neolithic was initiated there and in Brittany.

At this early date, the same sort of cultural fusion of neolithic with local mesolithic ways is not in evidence on Britain's North Sea side, though it was under way in Denmark by perhaps 4200 BC with slash-and-burn forest clearance. Britain's archaeology tends always to show an Atlantic continuity up the west coast, which reaches to the Northern Isles of Scotland, and a

North Sea continuity in the east; in Orkney and the Shetlands these conti-
nuities may mingle, overcoming the basic geographical divide. The earliest
evidence of the Neolithic in Britain away from the Atlantic outposts is dated
from about 4000 BC, and after about 3500 BC no purely mesolithic sites are
known. The Neolithic came to south-east England, probably from Flanders,
again more as an idea than as an influx of new people: the locals took to it
more or less as we saw the Ertebølle people in Denmark adopting elements
of it, because it all helped to maintain and expand subsistence. Without a
major immigration of new folk, the way was open to develop local versions
of the Neolithic that were not mere continuations of their continental inspi-
rations.

At first, the Neolithic in England was a phenomenon of the chalk areas
of the south-east, not necessarily because this region was any less wooded
than the rest of the island but more because, once cleared of trees, the land
was easier to till. A zone of cultural continuity, seen in its pottery products,
extended subsequently from Sussex and Kent right up to Scotland. It seems
to have been a time of mobile farming, moving on after a few seasons, with
no long-inhabited houses. The early Neolithic here was not so much about
settled living from the first (as happened quite rapidly in other parts of the
world) as about woodland clearance, by means of axes of polished stone,
and about domesticated plants and animals, with pottery and also some
signs of a greater ritual attention to death, at least for some members of the
community. The originally earth-mounded tombs and shrines (or mortuary
houses) of these first farmers in England resemble the timber longhouses –
and mortuary houses – of their continental counterparts, though there is
little or no evidence for such longhouses for the living on English sites. In
Denmark at about the same time, both long mounds and round ones
housed the graves of the dead. That the first farmers in England came
together in occasional gatherings is suggested by the circular enclosures
with interrupted ditches that date to these early times. These sites were
probably located in a sort of no man's land between the rival territories of
the farming folk, a special zone of ritual significance.

Innovations

Woodland clearance went on everywhere through the early and middle
phases of the Neolithic, on a slash-and-burn basis that demanded a good

supply of polished stone axes, for whose raw material flint mines were exploited in, for example, Belgium, and in Britain in Sussex. Later on, the place called Grime's Graves in East Anglia was extensively developed, where deep shafts with underground galleries running off them can be inspected to this day. On the continent there appeared a tradition of male burials with funnel-necked beakers, collared flasks and pottery cups that is thought to reflect the beginnings of a drinking cult (presumably of alcoholic beverages) which perhaps hoped to continue a popular everyday habit in the next world.

Meanwhile, the wider world outside north-western Europe was witnessing new developments that would in time reach towards our North Sea region. The hammering and casting of copper and gold, both to be found in the Balkans, was producing a range of prestige goods, more for show than use, before the alloying of copper with tin into the altogether more utilitarian material called bronze was achieved. Fine pieces of stonework were being produced, too, at this time – again for display and deposition with the dead as grave goods. Making bronze and casting it in two-piece moulds, for greater complexity of the final product, followed in south-east and central Europe. The plough was developed, and reached Denmark and southern Britain almost as early as 3500 BC; the wheel appears in the form of perhaps deliberately sacrificed examples in Danish bogs, from before 3000 BC; wool-bearing sheep were introduced to the shores of the North Sea at about the same time.

After 3500 BC megalithic tomb building, with large stone components inside and kerbs of stone outside the covering mounds, was under way in southern Scandinavia, north-west Germany and the northern Netherlands – at the same time as the practice thrived along the Atlantic coast of western Europe where we saw its beginnings going back a thousand years earlier. On the British side of the water, the nearest megalithic tombs to the North Sea are to be found in Scotland and Kent, while the absence of local stone supplies helped, perhaps, to discourage their construction up most of the eastern coast of England. In eastern England, there were earth mounds over neolithic graves and shrines, but none of these structures contained large stone elements. Similarly, the large monuments that were a distinctive development of the British Neolithic – circular enclosures with a ditch and usually an external bank, with at least one entrance and sometimes a setting of pillars inside – lack stone components in eastern England, sticking to the wooden posts of the earliest examples and never going on to anything like Stonehenge, even in its neolithic phase. An example of a wooden-posted henge structure near to the North Sea in eastern England is provided by the site of Arminghall near Norwich – there is really nothing like the henges in wood or stone to be seen on the other side of the North Sea. Such British henge monuments, with or without stones, were clearly ceremonial centres of some sort, social or religious or both. A great part of the ideology of these early and middle neolithic peoples in north-west Europe clearly centred on the tombs of the ancestors sited close to the homesteads and little village settlements of the time. These were communal tombs, often under long mounds and open to repeated interments from the communities with which they were associated. It is not at all obvious that this neolithic society showed any great differentiations of rank and status, though we don't really know what percentage of the population merited burial in the communal tombs, and the mortuary houses may have been associated with the funerary rites of top people of some sort, maybe chiefs or medicine men.

During the fourth millennium BC, a shift towards a less settled and more socially differentiated way of life becomes apparent in north-west Europe in general, with signs of more mobility of both goods and people. This shift was related to those social changes going on in south-eastern and central Europe that brought the plough, the wheel and eventually metal technology to north-west Europe. An emblem of changing times in the north is furnished by the appearance, in individual male graves under round mounds, of a set of grave goods that point to fighting and drinking as honoured social traits, for a section at least of a newly emerging order. The drinking is attested by the beaker-like pots in the graves and the fighting by stone battleaxes. At about one litre capacity, the beakers suggest an early preference in the north for beer drinking over the wine favoured in warmer places to the south-east. The round mounds, in place of the older long ones, have suggested to some archaeologists that their occupants were related to eastern peoples used to living in small round houses, or even in circular tents on the steppes. Wealth seems now to have been rather more invested in mobile livestock than in the fields of settled villages. Houses were now smaller and more scattered, not focussed on the ancestral tombs and cult houses of earlier times.

A new order

The core region of this later neolithic manifestation in north-west Europe covered an area south of the Baltic from Jutland to the River Bug in Poland. But this way of life soon spread widely to the southern shores of the Baltic and Scandinavia and to the Rhineland with related cultural complexes in Belgium and France. Britain appears for a long time to have remained a more old-fashioned region, going on with its tradition of communal tombs and agricultural settlements: though there were some developments in eastern England, especially in Yorkshire, which parallel continental innovations with single burials furnished with axes, maceheads, knives, even jet belt-fittings, all of which seems to indicate the promotion of individuality over the old communality. In the rest of Britain, including the eastern side of Scotland, local developments saw the elaboration of stone circles (and wooden-posted structures) that may have derived from the kerb stones of the older megalithic tombs: Avebury and Stonehenge in Wiltshire, and the Ring of Brodgar and Stones of Stenness in Orkney are examples. In the British Isles, the megalithic tomb tradition went on, in Ireland as well as Orkney, where we also have the extensive remains at Skara Brae of a whole village of stone-built and stone-furnished houses. The tombs show alignments to the midwinter solstice and the circles to, at the least, the midsummer sunrise: glimpses into the religious beliefs of the times.

The continental drinking and fighting tendency, manifested already in single graves with beakers and axes, developed in the Rhine delta region into the 'Bell Beaker Phenomenon' well before 2000 BC. The beakers were now bell-shaped pots, with impressed decoration that resembles woven textiles: residues found inside them prove that they once contained alcoholic concoctions. They were again deposited in single male graves under round mounds, along with other grave goods of a combative and horsey character. There are, to begin with, stone axes and arrowheads of flint, bone wrist-guards for protection in the course of archery, buttons for fastening leather jerkins, and bone cheek-pieces from horse bridles. The horse was a novelty brought in from the eastern steppes as perhaps mainly a draught animal for chariots but also evidently as a mount for riding. The chariot came west to Europe at this time, and also went south to the eastern Mediterranean and Near East.

The earlier graves of this bell beaker phenomenon of northern Europe still show only stone weapons but as time went by the bronze dagger came to the fore among the grave goods: north-west Europe was joining the Bronze Age already under way in central Europe. Once again, the question arises as to how much of an irruption of new people lies behind such an adoption of new ways of life and new technologies. Some archaeologists have speculated that the language group to which all Europeans now belong (with the exception of the Basques, the Hungarians, the Finns and the Turks), the grouping called Indo-European, came into western Europe at this period. Languages can be introduced into new regions, and come to dominate there, with the arrival of only small groups of people so long as they are in a position to make their presence felt. Perhaps only a relatively small number of adventurers, making common cause with ambitious locals, were able to come in and establish themselves in an eventually dominant role in the closing centuries of the old Neolithic, to usher in the Bronze Age of the territories around the North Sea. It was certainly all linked to a great increase in trade in these times, and the vital exchange of raw materials: and with raw materials went, no doubt, fashions and ideas.

The Bronze Age world

Bronze was an altogether more serviceable material for making weapons and tools than hammered and cast copper alone could ever be. Items of copper manufacture had always been of a rather special character, rare and not for everyday use. Bronze technology made practical the large-scale production of weapons, tools, ornaments – and specials, too, to serve as grave goods or be ritually deposited in the earth (bogs, mostly) as offerings to whatever were the gods and demons of those days. The craftsmen who made bronze must have been regarded as magicians in their own right, who knew the mysteries of creating such hot fires and mingling ores to produce the strange and desirable transmutation.

Neither copper nor tin were especially easy to come by in many parts of north-west Europe, so an extensive system of exchange grew up that pulled together the emerging world of the European Bronze Age. The copper sources were to be found in the Alps, the Carpathians, the Balkans and Ireland; the tin in Germany and central Europe, in Brittany and Cornwall. Over time, the long-distance trade of the Bronze Age called into being a noticeable cultural conformity of design in weapons, carts, horse equipment, drinking vessels, textiles and ornaments. In northern Europe, the Bronze Age saw a further spread through forest clearance into available areas of light soil, actually extending the range beyond what would be kept under the plough in later times, when improvements in that device allowed the ploughing of heavier soils. Some of the extended range of early Bronze Age clearance was abandoned in due course, which explains why so many Bronze Age burial sites are now to be found in charming wooded or heathland areas.

These Bronze Age tombs were finely heaped and furnished with fine grave goods, but their occupants had evidently lived in no fine halls and palaces of a permanent character. This was, indeed, a more mobile world, at least in continental Europe, with more wealth on the hoof and less in the way of settled community-living in attachment to the communal graves of the ancestors. In much of Britain, it seems the old ways were maintained for some time in resistance to the bell beaker ethos, despite the clear arrival of the latter in eastern Britain where beaker burials with just the same array of grave goods that you find at a site in, say, Holland have been excavated at, for example, Burghley House in south Lincolnshire. In time, a notable continuity of the beaker cultural phenomenon is evident up the east coast of Britain and across the North Sea: in this zone there are early signs of land division into individual fields and of the building of roundhouses rather than communal longhouses. From North Norfolk, on the North Sea shore at Holme-next-the-Sea, comes evidence of a ceremonial landscape of the Bronze Age, comparable in its way with Salisbury Plain's: an already excavated circle of fifty-five posts around an upturned tree trunk, precisely dated to have been felled in 2050 BC, is accompanied by another, larger wooden circle yet to be investigated. The barrows of East Anglia in the Bronze Age covered some very rich burials and there were ritual deposits of metal wealth in the Fens. This eastern region bordering on the North Sea, perhaps because it was the first destination in Britain of the trade from Jutland in widely-coveted amber, maintained strong links with the Bronze Age communities centred on Salisbury Plain away to the south-west. When the beaker presence first crops up in the region of Stonehenge and Avebury, its burials look a little marginal to the old and well-established ceremonial centres that had come down from neolithic times. After 2000 BC, the beaker burials got bigger and better and the rich Wessex culture emerged in this location so favourable to agriculture and pastoralism. The Bronze Age chieftains buried with much good stuff, including gold and amber, in their barrows on Salisbury Plain presided over the revamping of Stonehenge that turned it from a neolithic enterprise of earth banks and timbers into a mighty stone monument. But still, they were not living in any fine palaces that we know of. What houses of the time have been excavated, in southeast England not so far from the English Channel, are small, circular constructions in hamlets of up to ten households.

Across the North Sea in Scandinavia, where longhouses remained in fashion, people had made a slow start on metallurgy with imports rather than a home-grown industry, even copying bronze daggers in flint. But the Scandinavians took to Bronze Age technology with relish during the course of the second millennium BC. Instead of importing their finished bronzes from central Europe and Ireland, they began to export their own products both east and west. They imported their raw materials, tin and copper, and in return exported above all a very popular luxury item of the day: amber, the clear yellow fossilised resin of long-gone conifers. Amber fragments from the sea bed are washed up on the southern shores of the Baltic east of the Vistula and along the west coast of Jutland. So fancied was this material that its trade routes took it as far as the eastern Mediterranean. Furs, skins, animals (sheep in particular) and perhaps human beings as slaves were also traded out of Scandinavia for the sake of metal imports.

Boats and burials

The trade of the Bronze Age world needed boats: the Scandinavians, for example, needed them to get around among their own islands and to make their way across the southern Baltic and down the coast of Jutland to reach the Netherlands or cross to Britain. The inhabitants of Britain and the Netherlands needed them to trade – bronze axes have been found in Holland that were made in Wales (on the basis of metal analysis) in the British style. A boat found in Dover and dating to about 1500 BC shows what one sort of Bronze Age shipbuilding tradition could produce: it is some 12 m long with one end squared off. There is no evidence of provision for a sail and no signs of rowlocks: evidently it was a boat to be paddled and a suitable sort of paddle, in oak and of Bronze Age vintage, has been found at Canewdon in Essex. A piece of Dorset shale was found in the

Dover boat, pointing to coastal if not sea-crossing work. The wreck of another Bronze Age boat found off Dover, carvel-built of butted planks sewn with withies, contained an amount of bronze scrap that indicates cross-Channel trade and it has been estimated that the Dover boat itself could be paddled across to France in about five hours, calm water permitting. Interestingly, the Dover boat seems to have been carefully part-dismantled before abandonment: its plank-built sides are missing, having been removed by cutting through the stitching that held them together. Boats of an entirely different sort are depicted in rock carvings of the Scandinavian Bronze Age, on smooth faces polished by glaciers along the coast of Sweden facing the Skagerrak, and they are also modelled in bronzes of the time: they were evidently oared longboats made by cladding wooden frames with cattle hides, and their lightweight construction would have made them handy to carry overland. Their mode of manufacture was thus quite unlike that of the Viking longships of two thousand years later, but their flat keels and high sterns and stems give them something of the same look, especially when they appear to carry animal heads at their prows. One of them, sketched on a bronze sword from Denmark, uncannily resembles the Homeric ships of Greek vase painting, to which it is indeed rather closer in time – though again, of entirely different construction. The largest of these ships might have accommodated eighty men and still have been easy to pick up with its projecting keel extensions. Similar ships are shown on a tomb slab from south Sweden of about 1300 BC, along with the newfangled chariot and lines of mourners including people blowing lurs.

Six great bronze lurs, which lent their design to the wrappers of Danish Lurpak butter, were found in a late Bronze Age votive deposit in Denmark, as part of the long tradition in the prehistoric north European world of making costly offerings to the gods – and to these votive deposits, especially in Denmark, we owe a great deal of our archaeological information as well as some very striking archaeological pieces. There are horned helmets from nearly two thousand years before the Vikings (who never sported them), a magnificent chariot of the sun with a gold solar disk, and much gold all round. The top people of this late Bronze Age world in Denmark (where the best evidence is available, but also in southern Sweden and parts of northern Germany) were wealthy and powerful, and they had themselves buried in style. Not quite the style of their contemporaries at the eastern end of the Mediterranean, perhaps, but fine enough. Under their burial mounds, in their tree-trunk coffins, individuals of this Bronze Age élite were laid to rest in their best clothes of woollen shirts and cloaks, caps and – for a young woman's body – a sort of string miniskirt three millennia ahead of its time: it was quite warm in the Bronze Age. These may, in fact, be special burial clothes that we also glimpse on bronze figurines of an evidently ritual character. It was the tannic acid of the oak that preserved the clothing, as well as the hair and nails, even skin, of these Bronze Age people.

The making of special goods for ritual deposition, not in graves but as part of the long north-west European tradition of 'sacrificing' items in waters and bogs, is attested across the North Sea from Denmark in the area of the Fens. The Late Bronze Age site of Fengate has revealed the layout back in the thirteenth century BC of field systems that clearly supported an efficient pastoral economy. At the site of Flag Fen of about 1000 BC, when the Fens had got wetter and formed in part a shallow inlet of the North Sea from the Wash, a massive timber platform was constructed over the waters with more than a kilometre of timber posts linking it to the mainland. In peat beside the run of these posts (and along with animal bones and pottery) some three hundred metal articles were discovered – including rings and pins and also spears, swords and daggers and fragments of bronze helmets. Some of these items were pretty poor things, made just of tin in some cases: they were specials for the observance of the tradition of deposition. A similar situation of concentrated deposits of goods like these occurs along stretches of the Thames.

The end of the Bronze Age

At the close of Bronze Age times in Denmark, cremation overtook interment and the grave goods that went with the burnt bones tended to become fewer and paltrier. A new technology from southern central Europe was making its impact felt in new patterns of trade in the north-west European world; at the same time, farming – which had brought such advantages to these parts over the previous three millennia – was suffering as rather cooler and wetter conditions came on. The switch to cremation in the Scandinavian world matched a change going on to the south, with the arrival in France and Belgium of the Urnfield culture complex by about 1000 BC. The ashes of the dead were being buried in pits or urns in the ground, to fill whole fields as regular cemeteries, with a rich array of grave goods including swords, armour and bronze vessels, gold, amber, jet, glass and, after about 1000 BC, objects made of iron. Evidently, trade routes were extensive to bring some of these items into Urnfield graves. At the same time, there was a move towards the building of stockaded and fortified habitations, as though trouble was in the air.

In the north, in Scandinavia, the cremations were not specifically of Urnfield character, but the idea was the same – even if, sometimes, a meagre cremation might be put into a full-size inhumation grave. And sometimes burials were placed in ship-shaped settings of stone, particularly on the island of Gotland, arranged with raised 'sterns' and 'prows'. This practice foreshadows the spectacular ship burials of later times in the Nordic and Anglo-Saxon worlds.

At the end of the Bronze Age, there was more metal about than there had ever been, worked as sheet metal and in more complex moulds, as with the elegant technique of lost wax casting where a wax pattern of the end product (which can have a very detailed shape) is enclosed in soft clay and then melted out of the clay mould when the latter is fired. Into the enclosed mould the molten metal is then poured to reveal a fine casting when the mould is broken open after cooling. Multipart moulds were employed to cast the bronze figurines and the lurs of the Danish Late Bronze Age. And gold was much in evidence, especially in north Germany and Scandinavia, and in Ireland. All this wealth in metal points to the existence of powerful hierarchies, whose presence we discern in the construction of huge burial mounds in north Germany and notably in Sweden, with much bronze inside them. But the fact that so many of the cremation graves of the Late Bronze Age in these parts have next to no grave goods in them suggests not just a situation of élites and underdogs, richer and poorer, but also perhaps a shift in beliefs about the dead, who were now honoured in memory and perhaps in recitals of their deeds rather than in themselves as corporeally revered ancestors under their mounds. Their deeds may well have been bloody ones, in the light of so many swords and shields in the archaeological record and of the evidence of enclosure and fortification at so many settlements.

The gradual transition from bronze to iron as the staple raw material of the north-west European world after about 1000 BC (and especially after 700 BC) may have needed the importing of technological experience from outside – ironworking was pioneered in Anatolia after about 1500 BC – but it did not call for the import or farther distribution of its essential ingredient, since iron was widely available. It did demand that furnaces be run at very high temperatures, oxygenated with the bellows that had already been developed in the Bronze Age. If that technological epoch had brought cheaper and more efficient tools (and weapons), with metal-shared ploughs to increase the fundamental farming wealth, then the Iron Age delivered all that in extra abundance on the basis of its commonly available raw material. Far-reaching changes were to be the order of the day.

Chapter 3

Chiefs and emperors

Ironworking first appeared in Europe in the region of Upper Austria and Bavaria: its arrival may be said to mark the formal entry upon the scene of the Celts, with whom the people known by their archaeological type site at Hallstatt may be pretty confidently identified – though their ancestors had clearly been around for some time, perhaps back to the earlier Urnfield days. (Celtic-speaking people had probably also been in place on the Atlantic coast of Europe and in Britain from before 2000 BC: the Celtic tongues are a branch of the Indo-European language group.) Items of iron were at first a rare and precious commodity, but the ready availability of their raw material soon made them into everyday objects, with bronze coming to be reserved for the most treasured possessions and grave goods.

To the north of the Hallstatt culture's reach, on the North German Plain and in Jutland and southern Scandinavia, the Late Bronze Age persisted, though some pieces of iron manufacture (evidently traded from the south) do crop up in the hoards of goods that the northern peoples were prone to deposit in their watery sacrificial sanctuaries. Theirs was a wealthy, and socially stratified, style of life until the close of the Bronze Age, when imports of the metals on which they depended were suspended with the adoption of iron technology amongst their erstwhile suppliers in central Europe. West of the Weser and into the Low Countries, a late version of the Urnfield culture ran on. But Belgium soon experienced a solid input of the Hallstatt lifestyle – and, on the grounds of proximity alone, we can conjecture that Britain must have too. Indeed, Hallstatt material in the form of, for example, swords and buckets and horse equipment is not uncommon on British archaeological sites.

Both trade and warfare seem to have been rather local activities still, with no long-distance commerce except as a chain of local exchanges and no massing of large armies to engage in real battles. Though there were no grand market places or trading depots, goods could be passed on over large distances and a certain uniformity of manufacture for a widespread web of trade came in, for instance, in sword types which could be recognised from Greece to Sweden. There were wheeled carts and specially laid trackways for them to travel on: two such are known from Lower Saxony, that were evidently constructed in the same year (713 BC), to go by the tree rings of some of the wood used in them.

By 600 BC, iron was everywhere the standard material of metal manufacture, with sickles and axes as well as swords produced in large numbers. The swords were no doubt in demand, not just as prestige items but for practical, even everyday use. From the end of the Late Bronze Age, the construction of hill forts had been coming on, for example, in southern Britain (including the northern part of Kent on the North Sea) and Germany: huge communal enterprises to fortify hilltops with concentric rings of earthworks, inside which houses and stores were congregated. In the eastern zone of Britain north of the Thames, hill-forts were sparser but the prevalence of warriors is evidenced in, for example, the Yorkshire barrows. The fortress phenomenon reached its height in the sixth and fifth centuries BC, with fewer but probably more dominant hill forts later on. Times seem to have been really colder and wetter by now, with the loss of some land that had been brought under cultivation during earlier and more expansive years, and consequent population pressures. There may well have been an exacerbated competition among the élites who controlled these prehistoric northern communities as they came into ever increasing contact with the southern powers of colonialist Greece and then Rome: much of that competition would have centred on the slave trade with the Mediterranean world that depended on raiding among the suppliers in the north. There is evidence that a number of the hill-forts across northern Europe suffered hostile assault in these times, and the rich burials of, say, the Haine region in Belgium (from the eighth century to the fifth century BC) testify to the existence of the ruling élites. The previous fashion of cremation gave way to inhumation again, in timber-built chambers which often contained a wheeled vehicle in association with the deceased.

Classical connections

In these last few centuries BC, the Hallstatt version of the Iron Age was succeeded in many parts of central and western Europe (with eventual forays
wider still) by the La Tène phase, whose art style was to enjoy a long-
lasting manifestation in the Celtic world, right into the succeeding centuries
AD. This was a florid style of leafy curves and beasts both sinister and comic,
with an odd penchant for a stylised sort of human head. And alongside their
own products, the La Tène élites favoured Greek tableware and drinking
vessels imported up the Rhône valley from the Greek trading colonies of the
western Mediterranean. The Marne region, west of the Rhine, features the
chariot burials and Mediterranean imports typical of the La Tène culture;
in the south-east of England, something very like the pottery of the Marne
is found and there are chariot burials further up the eastern part of England
in the Wolds and east Yorkshire, though they are a little later and don't show
quite the same range of grave goods as the truly Celtic La Tène heartlands
do. As so often with the British island story, the Iron Age of the British Isles
was plainly keeping up in its way with continental developments but going
its own way at the same time. (In Shetland and Orkney and on the mainland opposite Orkney, the fortified family dwellings known as brochs witness to an Atlantic influence that had not come via the North Sea.)

In the late fourth century BC, a Greek from Marseilles called Pytheas
made his way up the Iberian Atlantic coast and into the Bay of Biscay; after
which he switched to local shipping that took him to the tin country of
Cornwall (already known to the Greeks by repute) and then round the top
of Britain via the Irish Sea; on his way home, he crossed the North Sea to
Jutland to see the amber coast before coming back through the Dover Strait
into slightly more familiar waters. The book he brought out to recount
his adventures, called *On the Ocean*, marked the beginning of the
Mediterranean world's real acquaintance with the North. His Ultima Thule,
by the way, was probably based on what he heard about Norway.

Life around the north-eastern part of the North Sea region was even less
influenced by La Tène developments in central and western Europe than it
was in Britain. An Iron Age that was developed out of the local Late Bronze
Age ensued in the north, with La Tène goods in evidence (as the result of
lines of exchange) and urn cremations. The Brä Cauldron found in eastern
Jutland is a Celtic import from central Europe into this non-Celtic zone,

and the astonishing Gundestrup Bowl with its lurid mythological imagery is another. The climatic downturn led to the abandonment of some cultivation, but also an extension into hitherto neglected parts (in Denmark especially) where fields were laid out as never before and rye adopted as a crop more suitable to colder and wetter conditions. In Holland, marshland was exploited in the same spirit. No doubt it all helped, but increasing population pressure led eventually to the first era of migrations from this general area that brought trouble to the Romans, as we shall shortly see. Meanwhile the longhouse tradition, to house people and cattle, continued in these parts – houses are known from the Netherlands and Jutland, grouped in villages that at this time show little evidence of great social differentiation.

Celtic society on the other hand, was clearly a highly stratified one, with an arrangement of nobles, warriors, priests (the famous druids), craftsmen and farmers. The nobles operated a client system to build themselves factions: in some places there were kings at the top, while other groups were more republican. States were starting to emerge in western Europe for the first time. There was a growth of real towns, called oppida by archaeologists taking their cue from Caesar and other Roman writers: for, by the last few centuries BC, the Romans were increasingly concerned with the doings of the Celts particularly in Gaul, and with other barbarians from further afield. These oppida were permanent settlements, often defended, where trade and manufacture of goods – in metal, pottery, leather, wood, enamel and glass – went on, assisted by the use of coinage adopted from the Mediterranean world. Wine was their other chief adoption. Oppida are not known from really northern Europe, but they do occur across from south-east Britain to Romania, and in some especially favourable places like rivers and river mouths (Colchester is an example) these oppida came to figure as real forerunners of the trading towns of Roman times and the Middle Ages, with industrial zones alongside palaces and temples. Their positioning, indeed, suggests the role of trade with the Roman world as a factor in their growth: in southern Britain, these sites often yield Roman wine amphorae in pre-Roman contexts.

Italy felt the impact of growing Celtic power as early as about 400 BC when the Celts intruded into the northerly region of the Etruscans (founding Milan, by the way) and sacked the city of Rome in the early years of its own climb to power. Celtic trade with the Mediterranean had opened up the Alpine passes to easy access, with the prospect of plunder in the south. (The Celts moved on Macedonia and Greece in the early third century BC.) The Romans were driven to put an end to Celtic power in northern Italy by the start of the second century BC. In about 120 BC, the Greeks in Marseille – who had long been trading into Celtic Europe – called upon the now powerful city of Rome to help them against pressure exerted from the Celtic hinterland. Thus the Romans began the involvement in Celtic Gaul that would bring Caesar his fame and power base in due course, taking Roman rule north to the southern margins of the North Sea.

The threat from the north

But it might be said that the real northerners, living beyond the Celts in southern Scandinavia, found the Romans before the Romans found them. The centuries of climatic downturn and population pressure that had afflicted the northern world since the end of its Late Bronze Age – itself in part a victim of Iron Age technological innovation in central Europe – finally led to migration out of the northern world. At just about the same time as the Celtic Gauls were pressurising Greek Marseilles the Germanic marauders we know as the Teutones and Cimbri (from Roman writers), and associated tribes from the same area of Jutland and the North Sea coast at its base, migrated south. They moved first through Moravia and Hungary to the Middle Danube, turning west in 113 BC to attack the little state of Noricum in the eastern Alpine region, which had close relations with Rome. A Roman army came up to meet them, and was defeated. The Cimbri and Teutones did not, however, press on south into Italy but turned into Gaul, where these migrating tribes from the North Sea defeated several Roman forces over the next few years. The Teutones were finally defeated at Aix-en-Provence in 102 BC and the Cimbri in the Po Valley in 101. (The Teutones have given their name to the whole phenomenon of the Germans, and readers may recall that Danish map maker who wanted to call the North Sea the Cimbric Sea.)

By the sixties BC, the German threat to Gaul was becoming newly apparent, and Caesar seized his opportunity to advance his army career, and next his political one, by gaining the Roman state's approval to annexe Gaul, which process was completed as far as the Rhine by 51 BC. By this time, Roman trade with Gaul was well-established, and a wine export route had been opened up that reached as far as southern Britain, via Guernsey, in the hands of local shipping from Gaul. Metals were picked up in Britain for export into the Roman and Romanising world. The Rhine made a convenient frontier for Rome in north-west Europe and at the time Britain itself was rather beyond the Romans' grasp. Caesar nonetheless made what were largely propaganda forays across the Rhine, and also into Britain in 55 and 54 BC, staying only briefly, though to rather more effect the second time, when he defeated a native confederacy north of the Thames and established a basis for future relations. The Roman presence was now in place at the southern end of the North Sea.

The Rhine frontier became something of a Celtic-Germanic tribal frontier in the Romans' hands, rather more definitively than it had been in easier-going days before the Romans took charge. The Celtic Gauls were progressively ever more Romanised, but the Romans became better acquainted with the Germans, too, especially close to their frontier. Both Caesar and then the historian Tacitus a century-and-a-half later took the trouble to describe something of Germanic tribal life. Their accounts, read in conjunction with an assessment of the modern archaeological evidence, tell us what we know about these now only semi-prehistoric people just beyond the limits of the world that historians like Tacitus inhabited.

The Germans were a continuum of individual tribes (speaking dialects of another branch of the Indo-European language family), among whom intertribal raiding was a way of life. Each tribe was ruled by an élite, as the Celtic tribes were, with a council under a leader the Romans called *rex* after their own kings of much earlier times. A war leader called a *dux* (Latin again) could be elected for military emergencies, which were evidently frequent. Tacitus says that:

> *the Germans have no fondness for peace ... and a large body of clients cannot be kept together except through violence and war.*

The Druids were the Celtic world's medicine men, but the Germans had something like them, and were addicted to the old-established northern religious observance of making offerings to the Other World via depositions in bogs and watery places. The offerings were not just of fine arms and ornaments or whole chariots, but of people too. Sometimes the people were the outcasts and criminals of their tribes, as Tacitus details, but sometimes they were evidently offerings to whatever gods (ancestors of Odin, and the rest of the Germanic and Nordic pantheon, quite possibly) the Germans went in awe of. Thanks to the preservative properties of the bogs in which these bodies were confined, we can rather uncannily look into the faces now of some of these barbarians of the Iron Age, from a few centuries BC to a few centuries AD. The most famous is the Tollund man from Jutland, with his sheepskin cap on his head and the noose that ended his life around his neck. Another striking face is that of the blindfolded Windeby girl. Another wears his hair in the Swabian side-knot that Tacitus tells us was the fashion of one tribe called the Suebi by the Romans. From a bog deposit of this time comes what may well be the world's oldest preserved pair of trousers, now in the Schleswig Museum. Tacitus also mentions a more northerly tribe, strong in men and ships, that we can identify with the Svear who have given their name to modern Sverige (Sweden). Pliny has a reference to an island area he calls Scatinavia, and we may note again the mention of Ultima Thule by Pytheas in the fifth century BC, which may reflect hearsay about Norway that he picked up on his travels in north-west Europe. (The Danes were originally a tribe in southern Sweden, too – and Norway got its name much later on, meaning quite simply 'the way to the North'.)

The impact of Rome

In the time of the first Roman emperor, Augustus, there had been a scheme to extend the Roman frontier beyond the Rhine and re-form it along the Elbe, Vltava and Danube. It was in part the prospect of enhanced Baltic trade, in amber and furs, that prompted this plan. But the idea was hard to implement in a terrain that lacked anything like oppida to take and control but did not lack forests for enemies to melt into. After some advance towards the Elbe, the Romans were heavily defeated in the Teutoberger Wald about 150 km south of the Elbe and the second emperor Tiberius gave up on a bad job after one last attempt in AD 16 and withdrew to the Rhine. Interestingly, the German *dux* who defeated the Romans had been in the Roman cavalry (a not uncommon career for Germans of the time): in AD 19 he made a bid for *rex* but was seen off by his own relations; the Roman version of his name was Arminius, Herman in his own Germanic tongue, from the same root word that gave the Romans their word for the entire territory of these Germanic tribes, Germania. Some of the best examples of Roman military gear that we possess today have been found in Danish bogs

– kit taken home by erstwhile mercenaries in the Roman army, or captured in conflict. And many a tribal leader liked to be buried with luxury items from the Roman world – like the coloured glass cups from a Danish grave of about AD 200, with bulls and birds depicted on them, or the silver drinking cups with scenes from Homer's *Iliad*. Roman wine-drinking kit, despite the manly contempt of the northerners for such thin potations, has been found in Norway and Sweden. What were evidently distribution centres for Roman goods appeared in places like Stevns in east Sjaelland.

Once the Romans settled on their Rhine frontier, with legionary camps along the river at Nijmegen, Xanten and Cologne (and the line continuing along the Danube from Regensburg to Vienna and Budapest), there were long periods of comparatively peaceful life and commerce for people on both sides of that frontier. Glass from the Rhine, the red Samian tableware from France, wine and olive oil from France and Spain and Italy: these were the goods the Romans traded out of the empire. The bolder Roman traders ventured in person across the Rhine, to engage in the trade of amber from west Jutland and the Baltic, sometimes to procure the wild beasts or slaves for the gladiatorial shows that disfigured Roman life. Some German traders crossed the other way into the Roman province and the frontier zone beyond the formal frontier came rather haphazardly to use Roman coinage in its dealings, as the coin hoards discovered by archaeology attest.

There was in the northern world outside the Empire a return to a richer and more socially stratified way of life that went along with trade with the Roman province. A village like the one at Flögeln in Lower Saxony has rather more in the way of developed metal workshops than might be expected of a simple barbarian settlement. Similarly at Drengsted in Jutland we find iron production on a scale beyond the call of local needs. At nearby Dankirke there was a store of luxury goods. The settlement of Feddersen Wierde, near Bremerhaven, includes one farmstead with a striking concentration of Roman imports, presumably in the hands of some local bigwig: coins, pottery and bronze vessels make up the collection. The main building here was of the well-established longhouse pattern of the north, but in this instance not divided into compartments for human beings, animals and perhaps a craft area as were other houses at Feddersen Wierde: it looks like a meeting-place, or hall of feasting – in a way very suggestive of the halls of the Anglo-Saxon and Viking lords of a few centuries later. The complex associated with this great hall consisted of smaller houses, and workshops dedicated to iron and bronze manufacture, while the rest of the village included other large and conventionally divided houses, food storage buildings raised on posts and more workshops including ones for wood-workers among whom were wheelwrights. Some of the cattle stalls could accommodate twenty beasts and half the animal bones at Feddersen Wierde belonged to cattle, along with bones from sheep, horses, pigs and dogs. Barley and oats, beans and flax are among the plant remains from the site. This remarkable village was founded as a mere hamlet on the coastal marshes of the Weser estuary in the first century BC; by the second century AD it had been enlarged into a village of fifty houses, on an artificial mound to protect it against flooding, and its houses were arranged in radial lines from an open space behind the mudflats that butted on to the estuary. It was abandoned in the fifth century AD when coastal flooding became too much for its occupants to go about their agricultural business.

During the centuries of Feddersen Wierde's existence, there was much occupation of the coastal lowlands of the northern parts of the Netherlands and of Germany and southern Jutland. The waterlogged conditions of the archaeological sites left behind have allowed the survival of a considerable amount of wooden material: scratch ploughs, fences, the lower parts of wattle walls. Arable farming was a crucial part of the local economy, but export into the Roman world was also very important: those cattle stalls, evidently enlarged from time to time, point to the supply of cattle and cattle products to the Roman province across the frontier, including leather for saddles, boots and army tents. The growing wealth and settlement concen-trations of barbarian north-west Europe led on to the emergence of major chieftainships and even state organisation among the non-Romanised peo-ples of these parts, with an increase in population pressures. These barbar-ians knew the Roman world's attractions and were becoming rich enough and well enough organised and equipped to contemplate more than raiding into Roman territory, spurred on as they were by the mounting pressures of their own populations (and of others to the east of them, outside our North Sea ken). Already in AD 162 the Chatti tried to move south into Roman Germany – it was a harbinger of great developments to come.

The Romans in Britain

When the Romans established their Rhine frontier at the time of the first emperors, they were (for several centuries, as it turned out) well-established on the southern margin of the North Sea, or Northern Ocean as Tacitus called it. Caesar had been to Britain twice and opened up relations with the coastal tribe of the Trinovantes north of the Thames. A trade developed between south-east Britain and northern Gaul, taking wine and olive oil to Britain, where a colonisation of 'Belgic' culture from northern France and Belgium had been under way from perhaps as early as c.100 BC. That process brought state-like social organisation (and the use of coins) to southern Britain, at least, well before it evolved across the North Sea in barbarian north-west Europe along the lines we have just seen. In these circumstances, it was natural for the Romans to think of annexing southern Britain into their empire alongside the similar populations of Gaul and the Roman province of Germania. The British were, moreover, rather making a nuisance of themselves as a stronghold of nationalistic Druidism, banned in Gaul since the twenties of the first century. In AD 43 the emperor Claudius invaded by Richborough near Ramsgate, very nearly on the North Sea – it is an inland site now, overlooking marshes that were once a sheltered anchorage. The Romans' initial intention was focussed only on the incorporation of south-east England, staying clear of the highland zones to the west and north. But by AD 70 (and after the suppression of the Boudiccan revolt centred in East Anglia) it was apparent that it would be necessary to go much further and, ideally, subdue the whole island. In the event, the Romans stopped substantially at the line of Hadrian's Wall, running west from the region of Newcastle today. Their frontier arrangements here, as on the Rhine, fluctuated from time to time with efforts to create a border further north, in the form of the Antonine Wall from the Firth of Forth where they maintained a fort at Inveresk on the North Sea. It is interesting to note that south of Hadrian's Wall the Romans managed to occupy an area of Britain well to the north of any part of Germany they succeeded in holding down, with a North Sea coastline much larger in the west, in Britain, than the one they controlled south of the Rhine in the east.

During the relatively peaceful and prosperous first couple of centuries or so of Roman presence on the North Sea, Britain and the Romanised provinces of northern France, the Low Countries and southern Germany traded extensively. We know of one Viducius, hailing from the Rouen area of northern France, who counted himself a Negotiator Britannicus (dealer with Britain) and seems to have enjoyed a very successful commercial career, trading from Colijnsplat in the Netherlands to York in Britain. He was one of a group of *negotiatores* who set up altars in a temple at Colijnsplat in thanksgiving for their safe and profitable crossings: he is recorded in an inscription found at York as a donor of temple gates. In this world of open North Sea trading, it is entirely possible that he ended his days in York. (Salt was one of the goods these merchants took from the Netherlands: they were often known as *negotiatores salarii*.)

The ships in which the cross-Channel and North Sea trade was carried on must have been a varied lot. At the quayside of Roman Colchester, for example, you might have seen very different ships from Gaul on the one hand and from the Low Countries and Germany on the other, products of quite separate traditions of shipbuilding. We have seen that dugout tree-trunk canoes have a long history in the North Sea region, and that skin boats on wooden frames are attested in Bronze Age pictures and models. Caesar mentions that Rhineland locals were using log rafts to cross their river in his time and two log rafts of the second century AD have been found near Strasbourg. The Greek document known as the *Massiliote* (Marseille) *Periplus*, a sort of sailors' handbook, reports the use of seagoing skin boats between Brittany, Britain and Ireland before Caesar's day; of course, nothing like that has survived, except perhaps as vestigial traces of such boats used in burials in the Roman period on south Humberside and in Fife. You might not think timber-framed skin-covered boats would ever be much use in really open seas, but Tim Severin sailed such a boat – going by traditional western Irish boat-building techniques – across the Atlantic via Iceland in 1976.

Progress with boats

Log boats have, not surprisingly, survived rather better in a few instances than skin boats were ever likely to: for example, at Appleby, Short Ferry and Brigg in South Humberside, from around 1000 BC. The Brigg boat was lost in a fire at Hull Museum in 1944, but records and photographs show it to have been made from a 15 m oak tree, with a rounded front and an otherwise open back end fitted with a caulked transom. It may have been a ceremonial item, but boats like it could have served for fishing and fowling and the transport of goods. The Brigg dugout could have accommodated a crew of twenty-eight paddlers, but you would hardly have put to sea in it. This log boat tradition has been, however, a very long-lasting one. A boat based on a single log 13 m long, from a tributary of the Humber but dated to about 300 BC, has the refinements of a composite bow construction, a fitted transom and wash strakes attached by pegging. Roman writers mention the use of similar boats in France and Germany, and two large boats in this style were found at Zwammerdam in the Rhine-Scheldt delta region. They were evidently river barges, with the sophistication of flooded wells, between watertight bulkheads, presumably for the transport of live fish. They may have been masted for sailing purposes. A Roman period altar from this region shows another sort of river barge or lighter, with curved-up prow and stern, loaded with wine casks. Lighters were everywhere used to tranship goods from seagoing ships for transport further inland – we can imagine such an everyday process going on, too, on the British side of the North Sea at Caister-on-Sea, from which goods would be sent up the river Tas to Caistor St Edmunds, not far from Norwich and once a busy Roman town where there are only fields today.

It was probably the fitting of wash strakes and also the repair of log boats that suggested the next stage of boat-building sophistication. (Though log boats were not finally abandoned in Scotland and Germany, for example, until the early years of the nineteenth century.) A log boat from Poole Harbour on the south coast of England, dating to the third or fourth century BC, shows the underside of its bow shaped to mimic the stem post of a boat built with planks and fitted with stem and stern posts: this rather demonstrates that plank-built boats must have been in existence at this time in this part of the world. (The process whereby the plank-building notion may have come about is illustrated in the repairs carried out to a much later log boat – of about AD 1300 – found in the former lake at Kentmere in Cumbria.) It was planked boats that were to have a long future ahead of them. A single plank is the earliest evidence of this style of boat-building, from a tributary of the River Severn and dating to about 1600 BC. The Dover boat we noted in the previous chapter is not much younger.

The three Bronze Age boats of about 1300 BC from Ferriby, Humberside, were constructed of abutted oak planks sewn together with yew withies and caulked with moss kept in place under a lath by the stitching of the planks. The bottom planks were carved to provide cleats for attachment to timbers across the flat bottom of the boat. (Another boat from Brigg, of about 800 BC, was of similar construction but with willow withies and in general of a less boat-like but rather boxed shape.) Such boats are reckoned capable of carrying up to three tonnes of loading, including their crew. The rather sophisticated Ferriby boats may well have been capable of inshore seagoing in quite rough seas, paddled by their crews.

It was boats very likely derived from this Ferriby style of the Bronze Age that Caesar encountered on the coast of north-west France in the hands of the Celtic Veneti in the first century BC. Strabo described them too: of oak planking, with flat bottoms and high bows and sterns, sailed with leather sails and anchored with stones attached to chains. Two coins of the British ruler Cunobelin, from just before the Roman conquest of Britain, show the same kind of boat, with deep hull, side rudder and square sail. (The use of a mast to hoist sail is first indicated in a gold model boat of the first century BC from Broighter in Northern Ireland: its steering oar and anchor are modelled too; it evidently represents a hide-covered frame-built boat that could be rowed as well as sailed.) Ships like those of the Veneti were more use in the coastal waters of the Atlantic and English Channel – and the North Sea, for that matter – than the Romans' own boats were, since their flat bottoms and shallow draughts allowed them to be got into not very deep waters and to be beached as necessary. There was evidently a lively trade between the southern and northern worlds by means of these vessels, with the Channel Islands as stopovers on the way: a boat discovered in the harbour of St Peter Port in Guernsey was of the Celtic sort, with mast and sail, though of Gallo-Roman date. Caesar admitted that his own oared ships were not as much use in the northern waters as the Gauls' sailed boats were, which moreover were higher-sided and hard to board in Roman fashion. When the two sides fought with boats off the Brittany coast, the Romans resorted to attempts to damage their opponents' rigging with grappling hooks.

But there is some evidence for the eventual use of ships of a more Mediterranean style in the waters of north-west Europe in Roman times: the wreck from the Thames by County Hall in London of the third or fourth century AD is a case in point. These boats employed edge-to-edge planking not sewn together but held with tenons inserted into the thickness of the planks and dowelled. The second-century AD seagoing ship from

Blackfriars in London illustrates another approach to boat-building in which the planks are not fastened to each other at all but rather nailed to wooden ribs with long iron nails turned over inside. This technique was also employed on boats for inland waterway use in the Rhineland region of the first to third centuries AD: these boats were long and narrow, flat-bottomed and barge-like, with low sides slightly rising at stem and stern. The clenched nails heralded a technique of great importance in the building of the Frisian cogs of medieval times.

Further north in non-Roman Europe, yet another technique of future importance comes to light in the Hjortspring boat of the third century BC, found on the island of Als, Denmark. This was a 14 m long paddled war-ship of the day (war canoe might be a better name), sacrificially deposited with a mass of weapons and military gear including 150 wooden shields and 138 iron spearheads. It was a sewn plank boat of lime, built up from a dugout sort of bottom with two strakes per side having overlapped edges in an early manifestation of the clinker-built style that would be employed on Viking boats and, later still, on the medieval cogs. (There is a similar boat, from Björke in Sweden, only half the length but with a higher free-board of two planks per side.) The clinker mode of construction made for stronger boats, able to stand up to the rough waters of the North Sea. The Hjortspring boat was symmetrical in shape so that it could be worked from both ends, with a lashed-on steering oar. Interestingly Tacitus tells us that the Germans' boats had 'a prow at both ends, so they always face the right way for beaching': another pointer to the future design of Germanic and Viking craft. The Hjortspring boat predates the seagoing migrations of the Angles and Saxons and Jutes by about seven hundred years, but the boat-building tradition at which it hints was to be very important to them in the times of trouble that overtook the Roman Empire on the continent and in Britain from the third century AD onwards.

Chapter 4

Settlers and traders

From the third century AD, the Roman Empire came under increasing threat from turbulent tribes on its frontiers. In the far north of Britain, a Pictish confederacy was on the up. Piracy threatened North Sea trade. In the region between the middle and upper reaches of the Rhine and Elbe, the Alamanni, as the Romans rendered them, rose to power – again as a confederacy, here of Germanic tribes calling themselves the 'all men' (and, incidentally, going on to give their name to the Germans and Germany in the French language). To their north, inland from the North Sea in what is now the Low Countries and part of northern Germany, the Franks were coming to be a factor at about the same time: they were already a part-Romanised body of people, in everyday habits at least. In turn, to their north, on the coast fringed with the chain of islands that runs from the Netherlands to Schleswig-Holstein, the Frisians lurked, with the Saxons across the base of Jutland, and the Angles to their north. North of them, the Jutes occupied the northern part of the Jutland peninsula. Across from them in southern Sweden, more Angles and the Svear and Gotar (Swedes and Goths to be) flourished, with the Norse emerging in Norway. Around the Alamanni, tribes with names that would resonate in later times were gathering: Langobardi, Burgundi, Vandali. The Langobardi from the base of Jutland would give their name to Lombardy; the Vandals hailed from the region of Vendsyssel in Jutland; the Burgundi came from Burgundarholm, the Danish Baltic island of Bornholm today.

Beginning in the first century AD, the Romans had maintained their British fleet, the Classis Britannica, at Dover as a support for their forces in

Britain and a protection for their trade routes between Gaul, Britain and Germany. (There was another fleet based at Boulogne.) By the end of the third century, a line of forts and signal stations had been established against Frankish and Saxon raiders: these were the Forts of the Saxon Shore, the east coast of Britain that faced the homeland of the raiders across the North Sea. In fact, they stretched from Porchester on the Channel coast to Norfolk, with opposite numbers across the North Sea as far north as the Old Rhine mouth. The massive walls of Burgh Castle in Norfolk give a good idea of what these forts were like – this one was big enough to be manned by five hundred soldiers operating in association with a navy unit in the estuary nearby. Increasingly, the fleets and local naval units were employed against the threat from across the sea, mainly as a mobile aid to land defences since interceptions at sea were difficult away from the narrow Dover Strait. There were Roman coastal defences on the Gaulish coast to the north of the Dover Strait and in the Low Countries in the region of Bruges and The Hague. The raiders were evidently no mean threat. Whoever precisely they were in tribal terms, they came to be known as Saxons when they began to threaten Gaul and Roman Britain. It seems that population pressures at home, and the push of peoples from the east, together perhaps with a loss of farming land to slightly rising sea level at this time, drove the northern peoples to their raids and migrations into the fading Roman Empire. Around AD 280, the Roman naval commander Carausius was reckoned to be taking bribes from the Saxons to let them through on raids (and then robbing them on their way home): in his difficulties, he revolted against the Roman Empire and set up a little empire of his own, consisting of Britain and a northern coastal zone of Gaul. He was usurped by his second-in-command in 293, who lasted for three more years before Britain was brought back under full Roman control.

In 359, a disaster on the Rhine obliged the emperor Julian to send six hundred transport ships to Britain for supplies to help the recovery of the Romans' position. Meanwhile, the threat from the Picts in Scotland and the Scots from Ireland grew. In 367, a simultaneous attack by most of the enemies, northern and eastern, of Roman Britain earned itself the name of 'Conspiracy of the Barbarians'. Roman reinforcements were sent in through Richborough. In the aftermath, Britain's fortifications were repaired and extended, with a line of watchtowers added on the north-east coast of England. But the writing was on the wall for Roman Britain, no matter how much most of its citizens might want to hold on to their Roman way of life.

By the middle of the fifth century, the Franks were in control of much of the Rhineland and the Meuse and Moselle valleys: their graves in this region from that time on mark a clear break with Roman traditions. When their leader Clovis died a Christian in 511, the Franks were in power in the old Roman province of Gaul, though the 'Saxons' too reached down into northern France. By this time the migrations to Britain of the Saxons, Angles and Jutes – and some Frisians too – were well under way. Some mingling of these peoples is thought to have occurred before they ever set off for Britain in a very determined way and, interestingly, it seems clear that many of their original settlements at home were entirely abandoned in the process of migration, with no new additions to their native cemeteries and a general depopulation of their old homelands. This was a time of deteriorating climate in northwest Europe, with frequent marine transgressions around the North Sea.

Germans in Britain

Archaeological evidence suggests that there were already Germanic mercenaries in the Roman army in Britain before the end of the fourth century AD, helping to man those forts of the south and east coasts that aimed to protect Roman Britain against raids from, ironically enough, the barbarian compatriots of these very mercenaries. By the early fifth century, there was sometimes a Germanic mercenary presence inland in Britain, too; and this presence remained after the Roman army formally pulled out of Britain in AD 410. The various local rulers of Britain in the wake of the Roman withdrawal must have relied on the mercenaries to some degree in their efforts to protect themselves against the Pictish marauders from Scotland who had seized their chance to raid down the east coast of Britain. Indeed, the British authorities may well have called over yet more mercenaries from across the North Sea to augment their defences – from the second half of the fifth century, there were certainly a great number coming in. This situation may be the inspiration for the legend of a British leader called Vortigern who called over three shiploads of Saxon mercenaries under Hengest and Horsa to see off a Pictish threat. The story goes that the Saxons subsequently set their sights on taking power for themselves and turned on their British employers, bringing over more and more of their fellows to wreck the Roman towns of south-east Britain and embark on a westward expansion into the bargain. The Britons are said to have fought back and defeated the Saxons at the end of the fifth century, leading on to some decades of peace during which the incomers settled down and formed themselves into kingdoms. (The legend of King Arthur appears to relate in part to a similar situation, where a leader of the Romano-British people faced up to going it alone against the incomers, but the Arthur story is mainly an invention of much later times.)

Writing in the early eighth century, Bede felt very sure that he knew just where the various immigrants came from across the North Sea and just where they settled in Britain. His claims go against the archaeological evidence that Angles and Saxons and Jutes were already somewhat mingled before they left their homes to cross to Britain; on the other hand, his assertion that their original homelands were quite depopulated by their leaving is born out by archaeology. Bede says that the Jutes from the northern half of Jutland settled in Kent and the Isle of Wight, together with the part of Wessex opposite the island; the bigger part of Wessex, and Sussex and Essex, were taken by Saxons from Saxony; the Angles who came from territory between the homelands of the Jutes and Saxons occupied East Anglia, Mercia and Northumbria. It seems unlikely that things were so clear-cut, but plainly the immigrants came from the region of Lower Saxony in the Elbe-Weser region of north Germany and adjacent lands in parts of the Netherlands and Denmark. And however mixed they might have started to be at home, they went on to become more so in Britain. The extent to which the existing Romano-British people of, say, East Anglia were ousted by the incomers is a matter of controversy. Certainly the Germanic language of the incomers was soon triumphant, whether because the speakers of Celtic and Latin fled or stayed and adopted the language of the new people. In northern France, the physical types of people buried with Roman or Frankish or Saxon grave goods are sometimes the same; in other cemeteries, there seems to be an intrusion of robuster, taller physical types. But the French language is essentially Latin-derived and not heavily influenced by the Germanic dialects of the original Franks and Saxons. A thorough ousting in East Anglia is suggested by the change of burial customs that brought cremation pots and grave goods with clear parallels across the North Sea, but any such ousting may still have left a lot of Romano-British natives around.

The pottery from the site of Mucking in Essex (land of the East Saxons) is very like pottery from Feddersen Wierde, the village on the coastal flats of the Weser estuary in Lower Saxony that we looked at in the previous chapter. Cremation pots from Spong Hill in Cambridgeshire are very like ones from the Elbe-Weser region. The jewellery and other grave goods in cemeteries on both sides of the North Sea are very alike. But the houses the immigrants built in Britain were not like the ones they abandoned back in Lower Saxony. Instead of the aisled longhouses with lines of posts down the inner space and room for cattle and human beings at each end (of, say, Flögeln or Feddersen Wierde), the houses in Britain were constructed with their stouter support posts in the outer walls and no obvious divisions for men and beasts. It has been suggested that the milder climate of south-east Britain made it possible to leave the cattle out. Structures seen on the continent in association with the aisled houses but not thought there to have served for habitation were developed in Britain in such large numbers, alongside few larger buildings, that it looks as if they were the actual dwelling-houses of the immigrants in their new home. They were often only about 6 m by 4.5 m and they had their floors sunk up to 1 m below ground level; hence their German name, Grubenhäuser. There were two hundred of them discovered in the excavations at Mucking, sixty at West Stowe in Suffolk. At all events, the Anglo-Saxons (as we can call them from this point) in England preferred to live in their own villages of little houses rather than attempt to take over the plentiful housing in the Roman style to be found in the decaying towns they had overthrown – towns were 'tombs for the living' in Anglo-Saxon eyes, though they did smash the sunken bases of their Grubenhäuser straight through the rather finer floors of Roman buildings in Colchester.

Consolidation and Christianity

The Anglo-Saxon conquests left the North Sea coast of Britain under Anglo-Saxon control as far as the Firth of Forth, where the old British population held on, with the Picts to the north of them. (The Picts would succumb to the Gaelic Scots in the ninth century, already in place from the top of northern Ireland across to the southern part of the Western Isles and adjacent mainland – the territory called Dalriada – in the late fifth century.) From the time of their arrival, with whatever temporary reverses they may have suffered at the hands of people like Vortigern and Arthur, the Anglo-Saxons expanded west, towards and into the British and Gaelic lands.

Of course, the way the Anglo-Saxon people crossed to England in such large numbers was in boats, in which they were no doubt anxious never to get too far away from land for too long. The sort of boats they rowed across in can be discerned in the Nydam boat, now in the museum in Schleswig. This oak-built boat of about AD 350 (and thus only just predating the major sea crossings of the Saxons, etc.) is one of those ritual deposits to which the pagan northerners were so addicted. It is the earliest complete hull we possess, though there was another one at Nydam made of fir planks, destroyed by fire in the nineteenth century. In line with its ritual purpose, the Nydam boat lacks certain fittings and there is no sign at all that it was ever used to sail or row.

Going by this wonderfully preserved oak boat (and the plans made of the fir one), we recognise a mature tradition of boat-building that produced large open rowing vessels – the oak boat is 24 m long, though only fifteen pieces of wood were used in its construction. Its five strakes per side run the whole length of the boat, overlapped in clinker style and fastened together with clenched iron nails. (Previously the boats of the northern world had featured sewn-together planking, but the boats of the Celts appear to have been nailed, like those of the Romans.) The hull of the Nydam boat is braced with wooden frames that were purposely grown to shape, to which the strakes are lashed by cleats carved into them. The ends of the strakes meet at massive stem and stern posts but there is no true keel, but rather a keel plank. Steering was achieved with a heavy side paddle at the stern that must have been lashed to the hull. The vessel was powered by fifteen oars, operated in lashed-on tholes, rather than sailed. Representations of boats on coins and other items, all a little later than the Nydam boat, do suggest the eventual use of masts on broadly similar vessels. (Perhaps the sail concept was derived from ships of the more southerly tradition of, for example, the Veneti.) Though the Nydam boat does not show one like it, a fragmentary figurehead with a mouth full of gnashing teeth was found in the river Scheldt at Appels in Belgium, dating to the fifth century. A recent discovery in a cemetery of this same date near Wremen, on the Weser estuary north of Bremerhaven, has disclosed two boat burials – one for a man, the other a woman – with well-preserved wooden boats of a type that would have served as ancillary vessels for the larger Nydam boat: they are log boats with built-on side planking, covered over with a tent-like arrangement of further planks to enclose the burials. They appear to be regular boats that had seen some use before serving as burial places.

All in all, the Nydam boat itself is judged well up to short sea voyages and generally represents the sort of vessel in which the Angles, Saxons and Jutes crossed to Britain a century after it was built. There must have been an awful lot of such boats to bring so many immigrants across the North Sea and depopulate the homelands they left behind. During the period of the mass migration to Britain, the emphasis of North Sea traffic must have been skewed away from the long-established contacts between Gaul (and the Romanised Low Countries and Germany) and Britain, especially since the newcomers were pagans introducing themselves in force into a society quite extensively Christianised in the latter years of Roman imperial rule. Like the native population of Britain in general, the Christian establishment rather retreated before the onslaught, holing up in the west to form the basis of the distinctive Celtic brand of Christianity in later times. But missionary enterprise from the continent was reasserted in the south-east after a royal marriage brought a Frankish Christian princess to Kent, with clerics but also masons and glaziers coming in to work in churches not just in southern England but in the north of England, too, as the rest of the invaders became converted to Christianity. There is evidence that places like the decayed Forts of the Saxon Shore were sometimes used as bases by the incoming missionaries. In time, the Christianised Anglo-Saxons were able to send their own missionaries across the North Sea to help with the conversion of their cousins back home in northern Europe, who maintained their pagan heritage much longer than the migrants to Britain had been able to. A wonderful pair of golden horns with pagan iconography and runic lettering (found in Denmark but now, alas, known only from drawings made before their disappearance in the early nineteenth century) witnesses to the continuing production of fine pagan cult objects in the northern world at a time when the successor states of the old Roman Empire were well and truly Christianised. The Saxon homelands in Germany were not converted till the late eighth century, at about the time they fell under the sway of Charlemagne whose own Frankish ancestors had been Christians for a long time.

Pagan survivals

The Scandinavians were to remain outside the Christian fold for a long time yet. In the sixth and seventh centuries, southern Sweden and the Baltic and Danish islands were on the receiving end of a trading line that stretched up from the Byzantine Empire centred on Constantinople: the eastern emperors bribed off their local threats with gold, which found its way up to the Baltic in enough quantity to embellish the homes and graves of the rulers of that region. Southern Sweden at this time was dotted with well-organised and fortified settlements, some of them quite large. At Old Uppsala, north of Stockholm, there are three enormous mounds and the two of them that have been excavated reveal themselves as the burial places, at about AD 500 and AD 600, of rulers of the Svear, the Ynglingas of both Norse and English tradition. The Uppland cemeteries at Vendel and Valsgärde of the late sixth and early seventh centuries attest to the trade this part of the world was conducting with both the Byzantine Empire far to the south-east and with the Frankish one to the south-west. The Vendel burials, with their shields and helmets, horse gear (and horses and dogs) are interesting for their use of ships as the chosen vehicles of the dead and their possessions: the ships themselves have not survived in these graves, but their shapes – of 9 m or so length – furrow the site to this day, a few kilometres north of Uppsala.

Some actual fragments of a late sixth-century boat have come to light at Gredstedbro in Denmark, but the boat which tells us most about the ships built at the time for use in northern waters has not actually survived at all in its own fabric, except for a few iron rivets with a bit of wood around them. Rather it has come down as a detailed impression in the ground which the most painstaking archaeology has been able to bring to light. It is the Sutton Hoo boat, from the site in East Anglia close to Rendlesham which was the home of the King of the East Angles and High King of the English in the sixth century. Like the Vendel ship burials, the Sutton Hoo boat was a funerary deposition, even if nobody was found in it, and the famous helmet that came out of it is very closely matched by one of the helmets from Vendel. There were, clearly, strong links between the rulers of East Anglia and those of Uppland and trade went on between the two areas, with Uppland sending its iron and East Anglia returning its grain, wool and leather – however the Uppland kings were buried as pagans, while the East

Anglian ruler went to his rest as some sort of Christian. Like the Gredstedbro fragments of the same age and pattern (and like the Nydam boat of two hundred years or so before), the Sutton Hoo vessel was a clinker-built ship with overlapping planks. Its frames were shaped to fit the hull and fixed in position with wooden trenails.

The ship exists now as a fibreglass cast made from the sand mould left behind by the decay of the original timbers – thanks to its having been filled with sand at the time of burial, both exterior and interior details are well recorded. What we see is a ship not a great deal longer than the Nydam boat, at 30 m (with a beam of 4.8 m), though its strakes are not single lengths like the Nydam's but rather riveted composites, nine of them per side. It has the same sort of stem and stern posts as the boat in Schleswig, with an iron-bolted stem that may represent a repair. There were tholes for forty oars, nailed on rather than lashed. Any steering oar with which the Sutton Hoo ship was formerly furnished was not found in the burial mound, but the side is strengthened to take it. Like the Nydam boat, the Sutton Hoo vessel was very likely not a sailing ship, though the location where a mast might have been fitted served as the burial chamber and may have been altered for that purpose. While the Nydam boat looks as though it was made specially for ritual deposition, the Sutton Hoo ship was prob-ably a royal vessel that had seen some everyday use before it ended up in the funerary mound of its owner. That man was almost certainly King Raedwald, who died in AD 625. He was a rather selective convert to Christianity, who maintained his Christian altar alongside the cult items of his own old gods: the Sutton Hoo ship burial was his traditional pagan send-off, and the reason why his body was not found in the boat may well be that Christian priests managed to insist on a burial according to their rites for his mortal remains if not his treasured chattels.

Wealth and trade

The treasure was certainly rich and impressive, a testament to the wealth of the East Anglian dynasty that controlled the international trade of their part of the world, whose key export was – as it would be for a thousand years – wool. In this mound overlooking the estuary of the River Deben in Suffolk, there was helmet, sword, shield, axe, scramasax (like a cutlass), spears, drinking horns, bowls, buckets, cauldrons. There was a great silver dish made a century before the burial by the Byzantine silversmiths of Anastasius in Constantinople; thirty-seven coins from the Frankish empire of the Merovingians date the burial itself. The helmet was almost certainly made in Sweden and, like the Vendel helmets, its design is ultimately derived from late Roman military inspiration. As most probably is the pattern of the stone sceptre with metal framework, which seems to mimic the general idea of Roman military standards. The rest of the fine metalwork from Sutton Hoo shows both Scandinavian and Frankish influences but is thought to be of largely local manufacture, in some cases exceeding in quality the products of the foreigners.

The Anglo-Saxons had come to England in ships and presumably they kept up, to some extent at least, their warship fleets after they settled in and began to expand their influence west and north. The Northumbrian settlers made sallies into Scotland and Ireland in the seventh century and must have needed the support of ships to do so. The Picts in the Scottish Highlands were evidently sailors too, while the earliest indications of fleet operations in Britain in post-Roman times seem to belong to the Scots from northern Ireland, expanding into western Scotland and the Isles in the mid seventh century. And, of course, trade also went on by means of shipping.

Though it is not mentioned in contemporary records, the Suffolk town of Ipswich on the River Orwell (only a dozen kilometres or so from the Deben) was, by the eighth century, a thriving international port that traded with the Rhineland, as its archaeology demonstrates. Southampton was another thriving port of the same period, though its trade went as much to northern France and ports like Quentovic as across the North Sea to the mouth of the Rhine. London and York were the other ports we know of in England at this time, though there must have been other small ports as well. The Frankish world in Merovingian and Carolingian times constituted a stable trading partnership, with the resumption of levels of trade not seen in this part of the world since the end of the Roman Empire. Coinage reform, establishment of factories, encouragement of markets all prompted the development of an international trading economy, which called in due course for bigger ships and better dockside arrangements with improved opportunities for control and taxation. These were fairly quiet times all round but the piracy that had plagued the world since late Roman times never quite went away (and would come back with a vengeance, in the form of the Vikings). It was often safer, as well as more convenient for transhipment, to site the ports of the day a little way inland on navigable rivers that offered access to the sea: ships were small and of shallow draught, carrying cargoes of small volume (even if sometimes of high value, like the wines that came to England from both northern France and the Rhine mouth). Ipswich was just the sort of port location favoured for convenience and security.

Dorestad at the confluence of the Lek with the Rhine was another such port of the times, able to communicate by sea with Britain, Scandinavia and northern France. It may have been within the Carolingian empire but it was a Frisian town and the most important trading centre of the north-west European world, with nearly 1 km of wharves on piles, until the middle of the ninth century when it was overtaken by Hedeby (on the Schlei in Germany), Ribe on the west coast of Jutland and Birka in Sweden. The Frisians began their far-flung trading career in the seventh century and there were Frisian trading colonies in London and York in the eighth century (Bede mentions a Frisian buying a slave in York in 679). They were trading to the Baltic at the same time, with outposts in Hedeby, Birka and eventually as far north as Sigtuna. The Frisians were an independent-minded body of peasant farmers who, despite their incorporation into the Carolingian empire and forced conversion to Christianity, really conducted themselves as a string of republics along the Frisian coast where the shallow waters of the Wattenmeer (Waddenzee in Dutch) separated the mainland from the Frisian island chain. Small wonder that these peasant farmers could turn themselves into accomplished sailors and maritime merchants.

A new sort of ship

It was the Frisians who developed the prototype of a ship that would meet the need for bigger carriers and come to the fore in later times as the characteristic vessel of the Hanseatic League, the cog. The basic design arose out of the same boat-building tradition that produced the Zwammerdan lighters from the Rhine and the Blackfriars boat from the Thames in Roman times. A mosaic and a tombstone from the Roman Rhineland show boats with a style of sail-setting and other features that foreshadow the cogs. Fragments of a vessel found in Bruges suggest the keelless flat-bottomed pattern of the later cogs, with steeply angled end posts. A seventh-century slipway of timber construction found in an ancient shipyard at Wilhelmshaven points to the existence of early cogs by that time: it was designed for flat-bottomed boats that were 2 m wide or more at the bottom. Fragments of a side rudder were also discovered there, of a type associated with early cogs (and of an oar, though later cogs were not rowed). This type of rudder was not fitted with a tiller handle but topped like a spade so that it could be worked vertically at the ship's side or trailed back from the side at an angle. Some coins struck in Hedeby in the late eighth and early ninth centuries, in imitation of Carolingian coins issued at Quentovic and Dorestad, show vessels with a cog-like general configuration. Interestingly, the Carolingian originals show another sort of ship of the times called a hulk, from the Old English 'hulc' that originally alluded to the hollow hold of a utilitarian cargo ship, no doubt of less than elegant lines. The Hedeby coins show flat-bottomed boats with stem and stern posts, some of them with the slight change of angle to the bottom at each end to help them unstick after falling dry with the tide: a very useful feature in the shallow Wattenmeer waters of Friesland and in tidal harbours in general. Some of these coins show the strakes of the vessels and even the nails in them – perhaps four strakes per side, to result in a comparatively low-sided boat at this stage, about 1.8 m high. In some cases, the coins seem to show a lug-like sail-setting that would take a lateral pressure from the wind, which was just what the rudder type required to operate. (This way of setting a sail seems to have been transmitted from the Frisians to the Vikings' ancestors at an early date, for some Scandinavian tombstones show it from the seventh century.)

No actual examples of the early cogs as shown on the Hedeby coins have been discovered, though cogs are mentioned in written sources of the Netherlands in the ninth and tenth centuries. Archaeology does pick up on cogs again in the Hamburg area from the ninth century on, not whole boats but instructive fragments including many cog nails: you don't need much surviving evidence to know a cog, and the twice-bent nails that held the clinker-build overlapping planks together are a sure sign. They crop up in Birka, in Sweden, in the tenth century. The only complete cog we know dates from the fourteenth century and is thus one of the last ones ever built, to be described in a later chapter of this book. Suffice it to say at this point that these flat-bottomed cargo boats pioneered by the Frisians were ideal vessels in which to sail the waters where they originated – the relatively calm waters of the Wattenmeer behind the West Frisian islands and eastwards behind the East Frisians to the tidal estuaries of the Ems and Weser. By sailing up to Hollingstedt, a cog could come within 16 km of Hedeby and be carried across the peninsula to what was, in the ninth and tenth centuries, a Viking town. The cog must have recommended itself to the Vikings of Hedeby to be represented on their coins, though not surprisingly they showed their own ships too.

The homeland of the cog on the flat seashore behind the Frisian islands was prone to saltwater flooding and farmland was hard to find. It was short of timber which had to be imported from the south to make the houses and carts of the Frisian farmers. It could also, however, be used to build ships. In return for their imports, these farmers raised cattle and at least two breeds of sheep, to produce their woollen cloths of high reputation at the time. In their own ships, the Frisians could take their goods to England and to Scandinavia, as we have seen, and also trade others' goods as middlemen to far-flung destinations. They took Rhineland pottery, for instance, to Kaupang at the entrance to the Oslofjord. The English, the Franks and the southern Swedes were trading heartily, too – but not so adventurously as the Frisians, so well-placed geographically to sail south to the Franks, west to the English and, via Hedeby or the Limfjord, north and east to the Danish islands and the lands of the southern Baltic. A day's sail across open sea could take them from the Rhine mouth to Ipswich, from the Swedish island of Gotland to Latvia. The pre-eminence in commerce the Frisians owned – until the rise of Viking power – gave to the southern part of our North Sea, for a time and locally at least, the name of Frisian Ocean.

Trading places

The Frisians appear to have operated with cogs to the east but with hulks to England, using both in the Rhine estuary. Both types were of shallow draught, 60 cm or less, and could thus easily reach inland trading places on navigable rivers. Those trading places need not be towns like Southampton and Ipswich, for the ships could simply be beached on any stretch of shore or sandbank that was convenient. No quaysides or quayside installations of any sort were absolutely required: so long as the ships were near enough to conduct trade, they could either be anchored in shallows or allowed to fall dry for refloating on a suitable tide after trading was done. No doubt there would be provision of wooden hards to prevent sticking in mud and help with unloading and access to dry ground. In many places, things went on like this till the eleventh century, when bigger ships and the growth of towns encouraged the development of deepwater berths at permanent wharves, where security of goods (and merchants and crews) could be enhanced and customs could be levied. Before that, there might be just a row of tents for the people from the ships and another row for their native trading partners, with the beginning of a sort of street between them. Where available, abandoned Roman coastal forts or seaside towns could be pressed into service, their ruined walls offering some measure of added security.

From the late seventh century onwards, in places where trade thrived, there was a growing tendency for the creation of landing places dedicated to particular ships, with their own attached storehouses (rather than tents) which could offer accommodation during trading visits and perhaps enable a permanent presence of the visiting traders' representatives. On the other side of the old tented street, the native traders followed suit with store-houses and accommodation of their own into which cartloads of their trade goods could be gathered to be ready for the ships when they came. Trondheim in Norway and Otterndorf on the Lower Elbe still show the remains of this topography. The great street of the regular traders would be supplemented with an open market area for more casual trade from ships with no permanent warehouse: when the established traders' warehouses came to dominate, the market places went over to local commerce. In this way the first significant additions were made to many an old (and ruined) Roman town, or – in regions away from the erstwhile Roman world – the first real towns were founded. Unlike the rustic environments inland where feudalism cramped human relations, the trading towns that looked to mar-itime commerce were relatively free and adventurous places where the mer-chants (and the craftsmen who flocked to them) could follow a livelier and more enterprising mode of life.

In the Frisian homeland, the new towns grew up on long artificial banks to keep them safe from the perils of the sea. Most were small, but some like Dorestad grew big and thrived, building up their own trading colonies in faraway places. In the eighth and ninth centuries, Frisians settled as resident traders in York in England, Birka in Sweden, along the Rhine in towns as far as Strasbourg: by the late ninth century it could be observed that the smartest part of town in Mainz was not the hallowed area around the cathedral but in the Frisian quarter along the river, where the prized Frisian cloth was to be had. It was more comfortable and secure not just to sail but also to trade and live in company with one's fellows and the Frisians pioneered the development of unions or leagues of fellow merchants who looked after one another's interests in a way that distinctly foreshadows the progress of the great Hanseatic League of later times. They negotiated for themselves privileged customs arrangements, for example, within the Carolingian empire – just as the Hanse would do subsequently, when their Frisian-derived cogs dominated Baltic and much of North Sea trade. But between the Frisians' trading heyday and the Hanseatic League's, there was to be a furious interruption in the shape of the Vikings.

Chapter 5

Raiders

The Frisians were not ousted by the Vikings, but rather overtaken by them, in the North Sea at least. Indeed, the Scandinavians probably owed their cog-like sail-setting to Frisian traders, who also introduced them to the idea of establishing trading colonies abroad, as when the Gotlanders founded their own depots on the southern and eastern shores of the Baltic. But the Vikings, of course, could be pirates as easily as traders, able to do pretty much as they liked in the North Sea as long as they lasted.

Among the seafaring innovations of the Scandinavians was a greater willingness to sail out of sight of land for days at a time, for which potentially hazardous practice their apparent possession of the lodestone might have come in useful, with its not always very reliable indication of magnetic north. (The proper magnetic compass is first mentioned in the twelfth century in an Italian context.) They may also have employed some sort of sun compass like a sundial, but for the rest it was a matter of dead reckoning on the basis of a profound knowledge of their ships, the tides, the currents, the soundings, the winds, the sun and stars, and the natural history of air, sea and land about them. With their capacity to sail on the open sea for extended periods they were able to cross to Britain from western Norway via Shetland from the late eighth century, doing away with the slow shore-hugging business of sailing down the Jutish and Frisian coasts before essaying the crossing to England. In the same spirit they went on to reach Iceland, Greenland and America, ramble down the Russian rivers to make direct contact with the Byzantine and Islamic worlds, and enter the Mediterranean at Gibraltar. The Frisians never matched this enterprise and lost their distinctive identity in the foreign ports they previously frequented by being absorbed into the local trading communities where once they had held themselves in privileged immunity. Back home, in the Christian dukedom of Lower Saxony where most of their North Sea outlets lay, the Frisians became the 'Saxon' merchants who would play their part in the eventual rise of the Hanseatic League. Meanwhile, one Ubbo, *Dux Friesonum* was to join a Viking raid on Britain in 868 and there were to be Frisian sailors in the navy of King Alfred. (The dialects of the English, the Frisians and even the Vikings, all derived from a common Germanic basis, were not yet so diverged as to be quite mutually incomprehensible.)

The Vikings' impact on Britain was very much in the piratical mould to begin with, made all the more disturbing (to the Church, at least) because they were still a pagan force in a more and more Christianised world. They have been dubbed the last blast of pagan Europe and they had a penchant for looting coastal monasteries, as they showed at Lindisfarne as early as 793. (There appears to have been some naval action against them on the part of Offa of Mercia at about this time.) Interestingly, on their first raid in England four years before, they had been taken for visiting merchants until they murdered the reeve of the king of Wessex, on the Dorset coast. There were further visitations by Norwegian Vikings on the south coast of England, sailing not across the North Sea but via western Scotland and the Irish Sea: in 840, the Wessex Kingdom dealt with thirty-three shiploads of them at Portland. The Vikings' seamanship gave them access to Scotland, the Northern Isles, the Hebrides and Ireland, in all of which they steadily infiltrated into the Celtic societies they found there. (It was to take them much further afield, too, of course.) Their warships have been called 'ocean-going landing-craft', capable of long sea crossings and also of handy manoeuvring in shallow waters, where they could simply be beached to commence land operations. We are fortunate to possess a number of preserved Viking vessels that include not only the snaky warship types but also various forms of cargo boat, too. They are all based on a style of open, rowed, clinker-built boat design that goes back to the sort of ships found at Nydam and dated to the fifth century, with many modifications and innovations.

Rowing boats and sailing ships

There are no sixth-century ship remains from the northern world, although a ship house found in Norway would have accommodated a vessel up to 25 m long and 4.5 m wide. Signs of the Scandinavian world's rise to sea power are manifested in the several boathouses, some going back to the fourth century, excavated in south-west Norway, and in the massive sea defences constructed in Haderslev Fjord in east Jutland at about AD 470, well before the building of the Danevirke across the base of Jutland that so vividly signals Danish impact on the northern scene. A link between the Nydam boats and the Viking ships can be discerned in the seventh-century pre-Viking vessel found at Kvalsund in west Norway. This boat was made of pine and oak, 20 m long, in the same general north-western tradition as the Nydam boat, but with rather more of the beginnings of a real keel and with tightly curved stem and stern posts that clearly point towards the classic Viking ships. There was proper provision for a steering oar in the form of a carved oak boss to which it could be lashed. No trace of a mast or fixing for it was found, so this was a rowing boat still. A smaller boat found at Kvalsund had stem and stern posts raked at a lower level in the manner of the Nydam and Sutton Hoo vessels. This design can be seen to have persisted in north-west Europe into the tenth century in the form of the Graveney boat from the Kent marshes, whose stem post is rather like a cog's. At 14 m x 3 m, the Graveney boat was not the sort of thing in which to cross the North Sea, but it may have made the short Channel crossing from Dover – unfinished querns on board were of Middle Rhineland origin, but of course they may just have been old ballast.

Apart from the Kvalsund remains, only shadows of boats (like the Sutton Hoo boat in essence, but not so well detailed) are known from the pre-Viking years in Scandinavia. The ships from the Uppland grave fields, shallow boat shapes with patterns of rivets, appear to have had end-posts more like Nydam than Kvalsund. The larger of the Kvalsund boats could have had a sail, and the employment of that innovation was the next step in northern boat design. In fact, masts with square sails are to be seen in pictures of boats on memorial stones from Gotland thought to belong to the seventh century; the setting of the sails adopted for the Vikings' boats may well have been borrowed from the Frisians. The first surviving evidence of a Viking ship with mast and sail comes with the astounding Oseberg ship of about AD 800, and takes here such a sophisticated form that some period of development clearly lies behind it. The Oseberg ship and its contents were deposited in a trench cut in the clay of the outer Oslofjord, covered over with a mound of turfs: in this way, an excellent state of preservation was achieved.

The Oseberg ship was the burial vehicle of a rich and powerful woman: a royal barge designed for river and limited coastal sailing, rather as the Sutton Hoo ship was, but broader-beamed at 5.10 m to its 21.5 m of length, with twelve strakes per side in clinker fashion. This was not a sinuous Viking warship. It had a true keel, while its frames were more in the way of floor timbers, with deck planking. There were oar ports in the gunwale strake, but this was also a sailing ship with hefty provision for its mast. This ship is now one of the prize exhibits in the Oslo Viking Ship Museum, along with the array of grave goods that it carried, including a large wooden sledge and a cart, which are decorated in a rather grotesque and morbid manner.

Also to be viewed in the same museum is the Gokstad ship, of the late ninth century and even more impressive. This is a more seaworthy vessel, capable of long voyages away from home – as the sailing of a replica of it across the Atlantic in the late nineteenth century amply demonstrated, when it was found capable of seven knots an hour in good conditions. The Gokstad ship has more freeboard than previous vessels from north-west Europe with sixteen strakes per side, and the sophistication of drop-in covers for its oar apertures. There were thirty-two oars in all. A warship of the mid tenth century has been preserved, in that same shadowy form as we have seen at Sutton Hoo and Valsgaerde, in a mound at Ladby on Funen in Denmark. This was a true 'snake-ship' of the Vikings, with a narrow flexible hull of only 3 m maximum beam to its 22 m of length. Evidently it could carry a sail if need be, going by the four shroud rings found in it.

Five ships in a fjord

The Norse sagas hint at the existence of a number of boat types and classes of shipping over and above the snake-ships in which the Vikings went to war. But we would be largely ignorant of these variants in any detail but for a remarkable find from Skuldelev in Roskilde fjord, Denmark. Skuldelev in fact represents a multiple-find site, with a pile of well-preserved ships that were deliberately sunk with a freight of stones to block the fjord in the tenth century. All five ships follow the same shipbuilding pattern, but each one is a different sort of vessel. Most damaged, because it was at the top of the pile, is a 30 m long warship of which only about half the hull has survived to go on display with its fellows in the Roskilde Ship Museum. It probably represents the mature Viking warship pattern better than anything else that has come down to us. (Analysis of its timbers show it to have been built in Viking Dublin.) A smaller warship, 18 m long by 2.6 m of beam, resembles the Ladby boat quite closely and is clearly very much the sort of vessel that the Bayeux Tapestry pictures in the hands of the Viking-descended Normans as they set about the conquest of England in the mid eleventh century. Such ships were fast and easily handled, capable of carrying and landing horses and of being simply beached and launched as convenient.

But along with these warship types, the Skuldelev scuppering includes a large merchant vessel, with a shorter and squatter hull than the snake-ships: it carries fewer oar ports and evidently relied more heavily on sail, without so much consideration for speed to get the contents of its large cargo hold to their destinations. This ship was 16.5 m long and 4.8 m wide, very sturdily built and decked fore and aft – the sort of transport vessel in which to take goods to and from Iceland, Greenland, even America: the 'Knarr' of the sagas. There was also a smaller coastal trader and some sort of small ferry or fishing boat.

With their warships and their merchantmen, the Vikings were well-placed to raid and trade and settle all around the North Sea, and beyond it. A century or more before the scuppering of the Skuldelev ships, the Vikings were rising to be the dominant sea power of north-western Europe, sidelining the Frisians and Saxons who found themselves rather reduced by their incorporation into the Frankish empire. This empire, under the Carolingian kings, extended from the Pyrenees in the south to the Baltic Sea in the north; its frontier with the Viking world ran across the base of Jutland. As we have seen, the Frankish empire had brought about a tremendous revival of north-west European trade, such as had not been seen since the end of Roman times. The Vikings in the north had a powerful incentive to trade with the empire to their south – and also to prey upon the ports and shipping that renewed economic activity had fostered.

The Vikings were first and foremost farmers, growing rye and barley and oats and keeping cattle (as well as hunting, fishing and trapping in their more northerly domains like their mesolithic predecessors of four thousand years before). The very topography of their land – of forests, lakes, rivers, islands, mountains and fjords – pointed them towards the sea and they were always under some pressure of population growth and availability of land to farm. Their tradition of inheritance by primogeniture meant that younger sons were always on the lookout for enterprise as warriors, traders and craftsmen (particularly of items of iron manufacture). Craftsmanship and trade led on, in favoured locations, to the establishment of commercial emporia like the town of Hedeby on the Schlei estuary, just north of the border with the Frankish empire across the base of Jutland (opposite the medieval and modern town of Schleswig). Hedeby was founded in 808 by the Danish ruler Gottfrid, beside an earlier, eighth century, Frisian settlement: the Frisians needed only a short portage from the coast opposite their northerly North Sea islands to reach the Schlei.

Viking voyages

The Vikings who went west to Britain and Ireland were mostly Danes and Norwegians, with Norwegians predominantly going to Scotland and Ireland and to the far west in Iceland, Greenland and Newfoundland. The weather was a little warmer in Viking times, with less winter ice on the northern sea routes. The Swedish Vikings naturally concentrated on the Baltic and the river routes from it into what would become Russia (named after them, the Rus, in fact) and into the Byzantine Empire and the Moslem world, as far as Baghdad. Thousands of silver coins of Arabic origin found their way back to the Baltic and the larger Viking world in the course of the Swedish Vikings' trade (in furs and skins and iron swords) with the east. Hedeby was at the centre of both east-west and north-south trading operations: within its 25-hectare walled enclosure (of the tenth century) at its sheltered harbourside, its houses and workshops left plenty of space for large open market places. The place was well planned, with its rectangular houses and interspersed workshops arranged in regular plots. (It did not, however, greatly impress a visiting Arab traveller, who wrote it up as a filthy place, full of barbarians.) Other emporia of the Baltic and eastern trade were places like Kaupang ('the Market') near Gokstad at the mouth of Oslofjord, Birka on an island within Sweden, Staraya Ladoga near St Petersburg, and Kiev, Novgorod and Smolensk. The ships that plied the eastern Baltic and the Russian rivers were essentially the same as the Viking boats we know, but locally they tended to set their masts in transverse fittings rather than in keelsons following the line of their keels, and to fasten their strakes with wooden trenails rather than iron nails. They could sometimes be rather bigger, too, than the ones built for the rougher North Sea and Atlantic, serving as 'mother ships' to smaller boats that went deep into the Russian hinterland.

The piratical and pillaging side of the Vikings was probably habitually exaggerated by the clerical chroniclers and the use of the word 'army' to translate a term used by the English, that did not necessarily mean more than a couple of score of men, further enlarges the impact of the raids that did indeed take place. While the Swedish Vikings were trading and settling (not always by the most peaceful of means) in the Slavic lands to their east and further down into the Byzantine and Arabic worlds, the Norwegians were sailing to the Northern and Western Isles of Scotland by about 800 – Shetland, Orkney and the Hebrides – and on to Dublin. At Jarlshof on Shetland a settlement with an aisled longhouse, divided into kitchen and living-room, with outbuildings consisting of a barn or byre, a smithy, serfs' quarters and – interestingly – a bathhouse, gives us a vivid idea of Viking life: people kept sheep and oxen, pigs and fowl in these buildings, and they also hunted deer, seals and whales and fished for cod. (Viking raids were a factor in the Picts' fatal vulnerability to the Scots from Dalriada before the ninth century was out.)

The Danish Vikings were regularly sailing west and south in search of plunder from about 830 onwards. Gottfrid built or extended the earthen bank across the base of Jutland that formed the Scandinavian world's frontier with the Franks. He attacked the Frankish coastal defences in Frisia in 810, and in 834. After the grandsons of Charlemagne had fallen out with their father Louis, making the mistake of employing Scandinavian mercenaries at the same time as running down their father's naval defences, the Danes sailed up the Rhine and sacked Dorestad. Frisia was under Danish rule for forty years and Dorestad's decline began. In 841 the Danes sailed up the Seine to Rouen; in 842 they assaulted Quentovic near Boulogne, which was the Franks' principal port for trade with England. In 843 they struck at Nantes on the Loire, where they settled on an island at the mouth of that river 'as if they meant to stay forever'. In 845, they burned Hamburg and sacked Paris, repairing their damaged ships with timbers taken from the church at St Germain-des-Prés. From this exploit they were bought off with an enormous payment in silver, the first time of paying the Danegeld. The Abbot of Saint Riquier has left us a vivid image of the Vikings' threat:

> *The Danes, those barbarians, out of the midst of their raised masts look to us like wild beasts in the forests.*

Vikings in Britain

As with their settlement at the Loire mouth, the Danes went beyond hit-and-run at Thanet in England in 850, overwintering there with hundreds of ships and attacking London and Canterbury in 851, before they were repelled off Sandwich in a sea battle that saw the English under Aethelstan take nine Viking vessels. ('Sea battle' would really be a misnomer for any naval engagement in the North Sea until the era of heavy guns – it was really just a matter before that of grappling at close quarters in waters as inshore as you could contrive. Ships were mainly for fast transport to a chosen scene of conflict.) The Vikings overwintered in England again, at Sheppey, in 855. By the 860s, there were more and more Danish Vikings lurking in the Loire valley and travelling further south down the French coast to Spain and the Mediterranean and thus out of our North Sea ken. Their pressure on England was redoubled, to the extent that their 'Great Army' was able to occupy East Anglia in 865, quite peacefully it seems: which points to payment of Danegeld. In 866, with reinforcements from the Seine, they pushed north to York. From there they went south in Mercia in 867 and were able to hold Nottingham against the combined forces of Mercia and Wessex, before they retired to York with their Danegeld. York was to become a major settlement of the Danes, sited well inland on a river in the way they liked things, with workshops, warehouses and accommodation: Lincoln was a similar if less ambitiously developed Viking town.

In 869, the Danes were back in East Anglia, now to face opposition from King Edmund, whom they slew and so promoted to sainthood. Next year they pushed into Wessex, but fell back to London with more Danegeld, to undertake the subduing of Mercia and the sharing-out among themselves of the erstwhile lands of the Northumbrians, where many of them reverted to their ancestral farming way of life. In 875, factions unable or unwilling at this stage to settle for farming congregated in Cambridge, from where in 876 they renewed their tussle with Wessex, with the help of Vikings from

Ireland. But King Alfred outflanked them and bottled them up in Exeter. Under the terms of a truce with Wessex, the Danes were allowed back to Mercia in 877, but promptly regrouped and returned to overrun Wessex, causing Alfred to flee to safety in his fortified base in the Somerset marshes. He in turn was able to defeat the Danes and impose a treaty upon them which resulted in a measure of peace for a while.

879 saw the Danes once more in East Anglia, where they shared out the land they controlled. From 881, the Danelaw was established as the easterly and northerly zone of England under Viking rule. Landless Danes who had given up on the Wessex venture went back across the southern North Sea to ravage Flanders over eight years. Some of them returned to harass Rochester in Kent in 855, but were seen off by King Alfred, whereupon they set about the Franks in earnest, besieging Paris, taking their Danegeld, pressing further inland and only being brought to book in 891. Back across the North Sea in 892, they were held in check by Alfred yet again. By 896 Danish Vikings in England who still had no land in Mercia or East Anglia, and no booty to keep them going, crossed back to the region of the Lower Seine and finally settled down there. A treaty with the Frankish king in 911 recognised their leader Rollo as ruler over the lands these Vikings had acquired; later deals in 924 and 933 saw the whole province around Rouen assigned to them, to become during the course of the tenth century the Duchy of Normandy, under Rollo's descendants. The Normans took on board Frankish religion and law and the feudal form of society, redeeming something of their past reputation as raiders by their generous sponsorship of monasteries. The powerful vassals of their dukes went on to build many castles in rather the manner they would employ in subduing England after 1066, and younger sons of their nobility (who would not inherit and perhaps had no taste for the Church) were to roam abroad on military exploits as far away as Sicily.

Bigger ships

In England towards the end of the ninth century, Alfred oversaw the building of a series of small fortified towns called burhs, that served both as refuges against raiding and as economic centres in peacetime: sited about 30 km or so apart, many of these burhs went on to become important towns of later days, like Oxford and Buckingham and Warwick. He had already met the Vikings in some small-scale naval engagements and his scheme of burhs was undertaken in concert with the operation of a fleet that could move around his coast as required: across the Channel, Charles the Bold employed similar measures against the Vikings in France. Alfred's fleet could not, however, keep the Vikings out of the Thames in 892 and 895. This experience caused him to undertake the building of larger ships than had been seen before: the *Anglo-Saxon Chronicle* says they were twice as long as Viking ships and higher, but steadier and swifter too, built neither on the Frisian nor Danish pattern but according to the king's own ideas. There were sixty or more of these high-sided warships. Alfred's navy could operate such daunting vessels to advantage, as they would never have to sail far over the Channel and North Sea whereas their Viking enemies, if they wished (as they did) to match the bigger ships, would sometimes need to bring these unwieldy vessels a long way with big crews to engage in a sea battle. Some of the benefits of the old Viking warships, smaller and handier, were lost in this naval arms race, which was to lead on at the end of the tenth century to such great Viking ships as Olaf Trygvasson's *Crane* of 995 and *Long Serpent* of 999, and Harald Hardrada's copy of the latter in 1061. The Viking tradition of shipbuilding issued finally, in the thirteenth and fourteenth centuries, in vessels with much more complicated rigging and built-on castles fore and aft: the sort of boat the English came to call a keel, depicted on Norman, English and Irish seals but rarely evidenced by physical remains.

Alfred's policies were rather successful: by 920 his son Edward ('the Elder') was ruler of all England to the Humber and at least nominal high ruler of the English and Danish kingdoms as far north as central Scotland, where the Scots from Dalriada had by now assimilated the Picts and were poised to take over what remained of the old British territory along the Firth of Forth. The Welsh princes similarly ruled under Edward's overlordship and he commanded a fleet of some hundred ships to patrol his loosely united empire. Indeed, the threat of their navy, paid for and manned by national levies, permitted the English to interfere in Frankish and Saxon affairs, before the Norman Conquest. As the Danish-descended component in the populations of the Danelaw settled down to farm and manufacture (which is perhaps what most of them had really wanted to do from the start), they naturally enough came to disfavour the whole idea of raiding every bit as much as their Anglo-Saxon contemporaries did. Unfortunately, a new round of raiding was in the air, as a result perhaps of a sort of economic factor. The supply of Arab silver to the Baltic and the wider Scandinavian world diminished after about 930 and all but vanished by 970, providing a new incentive to go raiding south and west in the old way. The Norwegians in Ireland harried the west coast of the British mainland, with their ambitions directed towards York, where the Wessex overlords sometimes let them alone and sometimes saw them off as opportunity was afforded. In the end, they rid themselves of the Norwegian kingdom of York altogether in 954 under Alfred's grandson Eadred, giving it over to the Earl of Northumbria.

During the course of the tenth century, Denmark became a unified (and Christianised) monarchy under Harald Bluetooth and his son Svein Forkbeard. At Jelling in Jutland, beside two pagan mounds, the church is believed to have housed the reburial of the last pagan king and queen of Denmark. A huge runestone outside the church carries the first appearance of the Christians' cross in this part of the world and was most likely carved by a mason from the north of England. The feudal system of land ownership and social relations was adopted along with Christianity and new towns like Roskilde were founded, with mints. The earthen frontier across the base of Jutland (the Danevirke) was extended and in northern and eastern Denmark four extraordinary circular fortresses were built at Trelleborg, Fyrkat, Aggersborg and Odense. It has been suggested that part of their function was to safeguard the tax revenue of the newly unified state, but the highly regular and indeed regimented layout of buildings inside, with workshops as well as barracks, looks less like a defensive arrangement than one intended to house and organise an offensive force. It seems that the first fruits of a renewal of raiding paid for these army camps and that raiding was their raison d'être, including raids on England. The Viking-descended Normans offered harbour facilities, and overwintering in AD 1000, to their marauding cousins.

A united kingdom of the North Sea

The English under Aethelred II (the 'Unraed' or 'ill-advised') offered feeble resistance to the Danes, who struck at Southampton in 980, Portland in 982 and Maldon in Essex in 991, where they were mauled but not defeated and had to be handsomely paid off. By 1001 the Vikings were riding high again. Aethelred made the rash mistake in 1002 of massacring all the Danes in England that he could get his hands on, including Svein's own sister. Between 1003 and 1006, Svein came across and harried Wessex and East Anglia, returning with greater force in 1009. Much Danegeld changed hands. Aethelred had ordered a bout of shipbuilding on a grand scale to counter the Danish threat, but defections and shipwreck took their toll on his fleet. In 1013, Svein took his own fleet to the Trent in the heart of the old Danelaw and, with the support of the northern lords, marched south and overcame Wessex. Aethelred fled to Normandy, to seek refuge with the Norman duke whose sister Emma he had married – of recent Viking descent, of course. Then Svein died and his son Knut retired across the North Sea in the face of opposition from Aethelred's supporters in England. With the assistance of the Normans (despite their previous helpfulness to the Danes), Aethelred was able to return to England in 1014.

But Knut was back in England in 1015, with the help and encouragement of his elder brother who was now king of Denmark. Aethelred died in 1016 before any conclusive victories had gone to either side and a partition of the country between his son Edmund Ironside and Knut was arranged. Edmund promptly died and England was left to Knut, who married Aethelred's widow. Over in Denmark, his elder brother obligingly died childless so that by 1019 Knut was king of England and Denmark which included the southern part of Sweden, with a not altogether secure control over Norway into the bargain. This first and only united kingdom of the North Sea lasted until Knut's death in 1035. (Scotland and the earldom of Orkney were not parts of it.)

Legend has this King Knut amply demonstrating his inability to rule the waves; and in truth, Knut can never have set out to create a long-lasting and united Anglo-Norse kingdom around the North Sea, if only because the routes available across that sea and the ships to ply them were not up to the task of holding such a political entity together. The old Vikings could indeed come and go across the North Sea but it was a frequently difficult, sometimes dangerous and always time-consuming business to do so, whether they went from Norway to the Shetlands and down the Irish Sea or by the less favoured route down the east coast of Scotland and north-east England to the Humber, or from Denmark down the Frisian coast to the Rhine delta and thence across to the Thames and Humber.

Crossing the Channel posed no such difficulties, dangers and delays for the Norsemen who had become the Normans of the Duchy of Normandy. It was to be these Frenchified Vikings from Normandy who would inherit the English part of Knut's domains. When Knut died, his son Harthacnut was in Denmark and distracted by troubles with Norway, newly independent under Magnus Olafson. Knut's illegitimate son Harald thus became king of England, but died after only a few years, so that Harthacnut came to the English throne in 1040, but without any children of his own to succeed him. He determined that the succession should go to Aethelred's and Emma's surviving son Edward (his own half-brother), who came to the throne as Edward the Confessor in 1042. Magnus Olafson meanwhile became king of Denmark, and then died in 1047, with Harald Hardrada ('the Hardruler') succeeding him. Edward's time marked something of a golden age for the English navy, which was based in London but usually assembled at Sandwich for annual manoeuvres, where it was well placed for both Channel and North Sea operations. It was manned by the semi-professional soldiers of the Fyrd, with the assistance we can only assume of a body of men with sailing experience. Sea power was needed to counter threats from Scotland, Wales, Ireland and Norway.

Harald Hardrada left it a fatally long time, nearly twenty years, to assert his own rights in England and when he did so, upon the death of Edward, the old Viking heartland of the Humber failed to back him and he lost to the famous King Harold (named as heir by Edward) at Stamford Bridge in 1066. Harold, of course, went on in short order to lose to Duke William of Normandy in that same year, to whom Edward had allegedly also promised the English crown. The Norman Conquest was accomplished with seven hundred ships, some of them built for the purpose as the Bayeaux Tapestry shows and some probably borrowed from the Normans' Flemish allies: they were troop carriers and horse transports rather than fighting ships. The Conquest brought these former Vikings decisively to power in England, with an extensive North Sea coastal presence stretching right up to Scotland. The Normans had succeeded, in other words, in doing what the Vikings never really achieved: perhaps because they had had their sights set all along on the acquisition of landed estates rather than on plunder and tribute. The Norman castles, developed as much in England as back home in Normandy, were constructed partly for defensive purposes (the one in Dover had to withstand the French in 1216) and partly to assert the power

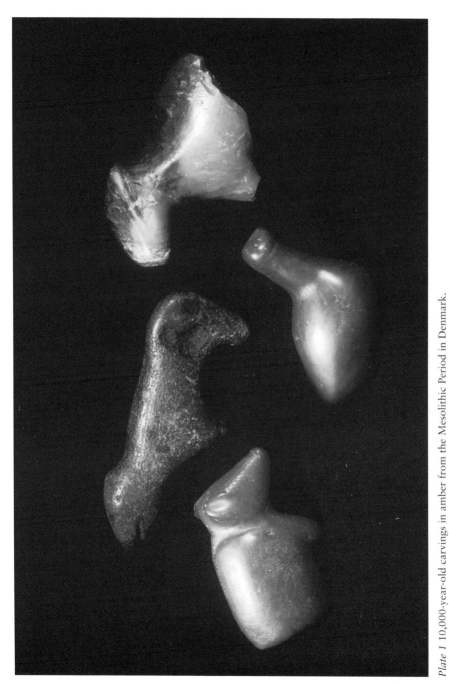

Plate 1 10,000-year-old carvings in amber from the Mesolithic Period in Denmark.

Source: National Museum, Denmark.

Plate 2 Megalithic monuments of the New Stone Age at Tustrup in Jutland.

Plate 3 The mark left by a wooden henge monument at Arminghall in Norfolk.

Source: Norfolk Museums & Archaeology Service. Photo by Derek A. Edwards.

Plate 4 A stone-built henge circle on Orkney.

Plate 5 Drinking pots and battleaxes of the late Neolithic Period from Denmark.

Source: National Museum, Denmark.

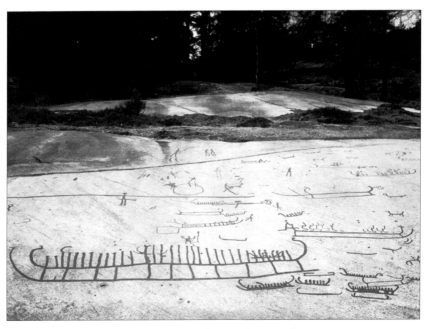

Plate 6 Bronze Age rock drawings of boats from southern Sweden.

Plate 7 Craftsmanship in bronze and gold from the Danish Bronze Age.

Source: National Museum, Denmark.

Plate 8 The ramparts of an Iron Age fort at Warham Camp in Norfolk.

Plate 9 The Gundestrup Bowl: a Celtic import into Iron Age Denmark.

Source: Photo by Ray Sutcliffe.

Plate 10 The head of the Tollund Man, most famous of the Iron Age bog bodies.

Plate 11 Roman cups in silver found outside the empire in Iron Age Denmark.

Source: National Museum, Denmark.

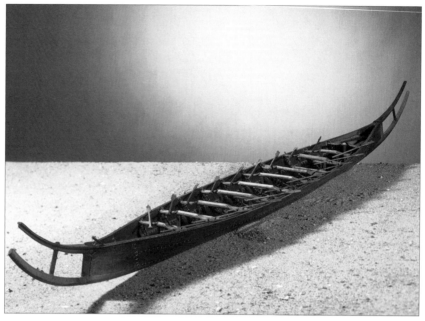

Plate 12 A model of the Iron Age Hjortspring Boat.

Source: National Museum, Denmark.

Plate 13 A Celtic ship on a coin of King Cunobelin.

Source: Institute of Archaeology, Oxford.

Plate 14 Richborough, the Romans' gateway into Britain, refortified in late Roman times.

Plate 15 The Roman lighthouse by Dover Castle.

Source: JAC Kinnear, © 2003 JTH Consulting.

Plate 16 Reconstructed Anglo-Saxon houses at West Stow in Suffolk.

Source: St. Edmundsbury Borough Council/West Stow Anglo-Saxon Village Trust.

Plate 17 The Nydam Boat from Schleswig in Germany.

Source: Photo by Ray Sutcliffe.

Plate 19 A helmet from one of the Uppland ship graves in central
Sweden

Plate 18 The Oseberg Viking ship in Oslo.

Plate 20 One of the Skuldelev wrecks in Roskilde.

Source: Photo by Ray Sutcliffe.

Plate 21 A reconstructed Viking barracks building in Denmark.

Plate 22 The monument of a medieval German merchant in Boston.

Plate 23 The Hanseatic cog found in the river at Bremen.

Plate 24 A model of the Bremen Cog, with seals of Hanse towns.

Plate 25 The Vasa warship on display in Stockholm.

Source: Photo by Hans Hammarskiöld for the Vasa Museum.

of the Norman kings in unmistakable terms. The New Castle on the Tyne was built to face the threat of conflict with Scotland, where King Malcolm Canmore (who had removed MacBeth) gave shelter to some of William the Conqueror's exiled enemies. His daughter, however, married Henry I of England, but this was not the end of Anglo-Scottish strife.

The only stretches of North Sea coastline that had remained for the most part beyond the attentions of the Vikings, in one form or another, were those that belonged to the earldom of Orkney, to the Scottish kingdom and to northern Northumbria, to the Wessex rulers south-east of London, and to the Frankish empire as far north as the base of Jutland (though with Viking inroads in the Rhineland and the East Frisian islands). It is to the fate of the Frankish empire and the emergence of the German half of it as the Holy Roman Empire, with its own piece of North Sea coastline, that we now turn to continue the story of human affairs around the North Sea.

Chapter 6

Merchants

The era of raiding in which the Vikings figured prominently in the North Sea region (with Magyars on the rampage in central and western Europe, Saracens in the Mediterranean) left Europe with an underpowered economy and a low level of population: some erstwhile major towns like Quentovic and Dorestad went under and never recovered. In 1000 the population of Europe stood at perhaps 30 million, but by 1150, it has been reckoned at quite possibly 40 or more million, concentrated mostly in England, France, the Low Countries and Germany. More land was being brought under cultivation out of previously forested areas, with new towns being built up. Local trade flourished again.

In the latter half of the ninth century, the West Franks (who were to become, mostly, the French nation) and the East Franks (likewise, Germany) had gone their separate ways as the fragmented and disputed succession of the descendants of Charlemagne took effect. The East Frankish crown went to the Duke of the Saxons in 919, and his successor Otto extended his power beyond Saxony (which already incorporated Friesland and Franconia to its south) over more of the German duchies, finally defeating the Magyars and conquering Italy, so that he was crowned Emperor at Rome in 962, as ruler of what later came to be known as the Holy Roman Empire of the German Nation. There was a series of dynastic switches in the leadership of this empire which saw successively Saxon, Salian, Hohenstaufen and Habsburg elected rulers.

In the Holy Roman Empire, there was an expansion to the east after the mid twelfth century to settle new lands, but much of the wealth of the empire was in the Rhineland, where Cologne became Germany's largest city, though not the only one by any means to furnish itself with a lavish cathedral. But while in other parts of western Europe kings of this time could begin to assert their executive powers over the declining feudal arrangements they headed (as they did successfully assert themselves in England and Sicily, and later in France and Spain), Germany's nominally overall rulers were obliged to accept that their realm would remain a collection of more or less independent principalities. (Just as they had to accept that their Italian domain would remain effectively splintered among city magistrates and tyrants.) The administration and the infrastructure needed to tighten any ruler's grip on Germany were simply lacking. In passing, we may note the limitations of the English and French kings' power, too: the French kings reasserted their rule over Normandy and the English-held parts of their country, but could not take Flanders; the English could not overcome the Scots.

In the tenth century, as we saw in Chapter 4, the old Frisian traders had come to be known generally as Saxons, still sailing their cogs on the old Frisian trade routes during the years of Viking predominance in the North Sea and the Baltic. Saxon merchants established a colony in Hedeby in 934, following the old company idea of private merchant guilds. By 1000 these 'Saxon' trading guilds were securing special status in foreign lands, as for example the Cologne merchants did in London. German traders began to show up along Viking trade routes, their presence recorded in Trondheim in Norway, even in Iceland. In return, there were Norwegian merchants in Cologne and Utrecht. Something of the international interchange of commerce can be seen in the records of the Norwegian port of Bergen in 1191, which attest to the presence of Danes, Swedes, Icelanders, Greenlanders, English and German merchants. Pottery of this time found in Bergen hails from England, the Rhineland and the Weser region around Bremen. Schleswig, the town which grew up to replace Hedeby, was visited by Saxons, Flemings, Icelanders, Swedes and Russians.

Most of the merchants now came from Christianised communities and their respective enclaves in foreign ports were often centred on a church of their own which acted like a sort of community centre and common warehouse too. Ships frequently sailed with a priest on board who conveniently doubled as a clerk to the trading enterprise. Trading privileges grew to be complicated and provocative; for example, in London around 1130, the merchants from Flanders were only allowed to stay for forty days, while the Cologne merchants suffered no restrictions and traders from Bremen and Antwerp could stay as long as they liked so long as they did not go beyond London Bridge; Norwegians could stay for a year but not go outside London, while Danes could go anywhere.

Hanse towns

The trading association that achieved pre-eminence in this situation was one that arose not in North Sea ports but in the south-west Baltic. Lübeck was the first wholly German town to be founded there (from 1143), in territory formerly occupied – if rather thinly – by Slavic people. There followed Wismar, Rostock, Stralsund, Greifswald, Kammin, Kolberg, and Danzig along the south Baltic coast, as part of a general push to the east, beyond the Elbe, that was fed by the growing population of northern Germany. Slav princes sometimes welcomed the Germans in to develop their domains, encouraging them by allowing them to live under their own laws in their colonies. (By the early fifteenth century, the Teutonic Knights in a rather less welcome fashion had reached as far as Courland and the Gulfs of Riga and Finland, overreaching themselves in the end to be defeated by the Poles in 1410 and thereafter to face decline. Their 'pacification' of the southern Baltic shores had helped to pave the way of the merchants, however.)

Trade was greatly enhanced by the north German expansion to the east – both by river routes into southern Germany, Poland and Central Europe and also by sea, starting with the cog-owning merchants of Schleswig and then Lübeck. With the cooperation and capital of inland merchants, these traders further developed the idea of the merchant union and an old German word for such association – Hanse (or Hansa) – came into vogue. The German maritime merchants of the Baltic were already known as the Osterlinge, or Easterlings to the English, when they established a Hanse depot at Visby on the Baltic island of Gotland in 1161.

The Hanse style of trading brought in such modern practices as book-keeping, sales on credit and commissions. The big merchants needed no longer to sail with their ships when they could do business by letter, with bills and receipts: a growing literacy helped, and was promoted by, this change in business dealings. Lübeck itself was a new sort of town, with the most liberal trading laws of its time and a self-governing status that put it outside the control of local princes and the emperor. Its very layout was new, with its merchants' houses in the town behind a defensive harbour wall and built along the roads that led from the harbour to the market area (chiefly for inland trade). Its topography and its constitution were widely copied in other Hanse towns. Their independence was not unique in the medieval world – most European towns were semi-autonomous 'republics' ruled by local aristocratic and mercantile interests – but the Hanse towns took their freedom of action further than most, especially as they came to act in league with one another.

Lübeck became both the port of emigration for emigrants to the east and the transit port for east-west trade in northern Europe. By 1259 a merchant union incorporated the three Baltic towns of Lübeck, Wismar and Rostock with Hamburg to the west, across the base of Jutland from Lübeck, with its river access to the North Sea. Hammaburg, as it was first called, had grown up at the confluence of three rivers, the chief of them the Elbe: it became an archbishopric in the ninth century under a son of Charlemagne and its fortress was built at about the same time to dominate the Saxon population around it (there was a sparse presence of Slavic people not far to the east) and secure the safety of the harbour. From the mid thirteenth century it functioned, in effect, as the North Sea port of Lübeck. (The Strecknitz Canal was cut in the 1390s to link Hamburg and Lübeck by water, but it involved so many locks with poor towpath arrangements that a barge could take a fortnight to pass through it.)

A century after that first union, the League of the German Hanse was formally established in 1358, holding its first general meeting at Lübeck in that year. More German towns achieved membership of the League: it was a standing rule that no town should be admitted that was not on the sea or a navigable river and did not keep the keys of its own gates. In the fourteenth and fifteenth centuries more than two hundred maritime and inland waterway towns were associated with the Hanseatic League, the largest on the sea or very nearly so. Lübeck's town seals show a cog, the old Frisian vessel that had proved superior to the Scandinavian merchantmen, with two crewmen in it, one of them in sailor's gear, the helmsman, and the other a well-dressed merchant with his fingers raised to swear his oath to the Union. The aims of the Hanseatic League were to secure commercial advantages wherever they traded, in the Baltic and around the North Sea, including the right to store their own goods in their own premises. League meetings in their principal cities took upon themselves the right to boycott the goods of ports or whole countries where they were not satisfactorily accommodated. Their association also helped against the scourge of piracy, particularly virulent in the late fourteenth and early fifteenth centuries, when the pirates played an ambiguous role both as maritime mercenaries available for hire and as random raiders between their bigger jobs. Some of them, like Klaus Störtebeker, achieved great popular fame in the manner of the much later Blackbeard in other seas.

The League abroad

Hanseatic foreign offices called Kontore (counting houses) were established in foreign ports, the first of them inside a fenced enclosure in Novgorod called the Peterhof. The second was in the more cosmopolitan town of Bruges (at 'The Assemblies'), which the League could reach from Hamburg and so take Baltic and eastern goods straight to the Flemish towns. The Flemish traders who had previously travelled up to Schleswig-Holstein for their goods were discouraged from further carrying in this area. From Bruges, some Hanse ships ventured south through the Dover Strait to Brittany and Portugal in search of cheaper salt supplies than they could find in Europe for use in the herring business, and even further into the Mediterranean. To Bruges came merchants from the south: they had been coming from Genoa since the late thirteenth century, joined by the Venetians in the fourteenth. For Mediterranean sailors, the tidal waters of the North Sea must have taken some getting used to: their charts and sea books soon became remarkably useful in their details of North Sea and Baltic topography and toponymy. (They settled in Southampton, too, and the Spanish joined them in Bruges.)

Along with their portolans, these Mediterranean seafarers brought knowledge of their own shipbuilding designs and techniques to northern Europe: in particular, the carvel style of shipbuilding, of which more later. Their presence contributed to the wide spread of a sort of international mixed Flemish-Italian architectural style from the Low Countries to the Baltic, seen in the decoration of the churches and town halls of the day. They also brought the compass, which they scarcely needed at home in the Mediterranean, to aid their Atlantic and North Sea navigations – the first mention of the use of a compass on a Hanse ship comes as late as 1433. The Venetians made high quality hourglasses in the thirteenth century but neither these nor the fine timepieces developed in the sixteenth century were good enough to be of much use in the determination of longitude. Astronomical tables were elaborated from the fifteenth century onwards, but a chronometer to arrive at longitude along with them would not be developed until the late eighteenth century in England. Fortunately none of these measures were desperately needed in the North Sea. Something else that commerce with the Mediterranean world brought to north-west Europe was altogether less desirable than shipbuilding and seafaring innovations: it was the Black Death, spread from the siege of a Genoese trading post in the Crimea to reach the western Mediterranean by 1348, the Low Countries and England the next year, Scandinavia and the Baltic in 1350. It recurred in the 1360s and 1370s, and in 1390 and 1400. It killed perhaps a third of the population of Europe, in some places three-quarters: it promoted the acceleration of social and economic change, including wage payment in place of feudal service and the breakdown of the old social rigidity. These processes were the background to the Hanseatic League's commercial progress.

In London, the Hanse merchants were welcomed into the same situation of trading privileges as the Rhineland merchants already enjoyed: eventually, the Cologne guildhall and the Steelyard were made over to the Hanseatic League as their third Kontor. (Steelyard perhaps derives from the Low German Stalgard, meaning a courtyard or sample yard.) There were subsidiary enclaves of Hanse privilege in Ipswich, Yarmouth, Lynn, Boston, Hull, York, Newcastle and Edinburgh. Lynn's enclave was established as early as 1271, well before the formal inauguration of the Hanseatic League, and its warehouses (of the late fifteenth century) can still be seen in a street running down to the river. Boston retains an evocative reminder of the German merchants' presence in England's east coast towns: the marble monumental slab of Wisselus Smalenburg from Münster who was buried in St Botolph's church in 1340. (The tower of that church – the 'Boston Stump' – is said to have been modelled on the cathedral tower of Antwerp, where English merchants moored at their own Engelse Kaai.)

Even a modest little port like Cley on the north Norfolk coast could house a chapel in its local church for Hanse merchants' use. Something of the power of those merchants is revealed by an incident of 1285 when a

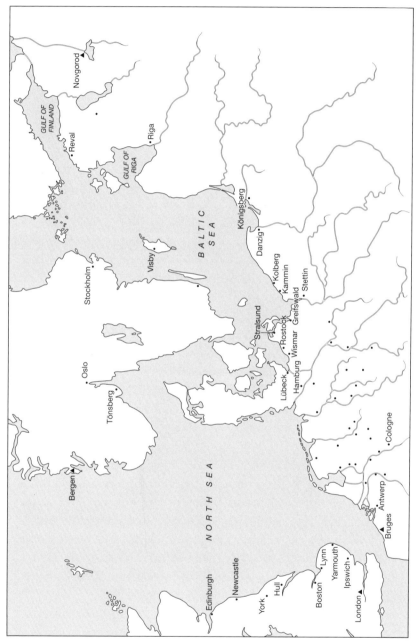

Map 5 Hanseatic towns on the North Sea and the Baltic: the major Kontore at London, Bruges, Bergen and Novgorod are marked

German ship in piratical style attacked a Dutch ship off the nearby small port of Blakeney: the Germans were caught and put in gaol, until (as a contemporary record puts it) 'a jury of Almain found at Lynn' got them out – in other words the German enclave at Lynn was able to interfere to secure the release of its own. Ports like Cley and Blakeney on the River Glaven in north Norfolk were typical, incidentally, of the many small ports that were dotted all around the southern shores of the North Sea in medieval times. They were devoted to local trade and trade across the North Sea, and fishing in that sea or down into the Channel and the Bay of Biscay, or as time went by in Icelandic waters, too. Their vessels could be hired or commandeered as transports, even sometimes as fighting ships, by the state powers of the day, before the establishment of national navies (though the Cinque Ports were the main source of 'warships' in England). For every major port of medieval times, there as a host of minor ones on both sides of the North Sea.

The power of the Hanse

The fourth of the major Kontore of the Hanseatic League was founded in Bergen on the Norwegian North Sea coast soon after London's. It was known as 'The German Pier'. Grain-short Norway had previously been supplied by the English, but when the English wanted to keep their grain for themselves, the Hanseatic League stepped in with Baltic grain: they developed stockfish (mostly cod) production in Norway in return, trading this commodity south to a Europe where every Friday was a fish-eating day. This was very much in keeping with the League's practice wherever it operated with clout: organising in central Sweden, for example, copper mining and in Danish Scania (southern Sweden) the herring fishery, to which they conveyed the necessary salt from Lüneburg in northern Germany, or from further afield down the Atlantic coast of Iberia in search of cheaper supplies – the fish trade was very dependent on salt. (The herring, for ecological reasons not now fully understood, left the Baltic at the start of the fifteenth century for the North Sea, where they kept up their seasonal progress from off Scotland in summer to Christmas in the Channel into the twentieth century.) As the Flemings also discovered, the Hanse was all about monopoly, backed with drastic measures when necessary. When, at an early stage, the Norwegians tried to shake the Hanse off, they were met with a stoppage of grain and a blockade of their own merchantmen. In the settlement of the dispute, the Hanse claimed exemption from taxes in Norway and unlimited access to all Norwegian ports south of Bergen. It was the Hanse monopoly in Bergen in the fifteenth century that first pointed the English in the direction of Iceland and then Labrador and Newfoundland as fishing grounds.

The chief enemy of the Hanseatic League was Denmark, with both North Sea and Baltic coastlines but short-cutted across its Jutland base by the League's land link between Lübeck and Hamburg. The Danes were victorious over the Hanse in 1362, but were themselves defeated by 1370, to the extent that the Peace of Stralsund subjected the election of the Danish king to the approval of the League. Hanseatic intervention in north-west Europe's affairs went on to include fighting – and recruiting – pirates who operated out of many a North Sea port (1390s), battling the Danes again until Danish customs charges in the Sound were lifted off Hanse ships from the Baltic (1435), supporting the English contender Edward IV in return for trading privileges (1470s), and forcing Denmark to prohibit navigation by the English and the newly thriving Dutch in the Sound (1470). The Hanse were, in fact, carrying on in the Baltic and North Sea in rather the same way as the Venetians were conducting themselves in the Mediterranean at much the same time. It is interesting to record that in the mid fifteenth century, half of the entirety of English trade – which was mostly in wool – was in the hands of the Venetians and Hanse between them, the latter carrying English wool exports all over the northern world, apart from the direct trade between London and Antwerp.

The League's various commercially driven struggles, going back to the Norwegian war, led on to the armouring of Hanse cogs with archers' platforms of the sort pioneered by the English in the twelfth century. At first, they were open raised platforms, but the Hanse went on quickly to enclose them and so create the first cabin arrangements on Baltic and North Sea vessels. Cabins were a benefit for trading ships in peaceful times, as well, but could always be handily converted for fighting purposes when merchantmen had to be turned into warships.

The last of the cogs

These cogs of the Hanseatic League have been well-known to historians, in a sketchy way, from the coins and town seals of the League's cities. Between

1962 and 1965, an actual cog was lifted from the silt deposits of the Weser, a few kilometres downstream of the centre of medieval Bremen, which was a League member from the start in 1358. It proved to be one of the last cogs ever built, only a score of years before the cog type was superseded by the hulk type as the standard vessel of the Hanse. The tree rings of its timbers demonstrate that the trees to build it were cut down in 1378.

Compared with the Viking merchantmen, the Bremen cog is a broader and higher vessel, 7.6 m at its widest and 4.2 m up from the keel, with sides too high to permit rowing: it has a single mast for one square-rigged sail. Though it is clinker-built and 23.2 m long, the cog is a far cry from the Viking snake-ships and stodgier-looking even than the Viking merchant vessels. Its broad keel meets the stem and stern posts at a marked change of angle, so that the cog is pretty much flat-bottomed amidships. Its ribs were evidently fitted into the pre-built clinker shell, which has thick strakes of some 5 cm, twice as thick as the Viking ships and three times as wide at 60 cm. The strakes are fixed together with iron nails, and iron clamps kept willow laths in place as caulking between the strakes. It all made for a stiff-looking and no doubt stiff-handling ship, which derives ultimately from that Germanic boat-building tradition that we saw with the Zwammerdam lighters and the Blackfriars boat of Roman times: the Frisian and Saxon merchants employed earlier examples of the type and took the cog tradition to Hedeby across the base of Jutland.

After about 1200, cogs are pictured in the seals of towns from Bruges to the Baltic. Documentary evidence and some wreck material suggest that the cog replaced boats of the Viking tradition after the twelfth century in the Baltic and Scandinavia in general, though some large and high-sided versions of the old Viking ship design were built before the cog eclipsed them; the northern tradition of boat-building that was taken to Britain by the Anglo-Saxons also issued in the medieval ships called keels that feature on some coins. In the Netherlands region, where many fragmentary cog remains have been excavated, cogs seem to have coexisted with other types like the keels and hulks which also figure on the seals of England and the southern ports of continental Europe: the hulk name relates to the hollow hold of one pattern of ship design and the keel name to the fundamental constructional feature of the other.

A seal of Lübeck of 1226 vividly sketches the appearance of the cog type in the thirteenth century, a century-and-a-half before the last ones like the

Bremen cog were built. The one on the Lübeck seal has curved stem and stern posts (carved like the ones on some Viking ships) with the strakes going over the end-posts in a non-Viking manner, and a side rudder. The stern rudder arrangement, going back perhaps into the late twelfth century, comes in on cogs shown on seals of Elbing in the Baltic (1242), Stavoren in the Netherlands (1246) and, very clearly, on the Stralsund seal of 1270, but it's a feature not seen on Lübeck seals till 1281. It seems that double stem and stern posts began to be fitted in some places in the mid thirteenth century, a feature which finishes off the strake ends hitherto brought over the single posts – Lübeck seals again do not show this design until 1281. The stern rudder was needed as the cogs got bigger. The first depiction of a square sail comes with the Stralsund seal of 1329. An actual wreck from the early thirteenth century, from Cape Skagen (Jutland), does not yet feature the square sail of the later cogs but is a bigger and better boat than the cogs evidenced by earlier finds, with a rounder bottom to ride better and higher sides (more strakes) to provide better carrying capacity. Another wreck from Kolding Fjord, of about 1180, offers evidence of the fitting of a stern rudder, well before its appearance on the seals. The high-sided Bremen cog is, in effect, a raised version of the earlier vessels shown on the seals and attested in fragmentary form in the wrecks with, as it were, an added storey above its protruding cross beams. The fighting platforms that were adopted after the struggle with the Norwegians show up on the Danzig (Gdansk) seal of 1299 and the Damme seal of 1309; the Stralsund seal of 1329 pictures a platform boxed-in beneath it to create a cabin, which afforded shelter to crew and cargo and a better view all round. The wonderfully preserved Bremen cog has benches along the walls of its cabin and a toilet facility at the back, sticking out over the stern of the ship. Such high-sided ships, of deep draught, were more suited now to specially built quaysides than to simple beaching. Harbours with cranes (of which there are pictures and some preserved examples in Baltic ports), beacons, defences, arsenals were developed. The Hanse's arsenals (naval shipyards) were outside town on peninsulas at Hamburg and Bremen, and on an island in the river at Cologne. The first mention of a light-keeper comes from Travemünde on the Baltic in 1316.

The Bremen cog was evidently not quite finished when it sank in its naval shipyard on the Weser in Bremen around AD 1380. Its forecastle, for example, had not been completed and there is no sign of its mast step. It

appears that a storm or an exceptionally high tide loosened the nearly completed cog from its construction berth and sucked it into the river and down
into the mud. This accounts for its excellent state of preservation, by which
we are able to inspect its windlass (never seen in the pictures on town seals
and needed to handle the bigger and heavier sail of the day), its cabin
arrangements, its constructional details – and a set of shipwright's tools
found in it.

The League in decline

The Hanseatic League outlived the career of the cogs with which the rise of
the League was so closely associated, the Bremen cog being among the last
of the type. Evidently the cog could not be scaled up in size to increase its
cargo-carrying capacity any further. Another shipbuilding tradition supplanted the cog style in the fifteenth century, one with another long history
behind it, whose early stages have been discerned in the small boat found
at Antwerp which is really no more than a log boat with two butted strakes
added to each side. Coins from Carolingian Dorestad on the Rhine of the
late eighth and early ninth centuries show rather banana-shaped boats with
a side rudder at the stem and a sail amidships, and possibly provision for
oars, that appear to continue this style. The Utrecht boat (found in 1930)
has its mast step about one-third of the way from the bow but appears to
be in general of the same type as the ones on the Dorestad coins. At 18 m
long, it's again a sort of log boat with – this time – three butted strakes
dowelled (trenailed) on to it, with vertical transomes at each end. It is
plainly a river boat and not any sort of seagoing ship, however. Another
boat from Utrecht, provisionally dated to the late twelfth century, follows
in the same general style; and from the same period there are church fonts
in Winchester and Bruges that show banana-curved boats, while English
coins and town seals of the fourteenth and fifteenth centuries show rather
similar ships, with stern rudders. The banana shape came about in the
absence of any heavy keel timbers to force a linear shape on these ships' bottoms.

These banana-like boats may be linked to the hulcs mentioned in late
tenth- or early eleventh-century laws of Aethelred II and the name goes on
being invoked in twelfth- to fifteenth-century documents. The town seal of
New Shoreham, formerly Hulkesmouth, appears to relate the hulc name to

such a type of boat. By the thirteenth century, hulks were already an important feature of French and English trade – the fourteenth-century seal of Winchelsea shows one with castles. By the early fifteenth century, and fused with elements of cog and keel design, they seem to have taken over from the cog types in north-west European waters, being built in the Netherlands only sixty years after the last of the cogs. No surviving example of a hulk has been found, but a seal from Danzig is thought to provide a particularly good likeness. Some of them, perhaps not surprisingly in the light of their conjectured origins in the Antwerp and Utrecht boats, were carvel-built with butted planking, which suited the general developments in shipbuilding of the time. The single-masted hulk was itself a relatively short-lived design in its mature form. By the end of the fifteenth century, three-masted ships with much more sail were the norm, now built first as strengthened skeleton frames rather than as strake shells, an approach permitting the construction of larger and stronger ships, which in the end could go on to support gun decks with gun ports. It was perhaps an input of southern Atlantic and Mediterranean shipbuilding developments, fused with the north-west European traditions, that created this new sort of shipping: certainly the carvel-build marked a departure from the long-lasting clinker pattern of the northern world, but the later ships' keel was adopted from the cog style. Carvel-build meant less timber was required to build the new ships and fewer rivets to assemble them. It was suited to the use of 'mass-produced' planking sawn by water-mills and the end product was a lighter, handier ship.

The Hanseatic League, once so powerful and commanding, faced decline from the late fifteenth century, having survived the slump in trade that came with the Black Death in the century before. This union of maritime traders that could formerly dictate policy to states and enjoy vast commercial privileges wherever it operated began to suffer reverses. The 1397 Union of Kalmar in all of Scandinavia had strengthened the northern nations against the Hanse; after 1492 the Atlantic trade of first the Spanish and Portuguese and then the English and Dutch (with some Scandinavian involvement) overshadowed the more locally restricted operations of the League; and in a time of general economic decline, famine, disease and accelerated social change, the migrating herring had deserted the western Baltic and the northern reaches of the North Sea. English and Dutch ships started to gain access to the Baltic and broke the Hanseatic monopoly. Ivan III of Muscovy closed the Hanse's Peterhof Kontor in 1496, though the

Steelyard in London was not finally wound up until 1598. The Swedes wrested control of the Gulf of Finland from the Hanse in the latter half of the sixteenth century. Bruges was eclipsed by the commercial rise of Antwerp on the Scheldt, with its better access to the Rhineland and the cloth towns of southern Flanders, to say nothing of its modern and flexible financial system. Again, the British and Dutch edged out the Hanse in southern and Mediterranean commerce. The League went on with its essentially coastal trade within a purely north European setting, and on a reduced scale, finally petering out as a formal entity in the seventeenth century at a time of general decline in Germany as a result of the Thirty Years War (1618–48). The consolidation of princely states like Brandenburg-Prussia did the Hanse no favours, either, as the century progressed. The Diet of the Hanseatic League met for the last time in 1669, though old Hanse relationships persisted, in a fragmented network now.

A new focus

By the time the League was wound up, commercial pre-eminence and maritime power had shifted back south, away from the Baltic, to the geographically well-placed Netherlands facing the southern part of the North Sea. The Low Countries straddle the estuaries of the Scheldt, Maas and Rhine rivers with access into Germany and via the North Sea to England and the Atlantic; at the same time they are well-placed for trade with the Baltic and with southern Europe. Their position brought some disadvantages, though, for the ships of the Netherlands could be denied access to the Channel by the English and westerly winds could prevent them getting out of their own ports.

In the fifteenth and sixteenth centuries, almost all sizes of seagoing ships of the day could pass inland via the Netherlands' complex network of waterways to ports in the interior, which were safer and more practical than ports in the flat coastal regions of this part of north-west Europe. In fact, of course, there had been important ports in the Low Countries since Carolingian times, with Dorestad at their forefront: subsequently Stavoren by the Zuider Zee had featured in tenth- and eleventh-century commerce, with Kampen near the mouth of the IJssel coming to prominence in the Middle Ages. It is interesting to note that the latter-day Hanse came to prefer trading with the Zuider Zee ports to going south down the unappealing North Sea coast of Holland to the ports of the more southerly estuaries.

In the fifteenth century, the Dukes of Burgundy built up for themselves a compact stretch of territory that ran north from their titular homeland and included Flanders and Brabant on the North Sea. They achieved what was in fact an independent state, in the richest area of north-west Europe, at the expense of France to their west and the Holy Roman Empire to their east. In time, their French fiefdoms in Picardy and Burgundy itself were lost to France, while the remainder of the Burgundian inheritance passed to the Habsburg emperor Charles V, who added further territories in the north-east in the form of the North Sea provinces around the Zuider Zee, including Friesland. (This Charles V was heir to four separate inheritances from his grandparents – in addition to the Netherlands, there were Sicily, Naples, Sardinia and Aragon, Castile, Granada and the West Indies, Austria, Tyrol, Carinthia and Alsace, to which he was able himself to add Milan and Tunis, Mexico and Peru, Bohemia, Moravia, Silesia and parts of Hungary. By the mid sixteenth century, his was a formidable reach of power and wealth.)

In the first half of the sixteenth century, the North Sea's coasts were in the hands, clockwise, of the not very united Scandinavian Union of Kalmar to the base of Jutland, the Holy Roman Empire in Lower Saxony and East Friesland, the Habsburgs in their own right in the Low Countries, the French in Artois (a short run, this one), the English and, finally, the Scots. The practical arrangements of these states had by now left much of the feudal system of social relations behind, with the universal Church weakened or supplanted by national versions and the powers of kings and princes greatly increased. New courts of law, new taxes, new machinery of government helped princes to their power; there were the beginnings of regular armed forces and professional diplomacy. The economy of Europe began to recover and the commercial classes in all countries were willing to accept the growth of absolutist royal power while it gave them security and freedom from civil war. Distinct foreshadowings of modern commercial arrangements can be discerned: in the Church's own erosion of its ancient prohibition of usury (interest on money); in princes' farming out taxes, coinage, markets and mining; in the establishment of banks and insurance provisions in Italy, Germany and the Low Countries; in the spread of manufacture by 'putting-out' of work to paid workers; in the growth of more and more associations of merchants. Nowhere was the progress of commercial arrangements to be better promoted than in the Netherlands.

Chapter 7

Dutchmen

Charles V, the mightiest European monarch of his time, abdicated in 1556, embittered by the failure of his imperial policies to hold his universal empire together in the face of the growth of nation states with their more separatist ideologies. His brother became the new emperor, but his son Philip (II) received the Spanish inheritance that included the Low Countries. In his domains, Philip would tolerate neither religious nor political liberty of any sort. Charles V had already persecuted Protestants in the Netherlands with heretics burned in Brussels in 1523. From 1565, Philip intensified the operations of the Inquisition in the Low Countries.

At this time, the Netherlands comprised seventeen provinces with a marked contrast between the French-speaking south and the Germanic-speaking north, which division more or less coincided with a religious border between Catholics and Protestants. At the same time a considerable divide in wealth was apparent between a prosperous bourgeoisie in the towns and an impoverished old nobility in the country. Moreover, every province and city was passionately attached to its own ancient liberties. There were more than two hundred cities in this, the first and most successful area of commerce and industry in Europe. It is very interesting to note that the provinces of the Netherlands brought the Spanish Crown seven times more wealth in taxation than all the silver from the Americas. Antwerp and Rotterdam handled something like 50 per cent of Europe's trade between them and Antwerp's Bourse was the centre of the European money market.

The eighty years Dutch War of Independence began in 1568 with the execution of two of the provincial Stadholders (viceregal lieutenants of the Crown) by Philip's 'Iron Duke' of Alba. Leadership of the opposition to Spanish rule was now focussed on the Stadholder William of Orange. Alba's replacement as Governor-General won back the southern Catholic provinces to Spain towards the end of the sixteenth century, but the northern provinces stood out with a proclamation of independence in 1581. William was murdered in 1584, and in the same year the seven republics that constituted the United Provinces met in the Hague under the chairmanship of the maritime province of Holland. Holland's pre-eminence among the United Provinces (it paid by far the biggest share into the central government and included the key city of Amsterdam) would see its name used to designate the whole Union: the 'Pensionary of the Council' appointed by Holland became (with five-year terms) the effective political leader of the new country. England openly supported the United Provinces against the might of Spain whose ambitions included the reconversion of the English nation to Catholicism. The defeat of the Spanish Armada in the English Channel came as a most welcome diversion of Spanish military capacity away from the Netherlands.

By the time of England's engagement with the Armada, ship design and naval armament had come a long way from the methods of the Middle Ages, when fighting ships were no more than castled merchantmen full of archers. Until the fifteenth century, northern ships had carried one square sail on a single mast, which could be very tall and of very large diameter. The *Philippa* as early as 1337 had carried a 30 m mast and Henry V of England's *Grace Dieu* of 1416–18 sported one twice that tall and over 2 m in diameter at deck level, the ship itself being almost as big as Nelson's *Victory*. The sail could evidently be reduced or increased in canvas area (as could the sail of the cogs, for that matter), but these single-sailed ships were always hard to handle, especially in confined waters like estuaries and harbours. The Mediterranean galleys that northern sailors encountered in the course of trade, travel and conflict appealed to military interests in north-west Europe for their capacity to be rowed under control in naval engagements, even if they might be sailed to the scene of battle. Cargo-carrying galleys were trading up from the Mediterranean to Flanders in the late thirteenth century and Philip the Fair of France ordered thirty war galleys in 1295. The English took to building 'galleys' of their own in the fourteenth century, but they were still clinker-built rather than of carvel-build in the manner of their Mediterranean prototypes. Gradually, the benefits in terms of economy of timber and lightness of handling led on to the adoption of the carvel practice of edge-butted planks, though essentially clinker style ships could still be built, in carvel mode, as late as the ill-fated *Mary Rose* of 1536. (Galleys had their disadvantages as cargo ships, requiring large rowing crews and provisions for them that crowded out the goods carried for trade.)

Carracks, caravels and galleons

In the fifteenth century, northern ships began to carry two (and later on, three or four) masts after the fashion of captured Genoese carracks, which themselves owed something to the later northern cog pattern as it had been adopted in the Bay of Biscay and then gone on to influence Catalonian, Genoese and Venetian ship design. Though they were of carvel-build in the southern fashion, Genoese carracks were fitted with the stern-mounted rudders pioneered by northern shipbuilders in the thirteenth century. Their sterns and stems were rounded in contrast with the stiffer lines of the North Sea cogs, though later Baltic cogs were more rounded, as depictions and wrecks found at Gdansk (Danzig) reveal.

The two masts of the newly developed northern carracks carried square-rigged sails, and the added mizzen mast a lateen sail of triangular shape which had originally been developed by the Arabs and helped in sailing into the wind, though it could be a handful in heavy weather. These late-medieval carracks could be up to 40 m long, handling more easily than their smaller predecessors ever had. They dominated fifteenth-century trade and took people to the New World at the end of the century. Smaller versions, handier for coastal trade, appeared in many forms.

But the heyday of the big carracks was over by 1500, in the face of a handier and initially smaller design that was pioneered by the Portuguese: the caravel, also multi-masted with two square-rigged sails and one lateen, but with a larger rudder at the blunt transom-built stern. These caravels were widely adopted in both Mediterranean and northern waters, cheaply built on frames in the carvel style, fast to sail and all in all the ideal ships of their day for trade, war and piracy. After the decline of the Hanseatic League, and of their Antwerp trade, the English traded to the Baltic in ships of the caravel design.

The first warships of the medieval northern world had been merchant-men convertible to naval fighting. Guns are recorded to have been first used at sea in an attack on Antwerp in 1336 and the first English ship with guns – three iron guns and a handgun – was the cog *Christopher* captured by the French at Sluis (a river outport of Bruges) in 1340. At about the same time as the Bremen cog was nearing completion in the 1380s, away in the Mediterranean the Venetians were equipping their low galleys (sailed or rowed) with slow-firing and wildly inaccurate bombard guns capable of firing stone balls forward from their single front decks. Not surprisingly, archery and hand-to-hand fighting remained the chief modes of naval conflict with these war galleys, though in due course small anti-personnel guns on swivel mounts were added and the bombards were mounted on carriages. For all their inaccuracy, these forward-firing guns had the merit that they could be loosed off from a distance in the early stages of an encounter rather than fired as a broadside only just before an attempt at boarding. At a time when the carracks of the day were equipped with guns that could not fire forward, a line of galleys approaching abreast had some initial advantage. The first gun ports are said to have been installed on a French ship built at Brest in 1501, though we may note that the old *Mary Rose* was bristling with them when she sank in 1540. In the early years of the sixteenth century, ports were opened in the squared-off sterns of warships for big guns ('stern chasers') to fire out of the back, chiefly in aid of shore bombardment; but thereafter ports were also employed for broadside use, below decks.

In the mid sixteenth century, a sort of galley-carrack hybrid was developed in the form of a design with low forecastle and high stern that could carry some more or less forward-firing guns (its 'bow chasers') as well as its broadside capability. Both the English and the Spanish adopted this galleon pattern, largely descended from the four-masted carrack in general concept and build. The English favoured a smaller, lower and so handier version of the galleon, with guns on carriages ported along the sides at various levels, and often large swivel guns on deck, too. The Spanish galleons were longer and higher, sometimes double-decked with raised foredeck and quarterdeck, going on to designs with multiple decks that needed a low centre of gravity to remain stable. Galleons in general came to rely on their broadside firing over any forward-firing capability they carried, foreshadowing the adoption of the 'line of battle' tactics in the next century. The arrangement of sails was elaborated at the same time for powerful performance, with divided sails on each of the masts and complicated rigging to work them. The aim of all the sophistication of gunnery was not, in fact, to sink the enemy's ships but to destroy their rigging, take out their gun decks, pick off their officers, close, grapple and board – in short, to take prizes! Ships like these had gone beyond anything that could be converted from merchantmen. Building and equipping them called for supplies of raw materials and even finished items that involved the vagaries of international trade. The Hanse had historically specialised in Baltic timber, pitch and tar; iron came from Sweden and Spain; hemp for ropes and sails might come from the Baltic, but the Bretons were master manufacturers of the finished goods; small arms, swords and armour were the specialities of the Low Countries and Italy; big gun casting was developed in Germany and the Low Countries.

The Spanish threat

When (along with at various times France, Spain, Portugal, Italy, Switzerland and Scotland) the Spanish-controlled Low Countries and Germany were counted among his enemies, Henry VIII of England brought in Flemish founders and turned to founding guns of his own in iron rather than importing costly bronze guns or the copper needed to make the bronze for himself. Big breech-loaders firing stone were the order of the day. The guns were as much for use on land to counter his enemies' ships' guns as for fitting into his own ships. Henry extensively fortified the southern and eastern coasts of England, building ramparts from which to fire his big guns: fourteen castles, of which Deal in Kent is the prime example, were planned though the northerly east coast ones were not built; there were blockhouses with two or more guns on the roof like the one at Tilbury in Essex; there were earth and timber bulwarks, sometimes behind brick and stone walls, as at Felixstowe and Yarmouth.

Henry VIII never, in fact, needed to man his coastal defences in earnest or fire his guns in anger or put his ships to sea in war, but his daughter Elizabeth did have to fight. The forts she built against the Armada were cheaper affairs than her father's, but her ships were better armed than those of the Spaniards in terms of range, power and sheer quality of the guns. Spanish ships had been operating under some difficulties in the southern area of the North Sea since Dutch Protestants out of Dover had taken Flushing, the only real deepwater port in Dutch waters. (In 1572, though, the Spanish were able to secure Dunkirk, and then Nieupoort in 1583.) The

Dutch, moreover, could frequently visit damage on Spain's ships and instal-lations by emerging from, and then melting back into, their country's net-work of inland waterways. Elizabeth's support of the United Provinces saw English as well as Dutch ships seized by the Spanish in their ports. Piratical exploits against Spanish interests in the New World and their raid on Cadiz made the English an even more urgent target for Spain's attentions. Piracy was rife at this time, backed in England by some of the greatest in the land. Pirates from North Africa and, as always, Dunkirk were also to the fore. It was in Dunkirk that the galley-derived frigate design was promoted from the end of the sixteenth century: shallow and fast with a lot of sail; and much favoured by pirates and privateers everywhere, and by the Dutch for cruiser operations in their coming struggles with the English.

Much of the early action between England's ships and the Armada fleet took place in the Channel in the summer of 1588. On 28 July, the English sent fireships among the Spanish ships now at anchor off Calais, waiting for reinforcements from the Spanish Netherlands under the watchful eyes of a Dutch squadron offshore. On the 29th, Drake attacked at close quarters and a nine-hour sea battle ensued. Wind drove the Spaniards on to shoals for a while and two of their large ships were grounded. When the wind changed, the Spanish could get away. The English ships ran temporarily out of ammunition but followed the Spanish fleet, forty of whose ships were driven into the North Sea while the remainder were battered by the superior English firepower with heavy Spanish losses. The Spanish com-mander lost his nerve and ordered his Armada to sail north on the southerly winds, to escape by going up and round the northern coast of Britain – in very stormy seas, as it turned out, for the weather seems in general to have been windier then than it is now. Only half of the remaining ships made the long and dangerous voyage round Britain and many were wrecked on unfa-miliar and unfriendly shores: they had not been designed for the conditions they met in northern waters. The weather and poor strategy on the Spaniards' part played as big a role in their débâcle as superior English sea-manship and armament. In the aftermath of the inglorious failure of the Armada, Spanish naval power suffered a decline and the Dutch rose to mar-itime pre-eminence. At the same time, the English Navy fell into compla-cent neglect and the French started to enlarge.

The skills of Maurice of Nassau as a military commander greatly aided the infant Dutch Republic in its repulsion of the Spanish from its territories: as did the Republic's seizure of Spanish (and Portuguese) trading stations around the world as the basis of the Dutch colonial empire to come, which forced Spain to trade with its upstart enemy and so help to finance the continuing war against itself. (The VOC, the United East India Company, was formed in 1602 to promote and protect Dutch trade with the Indian Ocean and it prospered mightily through most of the seventeenth century.) Unfortunately, struggles between Maurice and the Pensionary led to the execution of the first of the men England was to call the 'Grand Pensionary'; but Spain was eventually seen off and obliged to recognise the Dutch Republic in 1648.

The Dutch at sea

The sea was always a natural sphere of operations for the Dutch: to gain a living from, to escape by, to venture over. Dutch sea power was always at base a commercial enterprise, even in the times of unified defiance against Spain. Any one of the towns of the provinces engaged in the struggle might finance a fighting ship of its own, out of its commercial wealth. By the end of the fifteenth century, before the Spanish threat had arisen, the office of High Admiral had been created, with a Council of Admiralty that predates Henry VIII's Navy Board in England. The fleet that had come into being before the eighty years War of Independence was either largely destroyed or had passed into the hands of the Republic by the end of it. The Republic's maritime provinces maintained five separate admiralties – three in Holland, one in Friesland and one in Zeeland – which rather went their separate ways, looking after local trade and fishing. The herring, whose disappearance from the northern waters of the North Sea had done the Hanseatic League no good, greatly benefited the emergent Netherlands by appearing in plenty in the southern North Sea in the fifteenth century, perhaps as a result of changes in the Gulf Stream's impact on the North Sea's currents. The Dutch developed their Great Fishery in the North Sea on the basis of the herring – and the first moves were made under James I of England to tax them in English offshore waters. The Dutch might be willing to let their ships salute the English flag in the Channel, but they baulked at the fish dues and resorted to armed escort to avoid paying them.

Even the naval conflicts of the Dutch Republic that look political were really commercially driven in the interests of trade protection – like keeping the entry into the Baltic out of Swedish or Danish hands, or holding off the Dunkirk pirates, or fighting the first and second English Wars. The first of these conflicts, of 1652–3, was provoked by the English Navigation Act of 1651 that insisted (not for the first time) on the carrying of all goods to and from England only in English ships. The Dutch now faced a reinvigorated English Navy under Commonwealth direction: Charles I had lost his throne amidst a host of problems that included trying to collect taxes to improve his naval capacity. Cromwell's navy deployed the new line tactics of the day that maximised the use of guns and the Dutch with their smaller ships and boarding tactics did not come off too well in battles off Dungeness and Dover, north of Margate and east of Harwich. In the second war, between 1665 and 1667, the Dutch were to fare rather better, as we shall see. In these conflicts, incidentally, the capture of Dutch ships greatly enlarged the English merchant fleet and Dutch ship design was copied profitably.

Dutch trade

The trade that the Dutch Navy had come into being to protect was based on the exchange of goods between south-west Europe (France, Spain and Portugal) and north and north-east Europe, which meant the ports around the North Sea and the Baltic and even the White Sea over the top of Norway and Russia. (Of course, this trade commingled with Mediterranean and, increasingly, transatlantic and East Indies commerce in many of the ports of Europe.) It is estimated that perhaps two thousand ships were plying their trade under the Dutch flag in the seventeenth and eighteenth centuries, the largest of them carrying crews of up to twenty-five men. These crews were drawn, as parish records reveal, from all the countries of north-west Europe and sometimes beyond. Because the Dutch trade with Norway was the busiest commercial exchange of the seventeenth century, many Norwegian sailors ended up in Amsterdam, where a third of marriages involved foreigners: Germans at the top of the list, but Norwegians ahead of Danes and Swedes. (There was some migration of Dutch factors and representatives to Norway, but in nothing like the numbers coming the other way.) By the eighteenth century, the number of foreign marriages in Amsterdam was down to one quarter, but Rotterdam came up at the end of the century. Interestingly, a great many of the masters of Amsterdam ships were of Frisian origin.

The Norwegian trade of the Dutch brought away stockfish from Bergen (dried cod) and timber along with tar and furs, taking into Norway cloth, tiles, bricks, wine, tobacco, salt, cheese and spices. But the timber, in particular, that was taken out was always worth more than the imports brought in, so that money as well as goods changed hands. The English traders in Norway operated in the same way. Timber was in short supply in the rather forestless Dutch Republic, and much in demand to build dykes and drive piles in land reclamation schemes, to make casks for herring exports and, of course, to build the ships that carried all the trade goods around. Timber, moreover, was carried in Dutch ships to other places that needed it, including France, England, the southern Netherlands and Spain.

From Norway the Dutch got fir and spruce, and later oak also, as other supplies of this timber (in Germany along the Rhine, Weser and Elbe and in the Baltic region) declined over time. The timber trade was highly capitalised, requiring long-term investment in growing, cutting down, seasoning and transporting the bulky product: it was an ideal commercial operation for the Dutch who had developed the financial arrangements that could handle such investment, and also the wind-powered sawmills that could handle the raw material. The bulk of the Norwegian timber came from around the Oslofjord region in the south, but Trondheim (on the Norwegian Sea, to the north of our North Sea focus) was another good source, having a deep hinterland of wooded valleys.

The Dutch ships evidently made several trips a year to Norway, of six to eight weeks' duration including a couple of weeks in the Norwegian ports. Often specialised ships were used for the timber trade, with extra draught and gates in the sides at stem and stern to permit the loading of long lengths of timber. In the late seventeenth century, ships with steep stems and sterns, mainly fir-built, could be filled up with a lot of timber that contributed its own buoyancy. The Dutch ships were so good and so reasonably priced as a result of high production that the Norwegians bought them to trade with England, though at the same time they took to building ships themselves to evade their own laws against exporting their dwindling supplies of oak. It is estimated that by the end of the seventeenth century, there were three hundred big ships trading with Norway from the Dutch Republic, whose vessels sometimes engaged in direct trading, for example to France from Norway, as well as operating through Amsterdam.

In the latter half of the seventeenth century, the Dutch lost trade to an England that was coming to need more and more timber for its own ships, both naval and merchant marine, for its coal mines (in the form of props) and for its housebuilding, especially after the Great Fire in 1666. (A Norwegian bishop observed that many of his countrymen warmed themselves by that fire.) English forests dwindled and there was much call for Norwegian timber, to the point that over 40 per cent of the fresh timber used in England came from Norway. It was not so much at first to English traders that the Dutch began to lose ground as to the Norwegians themselves, in Dutch-bought ships or those of their own Norwegian build. Later on, the Danes got in on the act: from the 1670s on, it was Danes and Norwegians who were conducting London's timber trade, with a church of their own in town. Only from the first decade of the eighteenth century did the English themselves increase their own part in the Norwegian timber import business.

Commercial rivalries

Timber was not the only commodity that was traded by the Dutch and their rivals over the seas of northern Europe. Even such a characteristically English product as the clay pipes employed to smoke the New World import of tobacco became a typically Dutch item of manufacture and trade in the early seventeenth century. Pottery and ceramic tiles from the southern shores of the North Sea, along with cobblestones from the Rhineland and wine, oil and spices from further afield, were transported by Dutch ships to the Baltic and the White Sea, which had been opened first to English access (by passage over the north of Scandinavia inside the Arctic Circle) after the mid sixteenth century. After 1703, Russian ports flourished on the Baltic and the Dutch were prominent in the trade there. Timber, hemp, tar, glue (all important for shipbuilding), flax and grain were the goods taken west and south from the Baltic and White Seas. The Dutch almost exclusively took over the grain trade that had earlier been a mainstay of the Hanse, and supplemented the salt supplies of the Lüneburg mines in northern Germany, formerly promoted by the League, with cheaper Mediterranean imports. Records indicate that in the first half of the seventeenth century, Dutch shipping through the Sound that leads to and from the Baltic exceeded the amount of English shipping by twelve times. Later on, in the eighteenth century, the British were to catch up with this trade.

The British did not start to export their own salt, from their Cheshire mines, till the early eighteenth century, but they were exporting coal a century before that, though it was mostly Dutch ships that carried it to Scandinavia and the Baltic lands until the English Navigation Act of 1651 that provoked the first conflict between the Dutch and the English. Other goods that were conveyed around the North Sea included iron from Sweden (later Russia, too) and cloth from England, Germany and the Low Countries – an English ship that was wrecked at the entrance to Oslofjord in about 1630 was full of the lead seals once attached to bolts of cloth, together with spoons, pewter mugs, spurs and spectacle lenses. As time went by and the products of trade from distant colonies and far-flung lands started to figure in European commerce, there was tea, coffee and tobacco, silk, spices, sugar and potatoes, cotton and fine china and exotic timbers.

Both the Dutch and the British maintained large fishing fleets, after herring off the east coast of England and cod from the profusely supplied areas of the North Sea like the Dogger Bank. (The Great Fishery was in pursuit of herring and the Small Fishery of white fish, cod in particular caught by long line. The drift net and salting at sea greatly enhanced the trade.) The Dutch Republic, which had sailed a thousand or so fishing smacks and busses in the North Sea and traded herring to the Baltic using secretive methods of curing at sea, saw a relative decline in its fishing enterprise in the eighteenth century, as the British came on more strongly, along with Low Countries fishermen from outside the United Provinces, Danes and Norwegians. The Norwegians exported eels to the Dutch. (Of course, boats from North Sea ports were venturing much further afield at the same time, with both the Dutch and Scots as well as the English active in arctic waters after whales, seals and walruses.)

The ships in which the trade of the seventeenth and eighteenth centuries was conducted were developed out of the vessels of late medieval and early modern times, as were the warships we shall come to. Long-distance travel to colonies and trading partners in remote parts of the world required bigger ships for ocean crossings, as did whaling and seal hunting in the north and west. Purely North Sea trade could go on with coasters, of course, and a great many small vessels of shallow draught were constantly constructed to carry on the small-scale trade that did not require the big new ports for the big new ships: these little ships have scarcely survived to give us any actual relics of the shipbuilding traditions of their day, but documentary and pictorial evidence of all sorts of shipping increases through the seventeenth and eighteenth centuries. We know that the tendency from the late Middle Ages was to make more use of fore and aft sails and to lower the high castles of the medieval ships to consolidate a more seaworthy flush-deck design. From the seventeenth century, there comes evidence for the first time (though it must have gone on to some extent before) of ship design by planning on paper before construction, which was now aided by more in the way of mathematical calculation to avoid errors and wastage of materials. Warships were much more ornately turned out at this time, carved and gilded, to carry the prestige of their nations: they were, in fact, floating statements of the new-found importance of the concept of the nation-state. Trade protection by means of highly visible warships (and merchantmen, too, could well be armed and ostentatious) evolved into a nationalistic ethos of 'flying the flag' that came to be shared by all the maritime powers through the seventeenth and eighteenth centuries.

The Dutch were the leaders in commercial shipbuilding in the seventeenth century with their economical and practical three-masted freighters called fluyts which were developed out of the old carrack design. The British variant was the fly-boat. The Dutch are reported to have had perhaps ten thousand of these vessels, the largest of them trading to the Far East. Piracy and privateering prompted the installation of a gun deck in these merchant ships, so that they were hardly distinguishable from warships, as which they could double if necessary. Smaller ships might still be family-owned or funded by a small group of traders, farmers perhaps, to conduct their limited business. It was the Dutch Republic, where modern financial procedures allowed capital to be raised, that saw the formation of real shipping companies, employing captains and crews. Dutch ships were often bigger than English ones in the seventeenth century.

The prestige of the Dutch

Because of the early success of Dutch shipping, and the continued demand for Dutch officers and crews, the Low German dialect called Dutch was established as the common means of practical communication among sailors of all sorts, building on the closely similar dialect of the Hanse crews of yore: English words would come to be added to the repertoire of seafaring usage with the rise of British maritime power. The British could recruit their crews at home (by fair means and foul) and their naval culture was less cosmopolitan than the rest of seafaring Europe's, where crews and officers were always drawn from a wide base in many countries: the nationalistic habits of later times were hardly developed before the end of the eighteenth century.

In their heyday Dutch ships were the envy of the world, bought by owners in other countries and prized as spoils of war and piracy. Even when the Dutch yards were overtaken by the British, Dutch expertise was still highly valued – the interest of Peter the Great of Russia is one witness to that – and Dutch shipbuilders were hired abroad. Their manuals of shipbuilding and seamanship were widely distributed. Dutch influence on the building of ships outside the Republic can be discerned in the concept and building of the magnificent but ill-fated Swedish warship, the *Vasa*, that capsized in Stockholm harbour in 1628, shortly after construction. The Swedes had their own shipbuilding tradition, of course, that went back to the longships and cargo vessels of their Viking ancestors, but when in the 1620s they wanted to sail bigger ships out on the open sea they looked to the Dutch for inspiration and took on some Dutch designers to help build these ships. A few of these Dutchmen rose to positions of some eminence in the Stockholm naval dockyard, bringing in some of their own countrymen as shipwrights. The *Vasa* – salvaged in 1961 and impressively if uncertainly preserved in its own museum in Stockholm – consequently shows some Dutch influence in its construction and hull form. Indeed, its rather flat-bottomed configuration in the Dutch manner (they were used to operating in shallow waters) cannot have enhanced its stability even if it is deeper-hulled than Dutch ships were. A warship that was being built at the same time for the French in a Dutch shipyard was evidently furnished with a hull form similar to the *Vasa*'s.

Dutch financial and political involvement with the Swedes had come about in the early part of the seventeenth century after the Dutch and English together had by diplomatic pressure forced a peace between Sweden and Denmark-Norway which had built up its navy after a decline in the late sixteenth century and declared war on Sweden in 1611. The Scandinavian powers were always of interest to trading nations like the English and Dutch on account of their being in a position to interfere with the Baltic trade through the Skaggarak and the Sound. The Dutch came to disfavour the Swedes for a while when they put heavy tariffs on shipping into the east Baltic, but came round to them again when the Danes did the same on the Elbe and in the Sound. When the Swedes declared war on Denmark-Norway in 1643, they were able to charter twenty-two fully fitted Dutch warships and defeat the Danes at sea; the next year the Dutch sent forty-seven warships to the Sound to break the tariff regime.

The Danes lost territory in the outcome of this struggle, but the Dutch were keen not to see the Swedes press their advantage too far: when in 1648, at the Peace of Westphalia which closed the Thirty Years' War, the Swedes got control of the dioceses of Bremen and Verden, the Dutch – to whom these North Sea regions were commercially important – distanced themselves from the Swedes once more. As the Dutch fell out with the English over the Navigation Act, the Swedes courted the English, fought the Danes again and went on themselves to attempt to close the Sound to all foreign shipping. After a fierce sea battle in 1658, which was fought past Elsinore in the Sound, the Dutch won.

Conflict continued between Denmark-Norway and Sweden, with the interference of the English and Dutch till these two trading powers and France helped negotiate a peace in 1660. In the Third Dutch War with the English, the Dutch encouraged the Danes to attack the Swedes again and defeat them at Koge Bay, south of Copenhagen, in 1677. The Swedes had joined the English in helping France to blockade the Dutch as part of her scheme to overrun the Netherlands, as we shall see.

English and Dutch at war

When guns were first used on ships in the late fourteenth century, they were as much defensive weapons to deter seizure of the ships that deployed them as offensive measures against the enemies' ships, though they were used to bring down rigging to disable potential prizes. It was only from the first quarter of the seventeenth century that ship design accommodated guns that could be readily run about on wheels by virtue of the construction of a more level decking from bow to stern. It was British naval commanders like Blake and Monk with experience of gun battles on land who evolved new tactics at sea to make the most of the guns now available to the fleet built up by Parliament. Previously the idea had been simply to bring your ship as close as possible to an enemy ship and let fly, on an individual basis.

Now the requirement, set out in a new set of 'Fighting Instructions' by the English in 1653, was to keep all the ships of a squadron in formation, in line with the lead ship, and to loose off mass broadsides at the enemy from guns with longer range. In the first engagements of the naval wars between the Dutch and the English, the shallower draught and lighter ships of the Dutch did not lend themselves to the line tactics as well as the British ships did under captains familiar with the new necessities of line discipline.

But in the course of their naval wars against English trade protectionism, the Dutch did start to achieve their own successes. Early in the Second War, between 1665 and 1667, there was a minor engagement off Bergen on the Norwegian North Sea coast, when the town sided with fifty Dutch East Indiamen sheltering there on their way to Amsterdam against twenty-one English warships with whom the Danish-Norwegian king hoped to share the china, pearls and spices on board. The English suffered damage to three of their ships with six hundred men wounded or killed, while the Dutch took no harm to their ships and only a handful of casualties. (Ten towns-people of Bergen were killed in the bombardment of the town.) In the more substantial 'Four Days' Battle' that took place in the most south-western waters of the North Sea, between Dunkirk and North Foreland in Kent in 1666, the English lost seventeen ships and eight thousand men and the Dutch only broke off when English reinforcements arrived. Six weeks later at the end of July, the position was reversed between North Foreland and Orford Ness on the Suffolk coast when the Dutch lost twenty ships and seven thousand men. The English were now able to raid the coast of the Dutch Republic and destroy merchant shipping there. By this time, the English Navy could run to First Rate ships of a hundred guns, down to Fourth Raters with only thirty or so, or even smaller vessels.

Charles II of England, thinking he held all the cards, prolonged negotiations in the hopes of the best possible outcome for England – and laid up most of his ships and paid off their crews, against Monk's advice. The next year, the Dutch under de Ruyter sailed into the Thames Estuary and up the Medway, bombarded the fleet dockyard at Chatham, set fire to laid-up warships and captured the flagship *Royal Charles* with much naval equipment besides. (They took her home to rot in a backwater, though the stern survives in the Rijksmuseum in Amsterdam.) Now they were able to blockade English merchant shipping and to strike more or less at will – as it happened it was at Harwich, where they landed two thousand men to attack

Landguard Fort under cover of naval bombardment. (It had been designed by a Dutchman in 1625.) But the bombardment was too distant and the land force had to withdraw, leaving eight Dutch dead to one English. In the Peace of Breda in 1667, the British lost the East Indies and the Dutch the West Indies, along with the Hudson Valley in North America and the little town of Nieuw Amsterdam with a big future ahead of it as New York. The English did ameliorate their protectionist Navigation Act, but Charles went on wanting to rein in the Dutch.

Five years later, on hire to the French who wanted to seize the Netherlands, Charles was back at war with the Dutch. They, under William of Orange, opened their dykes to flood the advance of the French and de Ruyter was able to claim victory against the English Navy at the Battle of Sole Bay off Southwold, though both sides were mauled. In the peace this time (1674), William married Mary the Protestant daughter of Charles' Catholic brother, who lost his throne, as James II, to the Protestant pair in 1688 – to his credit it was said of him that he had built up a fleet good enough to bar his own return. (The French king, Louis XIV, made his peace with the Dutch four years after the English, getting nothing.) During the war, William had become Stadholder-General of the Dutch Republic for life: when he and Mary replaced James II, Holland and England were united under the personal rule of the new English king till his death in 1702 and the long commercial rivalry between the two countries was settled in England's favour at last. In truth, the struggle to maintain the security of its trade had left the uncentralised Dutch Republic in some distress, while the much more centrally governed English nation could forge ahead in the new century. After this time, shipbuilding was reduced in four of the five admiralties of the Dutch Republic, with Amsterdam alone remaining in full swing. The English, meanwhile, acquired the experience – partly because they had captured so many Dutch vessels in the first war – to build ships as cheaply and efficiently as the Dutch, and construction shifted from London and East Anglia to the north-east of England.

There was something of a Dutch revival after 1750, and throughout Dutch sailors and naval officers were widely in demand to man and instruct the navies of other states, Russia in particular, just as Dutch architects and engineers found plenty of employment abroad – like Vermuyden who drained so much of the East Anglian fenland. Dutch universities were among Europe's best, to say nothing of Dutch financial houses.

In the course of warfare in the North Sea, the Dutch and British would fight each other again, at the Dogger Bank in 1781 when the Dutch were in coalition with Spain and France, the latter in possession by this time of the world's largest navy; and off Kamperduin (Camperdown to the British, who won) in 1797, when the Dutch were again under French influence. For the whole latter half of the century, the French had posed a threat to Britain over more than trade: empire was at stake.

Chapter 8

Great powers

U ntil the mid seventeenth century, France – which has the shortest length of North Sea coast of any of the countries bordering that sea – was too preoccupied with internal and external conflicts to match the English and Dutch in the progress of their manufacturing bases and trade networks, or their prowess in shipbuilding and empire-building. From the middle of the century, slightly quieter times at home and abroad gave the French time not only to catch up with the English and Dutch but also to be thought to threaten the balance of power in Europe. The French army and navy were greatly enhanced, chiefly because France wanted to thwart the power of the Habsburgs, both Spanish and Austrian, who seemed to them to surround them on too many sides, including the Spanish Netherlands.

In the latter part of the seventeenth century, it looked certain that the Habsburg king of Spain would die childless and was likely to leave his piece of the Netherlands to the Austrian Habsburg line. The French took action against the Spanish Netherlands from 1667 to 1678, fighting the Dutch Republic too in 1672, which went on to widen the conflict in some of the ways that we saw with the involvement of the Swedes, the Danes and the English. At the same time, both the Dutch and the English feared French ambitions to get in on the business of securing foreign possessions and foreign trade, especially covert trade with Spanish America that the Spanish tried to prevent. In the War of the Grand Alliance between 1689 and 1697, England and the Netherlands fought the French in alliance with the Holy Roman Empire and Spain; the Peace of Utrecht (1713) that saw the end of the subsequent War of Spanish Succession gave the Spanish Netherlands to

Austria as France had feared. At about the same time, the Great Nordic or Northern War between Denmark-Norway and Sweden (with Russia and Saxony-Poland on the Danes' side) ended in a peace in 1721 that deprived Sweden of most of her southern Baltic possessions and Bremen-Verden: Denmark really got very little out of it in the end, except the decline of Sweden thereafter. But things were now rather nicely balanced in the Scandinavian world, in a way that invited much less foreign intervention in the future.

The rest of the eighteenth century witnessed a long struggle between France and Britain (England was now in full union with Scotland) for transatlantic power, in an ebb and flow that saw the British gain Canada and lose their American colonies. (They also drove the French out of India.) In contrast perhaps with its army, the British navy of the late eighteenth century was the world's best, with the largest battle fleet in the world and able to draw on manpower from the world's largest merchant marine. Standards of seamanship and gunnery were high, backed up by sound financing and administration. The French, for all their losses, maintained a great navy too, with both Atlantic and Mediterranean Fleets, and they actively pursued the development of ship design and shipbuilding technology, on the basis of the Dutch experience in these matters. The influence of French shipbuilding, at its peak in the middle of the eighteenth century, was widely felt. In general, the warships of the day might have lost some of their previous exuberance of decoration but they got bigger (almost as big as traditional methods of shipbuilding could permit) with steepened sterns and increased buoyancy to support their complex structure and enhanced armament in the shape of bigger and better guns. Boarding for the purpose of taking prizes lost its priority in naval tactics, the sophistication of sail arrays came on and anti-fouling measures like copper cladding below the waterline were sometimes applied. The French fleets were at the forefront of developments in warship design. But the French Revolution put a stop to all that and reduced them to a parlous state, from which they never wholly recovered.

The French Revolution also had far-reaching consequences for France's neighbours, among them both parts of the Netherlands. Shortly before the French Revolution, the Dutch Republic had fallen victim to a three-cornered fight between the Stadholder, the patrician families who controlled the Estates General and a bourgeois faction in favour of democratisation who called themselves the Patriot Party. In 1787, the Stadholder was helped by the rising power of Prussia (which had benefited from Swedish decline in the south Baltic) into a stronger position than ever with the Prussian defeat of the Patriots. In the same year, the Austrian Netherlands revolted against the Habsburg emperor's rule and then proclaimed the Republic of the United Belgian Provinces in 1790 – the name taken from the Celtic Belgae whom the Romans found in northern Gaul in the second century BC. Disputes between aristocratic and bourgeois elements among the rebels helped the Austrians to retake this part of the Netherlands by the end of the year.

The French revolutionaries sought to safeguard their national base with like-minded sister republics on their borders – one such was the Batavian Republic of the former United Provinces of the Netherlands, which flourished between 1795 and 1806, taking its name from the ancient Germanic tribe of the Batavi who had lived around Leiden at the Rhine mouth in Roman times. The Austrian Netherlands were annexed to France itself. When the French Republic was transformed into the Empire of Napoleon, the Batavian Republic was turned into the Kingdom of Holland. (After Napoleon, the two parts of the Netherlands were turned into the United Netherlands, from which Belgium broke away in 1830.)

The Napoleonic wars

The threat of Napoleonic France caused the British to strengthen their defences around the south and east coasts of England at Chatham and the Medway forts, at Tilbury and Dover. A string of Martello towers was built from Dymchurch on the south coast to Aldeburgh in East Anglia, as look-outs and a first line of defence. As a portent of dire things to come in the twentieth century, Napoleon was approached with a plan to invade England with a fleet of huge montgolfières (hot air balloons) carrying three thousand troops each. (The first crossing of the sea between England and France had been achieved in a hydrogen-filled balloon in 1785 by a Frenchman and a wealthy American.) No invasion by any means was carried out by Napoleon but he did attempt by decrees, backed by the partly recovered navy he had inherited from the Revolution, to exclude British trade from the large portion of continental Europe that he controlled. There was to be no import of British goods and no access to his ports on the part of British ships or any ships under the British flag, or even of anybody's ships that were known to have put in at a British port. In the course of the war against Napoleon, and his sometimes shifting alliances, Britain was sucked into hostile relations with not just France, but Denmark-Norway, Prussia, Russia and eventually Sweden, too. The Danes, in particular, had maintained a fleet which the British thought worth capture, sailing across the North Sea in 1807 to shell Copenhagen and secure forty or so Danish warships, together with gunboats and mortar boats.

British policy was to encourage trade with the ostensibly hostile ports of Napoleon's North Sea and Baltic allies by protecting every vessel in and out of these ports that sailed under any flag except the French one. The policy meant the use of false flags and forged ships' papers. And in fact, despite the French wish to impose their restrictive system, a vast trade went on across the North Sea throughout the period of Britain's struggle with Napoleon. Ships leaving British ports to do business across the North Sea assembled as convoys for protection by the Royal Navy during their crossing. Vessels from all along the eastern coast of Britain as far as Orkney were formed up into convoys off Norfolk and, at regular intervals of two to three weeks, they crossed to the Skagerrak and were taken under the wing of Britain's Baltic Fleet for further escort into the Baltic. When their business was over, they reassembled in the Baltic – with or without the blessing of the Swedes, as international politics dictated – and were seen safely out to the Skagerrak again.

During the sailing season through these years, thousands of crossings of individual ships were made in the convoys. Records perhaps surprisingly indicate that most of the ships were not under British ownership: some were American but the majority were of Scandinavian or Baltic origins, though not necessarily going under their own colours. There were some British ships under foreign colours, sometimes renamed to look like non-British vessels, and sometimes British owners bought foreign ships and crewed them with foreigners for this trade. In the late eighteenth century, the sailing barque was the common type of larger cargo ship. The Whitby collier was of this pattern, known for carrying coal in particular, and such ships were widely built as three-masters and, more latterly, two. (One of them went round the world under Captain Cook, as the *Endeavour*.) Large rectangular ports could be cut in stem and stern to carry timber. And, in fact, the goods traded out from the Baltic were chiefly naval supplies (the tar and hemp and so forth that the Baltic had always supplied, with timber from Norway, too) and grain. The Baltic and Scandinavian peoples desperately needed to trade out their products and the British in time of war badly needed the naval materials and profited by the grain trade: the Norwegians, in fact, were in the interesting position of getting grain for themselves from Denmark by courtesy of the British Navy's arrangements. Licences were issued by the British to permit their holders to join in this web of trade and enjoy the protection of the Navy, and only licence-holders were allowed to join convoys. The licences, of course, needed to be kept well away from the French authorities' eyes and were of no avail outside the convoys.

So, although the great sea battles of the Napoleonic Wars were not fought in the North Sea, it was all the same an area of intense and illicit economic activity throughout, which turned the French vision of a continental system to exclude Britain into something of an acknowledged fantasy. By 1815, war on land and sea had brought down Napoleon's empire and the British Navy had seen off the French, Dutch, Danish and Spanish Fleets. The British were now poised to take their own empire to its nineteenth-century zenith. The North Sea, the Baltic and the Mediterranean were no longer to be the necessarily dominant zones of European commerce: they remained important but in the context of a much wider world of maritime trade which often came into Europe through these seas rather than being generated in them.

The rise of Prussia

There were to be a few more national adjustments to the North Sea's margins in the nineteenth century. Norway was taken out of Denmark's hands in 1815, going to Sweden but with a separate government of its own (that led on to full independence in 1905). Belgium and Holland went their separate ways in 1830, as we have seen. Denmark lost Schleswig-Holstein to Prussia in 1866. And it was with the rise of Prussia and the unification of Germany that the German state came into its own on its stretch of North Sea coast, from the border of Holland to Schleswig-Holstein.

The experience of revolutionary social change as a French export, with the added episode of Napoleonic domination, fostered a degree of nationalism in the German world, in Prussia more than anywhere else. The rest of the loose association of German states might continue with very provincial ambitions, but Prussia – even before Napoleon – was set on a different course. The Prussian heartland south of the Baltic had been conquered by the Teutonic Knights in the thirteenth century and passed into the hands of the rulers of Brandenburg in 1618: with the fading Holy Roman Empire's consent, the title of King of Prussia was assumed by Frederick in 1713. His son Frederick II continued the policy of prudent finances and army conscription, with the acquisition of more territory at the expense of a partitioned Poland. Napoleon's victory over Prussia in 1807 prompted reforms in Prussia's army and government, and her subsequent part in the defeat of Napoleon brought her renewed territorial expansions.

From 1815, Prussia's westward acquisitions included part of Saxony, Westphalia and 'Rhenish Prussia' in the Rhineland. She now enjoyed both Baltic and North Sea access and set about consolidating her north German realm by bringing her eastern and western possessions together, filling in the gaps where other little German states persisted with a system of customs unions that made Prussia more economically powerful than Austria by 1850. The idea of a 'Great Germany' was mooted at this time, that would include Austria, but a rival tendency wanted to keep the old and still powerful force of Austria out of the union and instead forge a 'Little Germany' under Prussia. A period of Austrian-Prussian co-leadership of Germany ensued, with Prussia as the junior partner until Bismarck became the chief minister of Prussia in 1862. A North German confederacy was established that included the newly acquired territory of Schleswig-Holstein (from Denmark). This region across the base of Jutland had been taken under joint Prussian and Austrian rule in 1865, but lost by the Austrians when the Prussians defeated them in a war of 1866.

To the south-west of Schleswig-Holstein, the new city and port of Wilhelmshaven was named in 1869 (having been started in 1853) at an inlet of the North Sea coast of East Friesland: it was to be the Prussians' principal naval base, and that of united Germany thereafter until its destruction during and immediately after World War II. About 80 km to its north, at the mouth of the Elbe, is the North Sea end of the Kiel Canal which runs eastward for nearly 100 km to Kiel harbour on the Kiel Bight, thus connecting with the Baltic Sea. This canal was cut between 1887 and 1895 to do away with the need for German warships to sail north round the entire Jutland peninsula to reach the Baltic. Out in the German Bight, the tiny island of Heligoland – a pirate stronghold in the thirteenth century, then a Danish possession and later still a British one – was swapped by the British for the rather larger island of Zanzibar and so became German territory in 1890.

With the evident successes of Bismarck's policies and the ongoing expansion of her military and naval provisions, Prussia's ambitions as a great – and, indeed, imperial – power were becoming clear by 1870. Prussian rule already extended almost to France in the area of Lorraine and Alsace: when the Prussians defeated the French in 1870, this region was annexed and the southern German states were driven, really out of economic necessity, to join the new German Reich. And so, the victors' post-Napoleonic plan to counter any future French ambitions with a Prussian-led German presence on their borders had contributed in only a few decades to the rise of a unified and powerful German state. The British were inclined till the end of the nineteenth century and even a little beyond to view the French as still their greatest potential enemy in European and global affairs (and to take steps to keep up with the apparent threat from them in naval technology and coastal fortification), but in fact from the late nineteenth century until the middle of the twentieth century, it was to be Germany's imperial ambitions that posed the real threat. Any more fighting in the North Sea (which the British were still calling the German Ocean at the time) would be very largely a matter between Britain and Germany, with the North Sea featuring sometimes as the scene of naval conflict in itself, and sometimes as the vital highway – especially for Germany – to the rest of the world's oceans. Bismarck had not been wedded to the idea that Germany need be one of the world's top sea powers, but Kaiser Wilhelm II very much was, partly in envy of the maritime empire of his British grandmother, Victoria. At the same time as the construction of the Kiel Canal, a start was made on the building of warships for more than coastal defence.

Warship developments

Fighting ships had come a long way since the start of the nineteenth century, when the British and French were facing each other with huge wooden sailing ships firing not very accurate big-bore guns. These ships had taken traditional wooden construction as far as it could go, with linked forecastle and quarterdeck, roofed waist to make a continuous upper deck, and rounded stern and quarter galleries that were stronger, lighter and offered better gun positions. By the middle of the nineteenth century they might carry a hundred and thirty guns. Breech-loading replaced muzzle-loading and the rifling of gun barrels was developed for greater accuracy of targeting at longer range. The French had pioneered the use of explosive shells, proving their worth against Turkish warships in the Crimea, and requiring the general updating of coastal defences and their guns to meet this new threat. Meanwhile, a whole new method of propulsion had been applied to shipping in general and its advantages for warship use were soon appreciated. In the 1840s there had already been moves to convert some wooden warships to propulsion partly by steam and partly by wind. Despite the inveterate opposition of sailors to the idea of piercing hulls below the waterline, propeller-drive was preferred over the paddle-steamer design for the obvious reason of the paddles' extreme vulnerability to gunfire (though paddler warships were tried). The first purpose-built steam warship was the French *Napoleon* of 1852, beating the British *Agamemnon* by three months. By the late 1850s, armour-plating and gun turrets had been incorporated. By the 1870s, some warships carried no sailing rig at all. The first iron warship was the *Nemesis* of 1840 (built for the East India Company), but iron ships were deemed more vulnerable to gunfire than wooden ones. The British *Warrior*, begun in 1859, was iron-framed and armour-plated but the plates were backed with wood to take the force of gunfire: it was the first 'ironclad'. The French *La Gloire* of 1860 was wooden-built but iron-plated above the waterline. The first steel ship was built in 1865; by 1890 only one in five merchant vessels were of steel, but the warship application was becoming obvious.

Late nineteenth-century colonialism benefited from the use of cruisers that were good for far-ranging independent operations like policing and protecting trade routes and carrying out any necessary raids. At the end of the century the naval trend among the European Great Powers was to warships equipped entirely with big guns in the dreadnought style which soon made both the British and the German fleets' cruisers obsolescent, though the British boosted their cruiser component short of the dreadnought class with battle cruisers and light cruisers that were less well-armoured than the dreadnoughts but were fast ships to hunt down the armoured cruisers of the day. The Germans matched them with warships that were slightly heavier-armoured but lighter-gunned. Germany's intensive development of its naval power from the late nineteenth century, with North Sea bases just across the water from Britain, caused the British to extend their own naval provision away from their traditional Channel and south coast bases (to counter France and before her Spain) to the British east coast and the north.

The German Navy knew that the long supremacy of the British at sea meant that it was likely to continue at a disadvantage for some time. In particular the Germans feared a close British blockade of their North Sea bases and sought to avoid any major sea battle out in the North Sea in case they could not subsequently get back into their havens. The British for their part preferred a looser 'blockade' of the German bases, that would at the same time curtail the Germans' chances of getting far enough into the North Sea to reach any distant destinations and yet give them enough room to be tempted out and maybe engaged in a modest way on occasions. The British, as time went by and industrialised technology put new weapons in both sides' hands, feared submarines and torpedoes: rightly, though the Germans were in fact a bit slow to deploy them. Torpedoes and submarines were late nineteenth-century developments, the latter being perfected by the Americans under whose licence they were built by the British; the French persisted with them, too, and the Germans acquired them in 1906. For all that they had the superior navy, the British like the Germans had no great desire for decisive engagement: the Germans could not afford it and the British had no need of it. The upshot of this situation was that the naval action of the First World War in the North Sea was not as spectacular when it came as people had expected.

Battle in the North Sea

British ships (but not warships) had had a run-in with the Russians at the Dogger Bank in October 1904 when the Baltic Fleet of the latter was on its way – rather a long way – to fight the Japanese, with whom the British had been allied since 1902, in the course of the Russo-Japanese War. Incredibly, the Russians had fired on trawlers out of Hull under the misapprehension that they were Japanese torpedo boats. In early 1915, the Battle of the Dogger Bank between Germany and Britain was not a very major event either. For the Germans it was part of their strategy to take on elements of the British Fleet now and then, and for the British part of theirs to wait for the Germans to be lured out from time to time, wondering whether the Germans' North Sea Fleet would ever come out in force and offer the chance of another Trafalgar. The Germans' bases were at Wilhemshaven,

Bremerhaven, Bremen, and Hamburg; the British at Cromarty, Scapa Flow, Harwich, London, Chatham, and Dover.

The Germans did come out and fight in May 1916, at the Battle of Jutland, though rather inadvertently – they were not seeking a major battle but rather to entice a few elements of the British Fleet into a trap. What they got, without knowing it, was the entire British Fleet. When they realised the position, the Germans withdrew but the British blocked their way home: rather too cautiously so that the Germans slipped through their wake overnight, but not without a few serious engagements. When the British hoped to renew the fight in the morning, the Germans were gone. Although the British emerged from the fight with their general command of the seas intact, they took greater losses in both ships and men than the Germans did. Three British battle cruisers blew up because of poor isolation between gun turrets and magazines: most of the badly damaged German ships did not suffer this fate. The British lost fourteen ships in all and six thousand men, the Germans eleven ships and two and a half thousand men. Even so, the Germans never really challenged the British Navy again in the First World War and switched their concentration from major engagements with surface ships to the potential disruption of submarine attacks, fitfully backed up with rather unreliable Zeppelin patrols and raids on Britain from the air. The first Zeppelin attack came as early as 1915 and during the course of the war zeppelins dropped bombs on Tynemouth, Sunderland, Hull, Grimsby, Sheringham and Cromer, Yarmouth, Ipswich, Harwich and Dover. Hartlepool, Whitby, Scarborough, Yarmouth, and Lowestoft were shelled from the sea by German battle-cruisers. Although Blériot had made the first flight over the Channel in a heavier-than-air machine in 1909, military aircraft would not be crossing the North Sea to bomb towns, factories, dockyards and airfields until the Second World War. There was some U-boat activity off the east coast of Britain, too, but more of it in the Channel, the Irish Sea and out in the Atlantic. The British were obliged to recognise the submarine threat, and to acknowledge the inferiority of their naval gunnery despite their retention of overall naval superiority. The British Navy was, however, able to perform invaluable convoy escort duties and continue to operate a very successful commercial blockade of vessels bringing supplies to Germany via the North Sea, with a huge reduction of German imports that contributed materially to ultimate German defeat. The Germans' attempt to do the same for Britain by means of submarines in the Atlantic served to bring America into the war and hasten their defeat.

There was a plan to deal with the German Fleet, with air raids and then naval assault, to make sure that it could never emerge again for anything like a rerun of the Battle of Jutland, but the First World War ended before it could be acted upon. The German High Seas Fleet came out all right, to be interned at Scapa Flow in Orkney – and then scuttled by its crews in 1919 in an act of defiant dissatisfaction with the Versailles Peace. In the immediate aftermath of the war, there was for four weeks a Soviet Republic in Bremen in 1919 and an unsuccessful communist uprising in Hamburg in 1923.

The Second World War

Between the two World Wars of the twentieth century, treaties restricted the building of capital ships and the race was on to construct smaller cruisers with high offensive capability. Britain was at least as concerned with Mediterranean and Far Eastern naval affairs as with anything that might arise in the North Sea. The Germans' limited attention to naval matters was focussed on the Baltic and the Russians as a force to be reckoned with in their new communist garb. When the Second World War broke out, the German Navy was hardly ready to play any more aggressive a role in the North Sea than it had in the First. The plan had been to try and tie up an appreciable part of Britain's naval resources in the North Sea with a large force of (older) German warships, but in the event the Germany Navy was once more in no position to meet the British head on: it could chivvy the British and stretch their resources here and there but could not afford to come to major naval battle. In this fashion, the *Tirpitz* could threaten British Arctic convoys from its lair in the north Norwegian fjords, wasting British time and resources, but there was going to be little in the way of decisive engagement between fleets of surface ships. Instead the German Navy concentrated on submarine depredations, in particular, on vital British supply routes in the oceans beyond the North Sea.

The submarines' freedom to operate in the Atlantic, for example, was dependent on their capacity to come and go at will from their bases in the North Sea and down the Atlantic coast of France. British aircraft were effective against German submarines in the Bay of Biscay and the south-western approaches to Britain; and, as they had done in World War I, the British laid mines against the submarines in the areas of Scotland, the Faroes and Iceland. With the Germans in Norway, they could not repeat the line of mines across from Scotland to try and close the northern end of the North Sea to the submarines. The Germans, for their part, were forced to realise the importance of their North Sea Fleet in keeping access open for their submarines. Their North Sea territorial occupations brought them, in addition to their own stretch of coastline, France, Belgium, the Netherlands, Denmark and Norway.

It was the German occupation of Norway early in the war (April 1940) that brought about the nearest thing to a major North Sea naval confrontation that was witnessed in World War II. Along with the use of air power, the Germans made six simultaneous naval attacks on the Norwegian coast from Narvik north of the Arctic Circle down to Oslo. Possession of Norway was vital to the Germans to deny the British access to the Baltic, where Germany could be vulnerable, and to keep open the supply of iron from Sweden to the German war machine. The British countered the German attack on Norway in its central and northern regions, and sea battles ensued wherever the British could force them: with heavy losses on both sides. On the whole, the British – with clear naval supremacy – got the upper hand in these engagements, though the Germans with the *Scharnhorst* and *Gneisenau* sank the carrier *Glorious* at Narvik. What was very clear was that air power was now of the greatest importance in maritime conflict, as elsewhere in modern warfare: aircraft carriers, which had not been used in World War I though seaplanes had been serviced from boats, became the capital ships of World War II (and thereafter). From land bases hosts of bombers and fighters, and in the end flying bombs and even some missiles, would cross the North Sea before the war was over. Meanwhile, the southernmost stretch of the North Sea saw the successful evacuation of the British Expeditionary Force in France, and allied troops, in the early summer of 1940, by means of a host of civilian craft as well as naval vessels: from Dunkirk, that pirate base of earlier times. Britain's own coast came to bristle with anti-aircraft guns, observation posts, searchlights, minefields, barbed-wire and booms, in a way that will never be seen again in our present age of nuclear bombs and missiles.

The British could not get the Germans out of Norway and consequently could not cut the supply of ore from Sweden. Though they went on raiding the Germans in Norway with carriers and aircraft till the end of the war, they did not succeed in tying down an inordinately large number of German troops in this part of the world, as they had hoped. The Norwegian Sea and the Arctic waters saw increasing naval strife as the Germans tried, with aircraft and submarines and sometimes the *Tirpitz* and *Scharnhorst*, to attack the convoys to Russia that went over the top of Norway to the White Sea. At the same time, the war against the German submarines shifted into the Atlantic as their range increased to make attacks possible on Atlantic convoys.

Britain was still in a position, as it had been very successfully in World War I, to impose a commercial blockade on Germany; but it was not so effective this time, when a longer line of blockade was demanded by the German presence from Norway to the Atlantic coast of France, and when the Germans could draw for a long time on the resources they were plundering in eastern Europe. In the end, it was on land and from the air that Germany was defeated when the Soviet Union counter-attacked into the heart of Germany and the Western Allies, with the industrial might of the USA behind them, invaded German-occupied Europe across the English Channel.

Pursuits of peace

After the Second World War, it was to be the rise of Soviet naval power that was at issue, in a much wider context than the North Sea. The Russians had secured their access to the Baltic in the eighteenth century, and consolidated their position with territorial gains as a result of World War II. But the Baltic – necessitating passage out into the wider world via the Sound, the Kattegat and the Skagerrak – was not of so much use to Russia as the Barents Sea, with its port at Murmansk less than 200 km from the Norwegian border. Russia's only open access to the world's oceans is afforded by passage out of the Barents Sea and into the Norwegian Sea, north of the Arctic Circle. This route constituted for the old Soviet Union both its enemies' potential way in and its own way out. This part of the world was consequently, over many decades (and still to some extent, after the collapse of the Soviet Union), an area of open and covert operations for the navies of the postwar superpowers, especially for their submarines.

In the North Sea, the preoccupations of the superpowers and their allies were rather pushed into the background by what now looked like strictly local squabbles, often over fishing and to some extent, as time went by, over the oil and gas reserves that came to light in the North Sea basin. It has been a matter of policing rather than fighting, in what is now one of the world's busiest seas in one of the world's most highly populated and industrialised regions. Both population density and industrialisation go back a long way in the North Sea's surrounding lands, especially in the Low Countries and Britain. In these places there was an accelerating tendency from the sixteenth century onwards towards very efficient and commercialised farming, with fewer farms than went on being the case elsewhere in Europe (as it does to this day) and fewer persons engaged in farming. It was a process that 'freed' large numbers of people to flock into the growing towns of these places and get themselves jobs – a new concept in human economic relations – in the burgeoning industries of the times.

The Dutch pioneered the reclamation of land, with a willingness and capacity to invest in the business; in the course of reclamation, they discovered the idea of the rotation of crops by noting the beneficial effects of plants like peas, beans and clover that could restore nitrogen to the soil, though the chemistry and biology was not understood till much later. The English took up these agricultural innovations and extended them, with better ploughs and the use of the seed-drill. They developed schemes of irrigation and drainage on a massive scale in some places, like the fenland areas of eastern England and the borders of the Wash that face the Low Countries across the North Sea. By 1750, England was exporting 17 per cent of its food production and could afford to embark on the industrial revolution, which inventive and entrepreneurial elements in its society were clever and ambitious enough to devise. Among the most crucial of the technological innovations of that industrial revolution was steam power for pumps, mills, trains – and boats.

Chapter 9

Enterprises

B ritish experience with the use of steam in mills and mines and for purposes of traction was first applied to the business of water transport in
the form of canal and river boats: a successful paddle steamer (the paddle was
at the rear and wide) was operated on the Firth and Clyde Canal in 1802; by
1812 there was a regular passenger service between Glasgow and Greenock
on the Clyde. The idea was cautiously extended to first coastal operations at
sea and then to crossings of the Irish Sea and the Channel. The boats involved
were all paddle steamers working at low steam pressures. Crossing major
seas, among which the North Sea could be counted as far as the first
steamships were concerned, was another thing altogether, demanding bigger
and better constructed vessels with more powerful steam engines. Those
more powerful engines needed to show a better ratio of size to driving
capacity than the first steam engines developed for boats could muster. In a
paddle steamer, the big engines of the day moreover took up too much space
in just the place in the boat where space was at a premium, amidships. And
while the energy that powered a sailing ship came free (when it came) and
did not have to be carried on board throughout a voyage, the fuel that drove
the steamers had to be loaded in quantity at the start and maintained in suf-
ficiency till the end, taking up yet more space. Because steamships cost more
to construct and more to run, it was to well-heeled passengers and luxury
cargo that the first operators looked, along with the conveyance of mail
which was always an indication of the attractiveness of a route.

London, Calais, Ostend and Rotterdam were brought into steamship
connection in the early 1820s. Sweden and Germany were linked across

the Baltic in 1822. Hamburg, judged to be a profitable destination for ships from London (it was the world's third largest port after London and New York), was achieved by 1826, with weekly sailings by the General Steam Navigation Company. Hull to Hamburg followed in 1828, in the hands of local shipowners in Hull. Then came Hull to Rotterdam and even to St Petersburg via Copenhagen, and a short-lived Hull to Gothenburg service in 1834. Amsterdam and Antwerp edged into the steamship network, with no further British ports opening up to steam for a while.

The fact was that these paddle steamers were large boats for their time, made wider by their paddle boxes, and not always very well suited to the ports of the day. They were subject to the tides for their access into ports, their widths restricted by harbour entrances, and they often had to be loaded (passengers as well as freight) from small boats. On the other hand, by and large the steamers were more reliable as to times of departure and durations of journey than sailing ships could ever be. But they could be slowed up and run out of fuel by adverse weather and, of course, they could break down. And it has to be said that the stormy North Sea could not infrequently give the early low-powered steamers a hard time, when they would let out their anchor chains to drag on the seabed to stabilise them and the crew might pour out oil to lessen the force of a breaking sea: crossing the Sunderland bar just south of Newcastle-upon-Tyne was evidently a 'four-gallon job'.

By 1840, the Hull to Hamburg and London to Hamburg routes were served by twice-weekly sailings, and the Hull to Gothenburg service was essayed for a while. It was plain that here was a modest growth industry: German and Scandinavian services were developed at home, making it possible to go from England to Hamburg and then on by local mail steamer to Copenhagen via Kiel or Lübeck and so to Gothenburg in Sweden or Christiania in Norway (which would one day be called Oslo). Bremen in Germany and Harlingen in the Netherlands were added to the steamship ports of North Sea Europe: 1847 saw the founding of the Ocean Steamship Navigation Co. in Bremen with American capital, and also the formation of Hapag with the involvement of over forty companies in this Hamburg-American Packet Co. By the late 1850s, there were more sailings to St Petersburg and you could get to Hamburg from Leith and Newcastle as well as from London and Hull.

Boom years for steam

The late 1850s saw something of a boom in northern Europe, with advancing industrialisation and the rapid spread of railway networks. (And, interestingly, a new form of communication altogether, with a vast future ahead of it, was inaugurated in the North Sea world in 1858: the laying of a submarine cable for telegraphy, between Weybourne in North Norfolk and the East Frisian island of Borkum. Now there are nine cables to the Continent across the Southern Bight, three from Yorkshire and one from Scotland to Norway and another linking the Northern Isles to mainland Britain.) In the steamship trade, more companies were formed with more sailings and more competition. There were important technological developments. Iron hulls were adopted, stronger and more watertight: the first iron-built seagoing ship operated between London and Paris from 1822. Screw propellers, pioneered in the *Archimedes* from the Screw Propeller Co. in 1838 but initially distrusted because they involved piercing hulls below the waterline, were developed into a means of propulsion more efficient than the old paddles and better sited with their improved engines in a more convenient part of the ship, liberating space for cargoes and passengers. They were also less subject to states of the sea, even if paddles could deliver more speed – an advantage which prolonged their career for a long time in cargo and passenger ships where their vulnerability was of less importance than it was in warships. The trend of all these developments was towards ships for North Sea use that offered better cargo capacity and still some space for passengers. They were expensive, but could soon pay for themselves.

The mid nineteenth-century shipbuilding boom in Britain tended to the construction of wooden ships in the south and iron ships in the north: some vessels were a mix of iron frames and wooden planking. Specialised designs emerged, from bulky cargo vessels to sleek, fast ships. Sail was still favoured for non-urgent bulk cargo, and the last of the great cargo sailing ships were big steel barques with a huge amount of sail in very complex settings. But even with highly skilled crews, these big sailing ships could not compete with steam – they were too slow to make their crossings and too slow to turn round in port with solid ballast when steamships used water ballast. More ports joined the North Sea steamship network (at the same time, of course, as ports elsewhere came on): Hartlepool, Goole upriver from Hull, Grimsby, Lowestoft, Harwich, Bergen, Dordrecht, Kampen and

Amsterdam on the IJsselmeer. The booming railway companies invested in steamship routes (and built up ports), involving Grimsby to Antwerp, Rotterdam and Hamburg, and Harwich to Antwerp and Rotterdam. The railways of the countries on the eastern side of the North Sea were fuelled by coal from the western side in northern England, with timber going back the other way. Regularity and reliability, when all went well, were the attraction of trade conducted by steamship in this fashion, with no need to take too much account of the weather. Before the railways came, sailing coasters carried grain, cattle feed, fertiliser, cured herrings, passengers as and when required and, above all, coal up and down the east coast of England and even across the North Sea. (Coal could be a dangerous cargo, capable of spontaneous combustion and the production of explosive gases.) Among the effects of the railway linkage with the steamship ports was a reduction in the number of ports all round, with the loss or drastic downgrading of smaller ones, and also an isolation of the ports from their surrounding communities; seafaring became less a part of everyday life, even for people living quite close to ports, than it had always been.

The steamships continued to increase in size in the latter half of the nineteenth century, with more fuel-efficient engines and lighter steel construction. Superstructure grew amidships, with raised forecastle and poop extended to bridge, to form the basis of the 'raised quarterdecker' pattern. The British were to the fore in the building and running of these ships, until owners in Scandinavia, Germany and the Netherlands started to acquire British ships and then have their own built at home. Sailing ships continued to ply their trade alongside the steamers, but their numbers declined and the North Sea became the first of the world's major trading waters to go over mainly to steam, a circumstance to which it was well suited both for passenger trade and the conveyance of general cargoes over its relatively short crossing distances.

Consolidation

National interests, not least prestige, and the links with railway companies led to the formation of bigger shipping companies, as amalgamation and takeovers turned the older situation of small private companies into shipping giants. Well-to-do travellers, whether for business or pleasure, required high-class circumstances for their journeys around the North Sea: first-class railway connections to the ports, and crossings as short as possible in first-class accommodation. It meant that operators of the long hauls, say from Harwich to Hamburg, needed to make their services highly attractive to keep going. The Dutch from Flushing and the Danes from their specially built new port at Esbjerg were sending their luxurious paddle steamers, serviced by rail, to Harwich and the Great Eastern Railway Company decided to build themselves a new port there to cut out the walk from boat to train for newly arrived passengers. Thus was Parkeston Quay created in 1883, to which other companies soon transferred their Hamburg and Gothenburg runs, still in place today. The Hook of Holland's port and the Riverside Quay in Hull were realised in the same spirit.

North Sea crossings in the southern zone (apart from the Port of London) were based on frequent passenger-orientated sailings; to the north, things were cargo-angled with the conveyance of passengers as a bonus as and when required. Hull and Newcastle were connected to Bergen, and in the 1870s and 1880s Scandinavian emigrants on their way to the USA would come into Hull, Grimsby or Leith and travel on by train to Liverpool or Glasgow to set sail for America. Later, people from eastern Europe would travel via Germany to Britain on the same mission, although there were also by now direct sailings to America from North Sea and Baltic ports. (Bremen's 'Pier of Tears' saw the greatest volume of emigration.) In 1887 a purpose-built ship was dedicated to the tourist trade in the Norwegian fjords.

As to freight, there was a thriving trade in shipping cattle and sheep around the North Sea, especially from Denmark until an outbreak of disease in 1892. The Danes also joined the Dutch in the export of dairy produce, introducing refrigerator ships for the purpose from Esbjerg to Harwich and Grimsby, later from Copenhagen too. The Finns also participated in the dairy produce trade, to Hull. In the reverse direction, Hull, Grimsby, Yarmouth and Lowestoft exported loads of dried herring to Germany and various Baltic ports.

While the British and German Fleets of the early twentieth century were gearing-up for naval warfare, the commercial shipping of the North Sea was increasingly equipping their now mostly screw-propelled vessels with more and more in the way of superstructure to accommodate dining saloons, lounges, smoking rooms and lots of smaller private cabins in place of the previous four- or six-berth arrangements. By 1914, the services offered were highly reliable and safe, with more passengers and freight. The steamship had opened up the North Sea to travel, communication and the conveyance of goods in a way that no previous age could have ever conceived possible.

Steam was much slower to make its impact on the fishing industry that went on alongside the growth in cargo and passenger trade through the nineteenth and into the twentieth centuries. Since the fifteenth century, the herring fishery had been the most important aspect of the exploitation of the North Sea's resources, almost to the point of eclipsing all other catches. Each year the herring were followed from the Shetlands to the English Channel, especially by the Dutch for several hundreds of years until they lost ground in the eighteenth and early nineteenth centuries, after which the Norwegians, Scots and English rather took over. Herring continued to be taken by net and cod by long line until the English pioneered the widespread use of the trawl.

Fishing in force

It was fishermen from the Channel coast of England who really promoted North Sea exploitation in England. In 1833, they set themselves up in Yarmouth; from 1843 they were in Hull, after which the Scots came to the fore. A prodigious catch off the Humber soon saw a fishing vessel come back to port shining like silver with fish scales all over it, to earn the place of this bounty the name of Silver Pit, which it still bears. Railway access, and transport by rail to inland markets, made the Humber a good place to fish out of, and the whole region of the fishily prolific Dogger Bank passed into the hands of the Hull and Grimsby fishermen, who prospered. Whereas the Yarmouth and Lowestoft boats might still go out singly under local ownership, the fleet system was soon developed out of Hull and Grimsby, capitalised by more than just local interests.

In fleets, the fishing boats would now stay out at sea for weeks at a time, their catch being taken home by associated carriers to which steam power was sometimes applied. Not surprisingly, overfishing soon ensued. By the 1860s English trawlers (themselves still sailing boats) were intruding into German coastal waters, and shortly thereafter into Danish ones. Their trawls seriously interfered with the long lines traditional for fishing in these places.

The English fishermen earned themselves a bad name on the other side of the North Sea, especially when they occasionally landed and killed sheep and horses on shore, though some Danish fishermen joined the English boats. The Germans saw how well the English were doing out of fish that they themselves need not go more than a fraction of the way to acquire, with an eye on developing an inland market of their own for their own fish. It was not only the English who were stealing a march on them: Norwegian, French and even American boats were fishing for cod (to supply the market in Catholic southern Europe); Scots, Dutch, Norwegians and Swedes were taking herring. The Germans were not even getting their hands on their own coastal and Frisian island fish, let alone venturing further afield. But German ambitions in this area were slow to bear fruit, since they were not experienced in the fishing methods of their rivals and an internal market could not be generated overnight. Towards the end of the century, with the availability since the eighties of steam trawlers, they did make their mark.

The first British steam trawlers started operating out of Hull and Grimsby in 1882. By the early 1900s, these ports were employing more steam trawlers than the rest of the North Sea's fishing communities could muster together. From about 1900 steam drifters, using the drift net methods adopted from the Dutch, were able to pursue the herring shoals all the year round, unimpeded by wind and tide. The era of falling catches was thus initiated. The Danes by the same time were using steam engines to haul the seine nets they used to catch plaice off west Jutland and trying out trawling, which they were not to fully adopt until the 1930s. English, German and Swedish fishermen went after plaice in Danish waters until the Danes woke up to the value of their own fish resources.

The fishing methods employed in the nineteenth century have gone on being used into the early twenty-first, though with a welcome reduction in the hard manual labour of earlier times and with better means for finding fish and communicating at sea. Trawling continues and long line fishing has been revived; seining has been developed in Scotland and England. Fish stocks, as everyone knows, are now being fished down to dangerously low levels, though there is an ongoing dispute between marine biologists and fishermen as to the levels at which real danger arises, complicated by national claims about the extent of territorial waters and political directives from the European Union that arouse constant disagreement. The purely coastal concept of territorial proprietorship over the waters of the North Sea has gone for good, not just as a result of fishing rivalries but also because of the discovery of oil and gas reserves under the North Sea since World War II. The exploitation of these discoveries, incidentally, has frequently got in the way of fishing interests.

Post-war change

Only neutral Sweden emerged from World War II with its merchant fleet intact: all the other countries around the North Sea had lost many ships and neglected the maintenance and repair of such shipping as survived the war. Trade had been all but suppressed in most areas, except for aspects of Sweden's dealings. Post-war reconstruction, despite economic difficulties all round and protectionist imposition of quotas and licences, saw a great upsurge of North Sea traffic from the late forties. At first, in the dearth of available ships (though Sweden concentrated on shipbuilding), many wartime vessels were pressed into commercial use. Steam-engined escorts might be fitted with the diesel motors from wooden minesweepers and turned into serviceable cargo boats: equipped with refrigeration facilities, they could convey frozen fish to Britain. Former landing-craft were converted to coastal freight trade. But new ships were badly needed and that meant the renewal of the destroyed and neglected yards of most of the North Sea shipbuilding nations. The world trend was away from the smaller ships of the North Sea, in favour of larger tankers for example, and steel was in short supply: so there were economic considerations that sometimes went against the needs of North Sea shipping.

The standing of many of the North Sea's ports had been quite drastically altered by the experience of the war. Hamburg for a while was down, and Antwerp up. The input of American money in the shape of the Marshall Plan helped to rebuild a number of German ports from the late forties on. Bremen was quickly rebuilt as a supply port for the occupying Americans, already confronting the Soviet Union across the base of Jutland in East Germany. British and Scandinavian ports did not enjoy such advantages.

After the war, the coal trade of the inter-war years continued in small ships as before, though declining in the face of the rise of oil and in some places hydroelectric power sources, and timber from the Baltic continued to be conveyed west in small ships. In the mid 1950s, about half the vessels in the North Sea were still engaged in shipping Baltic timber and British coal, while the Germans and Poles were also carrying coals to Scandinavia.

Industrial reconstruction led to an increased trade in aluminium and iron, with larger vessels specialised in ore transport beyond the confines of the North Sea. Car exports became a significant aspect of trade, as well as agricultural vehicles and machinery. Interestingly, the conveyance of mail that had been a mainstay of nineteenth- and early twentieth-century shipping, indeed a test of its viability in many cases, increasingly went to the airlines as they expanded their operations greatly in the post-war years.

That old seafaring nation of the Netherlands, once so commercially and politically powerful in the maritime sphere and renowned for its shipbuilding expertise and the skills of its naval engineers and crews, came back to the fore in the design and construction of ships in the post-war years. Where pre-war ships had mostly been single-deckers with hatches to load and unload their cargoes (especially in the case of coal) by grabs, various new designs of coasters were developed by the Dutch for the timber trade in which they were particularly active, as they were increasingly in the porcelain-clay trade between south-west England and Scandinavian destinations. The fiercely competitive circumstances of these boom times, in which British and Scandinavian shipping suffered a relative decline, led to the design and construction of ever handier ships for North Sea trade: from steam to diesel, from single-deckers to shelter-deckers. The Dutch coasters, with small diesel engines, small crews, low tonnage and lots of space for cargo set the style for the so-called 'paragraph ships' of post-war years. After the war, there was a revolution in shipbuilding that saw the adoption of strictly utility designs, and manufacture by welding in place of time-consuming and labour-intensive riveting.

In the 1950s, West German shipping companies came to the fore, with their new coastal motor ships and cheaper crewing costs, again to the detriment of British and Scandinavian interests who operated with larger crews governed by the tonnage of their older vessels. The incentive arose to build ships of lower gross tonnage but greater loading capacity. It was Dutch, German and French yards who led the way at the beginning, selling their ships to the Scandinavian companies, who went on in time to build their own to the new specifications until the Norwegians came to dominate in this field. The Dutch started to lose ground, the Danes came up, but West Germany remained very competitive in North Sea shipping.

Shipping innovations

The political settlement that was achieved after World War II saw the North
Sea ringed, with the exception of traditionally neutral Sweden, by nations
in alliance with the USA. Economically, the creation of the EEC (European
Economic Community) in 1957 – of originally six members and nine by
1972 – carried great implications for North Sea trade, with the membership
of France and West Germany and then Britain, together with the
Netherlands, Denmark and Belgium. The free trade association called
EFTA, which included Norway and Sweden, was set up in 1959 and established industrial free trade arrangements with the EEC in 1973. These
economic unions fostered expanding markets, but the transport of goods
between them came to rely less on shipping than on rail and, increasingly,
road transport which often offered the attraction of door-to-door delivery.

The business of loading and unloading ships started to make sea transport, where avoidable, look expensive in time and money. Seafarers and the
people who built their ships for them were traditionally averse to putting
holes anywhere in a ship – we've seen that propellers were resisted for that
reason. The aversion extended to apertures on deck, which were however
inevitable in cargo ships, particularly as superstructure grew. They might be
points of structural weakness and they might potentially let water in, but
hatches were unavoidable. They were hard to render watertight without
hindering their use, and the instinct was always to keep them small.
Loading and unloading were consequently time-consuming and labour-
intensive operations: therefore expensive. The response of shipping interests
in Europe in the 1960s was to concentrate on centralised bulk cargo ports
– like Rotterdam, Bremerhaven, Antwerp, and Gothenburg – well served by
road, rail, rivers and canals, so that goods could be collected in them for
export and diffused out of them for delivery, in conveniently packaged
form. At these main ports new methods of loading and unloading were
developed, with the building of bigger ships that could make the most of
them. Pallets could be loaded and unloaded through side, bow or stern
doors by fork-lift trucks. In the late sixties the use of large standardised containers (the idea was developed in the USA) led to a great extent to the
replacement of the old multiple lift-on lift-off procedures with single roll-
on roll-off arrangements, inspired by wartime practice and doing away with
much of the old workforce of dockers in the process, with both social and

sometimes political consequences. Containers could be craned as well as rolled, of course, and some ships were designed to accommodate both methods: the key to the container revolution was the standardisation of container dimensions so they could be stacked in guides in the ships, with mandatory corner strengthening that permits stacking up to a dozen or more containers deep. Whatever the labour problems they entailed, dedicated container ports spread around the shores of the industrialised lands bordering the North Sea and their success meant the end of the old cargo liners and the decline of the non-specialised smaller ports. Since the 1970s there has also been a further growth in the coaster scene, with vessels intended for both sea-crossing and inland waterway use: shallow-draughted, fitted with masts and even wheelhouses that can be lowered as required (hydraulically in the case of the wheelhouses) and equipped with container capacity.

Bulk cargoes of iron ore, bauxite, coal, cereals and phosphate continued to be important features of North Sea trade by shipping in the late twentieth century, but the demand for petroleum products also required the use of ships for the transport of oil and gas and other oil-derived materials. Oil had long been imported into north-west Europe by ship from distant parts of the world: the discovery of oil and gas reserves in the North Sea gave some of the nations of this region a boost to their own supplies and a role in the world economy of oil and gas production. Britain and Norway in particular have benefited from the discovery of oil and gas in their territorial waters that can be piped directly to their shores from the rigs out at sea. But tankers, too, have their place in the transport of these resources. North Sea gas, which became a valued commodity after the fuel crisis of the early 1970s, is transported in a highly refrigerated state to reduce its volume on board tankers. The transport of chemicals of all sorts has resulted in some very specialised designs of shipping, able to carry different products in separate tanks. The operators of the Bremen cog at the end of the fourteenth century would have been amazed to go over them. Today's huge bulk carriers and tankers are constructed on the basis of extensive prefabrication of large sections of each ship and the automated manufacture of many components. Construction goes on in enormous docks with cranes to assemble and launch the great ships. Europe's part in shipbuilding today is rather confined to the sophisticated liquified gas carriers and large cruise ships – more everyday shipping has gone on to be built in Japanese and then

Korean yards, with China, Indonesia and Malaysia on the up. At the same time, there has been a decline in national merchant fleet operations since the 1960s as 'flags of convenience' have rather taken over. Britain has gone from having the world's largest merchant fleet under its own flag to ranking at thirteenth by the end of the last century. The Netherlands and other European countries have gone the same way and there is now a proposal for an EU flag that would at least supplement the national flags and FOCs.

Travel and trade today

In the midst of all the industrial carrying that still goes on by ship in the North Sea, the importance of the transport of people has assumed a new character in the age of mass tourism. While persons on business, or travellers to tourist destinations well inland, must almost always prefer to travel by air, a sea voyage very often recommends itself to those in search of a more relaxing holiday or who want to take their car with them. The Scandinavians pioneered the car-ferry notion in the Baltic (some of the latest vessels can carry thousands of cars on multiple decks) with bow and stern doors to operate the first-on first-off procedure. 'City breaks' from Harwich will take you to Danish and German North Sea ports like Esbjerg and Cuxhaven, from Newcastle to IJmuiden in Holland, or Kristiansand in Norway and Gothenburg in Sweden and so on to the Sound and Copenhagen. If you take your car, whole worlds in the hinterland of these ports are opened up for exploration to the detriment of the railway services once linked to them. In more relaxed style (and mercifully carless), you may cruise the Norwegian fjords or the Baltic, with the delights of Stockholm, Riga and St Petersburg in store as well as a host of on-board entertainments. The travel business has been significantly extended in this way.

The trend in both merchant shipping and in the passenger trade has been towards fewer and larger companies than before, as in so many aspects of global economic life. Europe's trade was concentrated before the discovery of the New World in the Mediterranean, the North Sea and the Baltic, together with the Atlantic coasts of Western Europe (whose ports came to the fore with the transatlantic trade). There has been a shift of the world's trading centre of gravity to the Pacific and Indian Oceans in modern times, with the European nations owning less of the world's shipping than they did. The supertanker phenomenon goes with this shift. The logical conclusion of technical developments in the navigation of such ships will be the sailing of the world's seas with huge, uncrewed vessels under satellite guidance backed up by computerised on-board automation. Already, the fitting of electronically controlled systems for rudders, propellers and side thrusters has vastly reduced the role of the traditional tugs that guided ships into port (though tugs fitted with all the latest aids have found new duties in the salvage area and in the business of supply and back-up to the oil industry).

From the beginning, the habit of going to sea in ships has brought on a host of associated practices and devices: probably the very first ventures in dugouts and skin boats relied on beacon fires now and then to get them home. Watchtowers and lights were employed in northern waters by the Romans – there were lighthouses at Dover, Boulogne and in the Yare Estuary, for example. The citizens of Charlemagne's empire on the North Sea looked out for the Viking threat in the ninth century. Some Norman castles were sited to oversee maritime matters – at Dover again, and Orford in Suffolk and Castle Rising in Norfolk. There were beacons at Ostend and in Walcheren (at the mouth of the Sheldt Estuary) and at Travemünde down-river from Lübeck in the later Middle Ages. By 1600, there were at least fifteen lighthouses on the Baltic coast as far as Riga. Lowestoft got its first light in 1609. Along with the lights went buoys and channel markers, pilot boats and, eventually, tugs. The more ships there were, the more ship-wrecks to be dealt with: by going to the aid of the threatened crews, by salvaging (and looting) the cargoes, by removing obstacles to shipping. Lifeboat work was local to begin with (and not always undertaken for the best of motives): it has retained something of its local and voluntary character in Germany, England, France, Norway and Sweden, but been put on a more state-run basis in Denmark, the Netherlands and Belgium. The French Société Humaine des Naufragés was formed in 1825; Britain got its Royal National Lifeboat Institution in 1849; the Deutsche Gesellschaft zur Rettung Schiffbrüchiger was set up in 1865. Excise men, meanwhile, turned into coastguards, with radio, radar and rescue helicopters among their resources.

While the purely tourist aspects of the North Sea's traffic would have astounded the sailors of all ages before the nineteenth century (and the vessels' means of propulsion and navigation even more so), the basic idea of crossing the sea in ships would have been instantly comprehensible to every seafarer since neolithic times. Exploiting the sea's resources in the form of fish would have similarly recommended itself. What the people who lived around the North Sea and sailed over it at any time until half-a-century ago would never have bargained for was the wealth that lay beneath it, in a form that nobody had any use for until little more than a century ago and itself the result of natural processes in the geological history of the world of inconceivable antiquity: in a word, oil.

Chapter 10

Industries

Petroleum is a product of life, or rather of the decomposition of living organisms – marine organisms, in fact. In remote geological times, there was a sea roughly where our North Sea rolls today with the requisite life forms in it to generate the oil and gas we find under the sea in our time. The remains of the tiny organisms that lived in that old sea sank to the bottom over the years, joined perhaps by the remains of land organisms carried down to the sea by ancient rivers, to mingle with the sands and silts that settled there. The same process goes on today, but it takes a very long time to create the conditions for oil and gas generation: from tens of millions to hundreds of millions of years. The Upper Carboniferous coal measures that are the main source of the North Sea's gas fields are some 300 million years old, with some others generated in Triassic times about 200 million years ago. Jurassic rocks of down to about 150 mya are the source of the northern part of the North Sea's oil and probably the central area's too.

The sediments forming on the seabed during these remote geological epochs grew thicker and thicker, and heavier and heavier, sinking deeper into the floor of the ocean with more deposits always building up on top; in this process, the pressure on the sediments below grew thousands of times greater and their temperature rose by hundreds of degrees, until these deposits of mud and sand themselves hardened into shale and sandstone. The shells of the erstwhile living things mixed in with the mud and sand hardened into limestone and the rest of the organic remains were turned into petroleum.

Petroleum has liquid, gaseous and solid components, varying from a thin consistency like gasoline to something too thick to pour easily. Some gaseous compounds are usually dissolved in the liquid; if large quantities are present, then the petroleum deposit will be associated with a deposit of natural gas. Once formed, the crude oil and natural gas rose up into the sediments above the layers in which they were formed, unless and until they became trapped under denser rock, to form a reservoir. The Permian sandstones of 250 mya performed this duty for the gas and, after about 100 mya, the Upper Cretaceous put thick limestone and chalk deposits over almost the entire area of the future North Sea (which deposits can be seen on land in Denmark, Germany, Holland, Belgium, France and eastern England). Some oil might always reach up without obstacle, so that there are surface or seabed flows today and bitumen lakes in some parts of the world, while natural gas sometimes escapes in a similar way.

Surface finds of crude oil have been exploited historically to caulk boats and waterproof clothes, or light torches, but it was a small-scale and localised business. It was not until the nineteenth century that any substantial use for the oil was developed, when a cheap source of lamp oil was to be appreciated by people who couldn't afford whale oil or town gas. By the middle of the century, a process for producing kerosene from crude oil gave those people the fuel they required and it became apparent that distillation of petroleum might lead to a range of useful products. In the 1860s oil was shipped from America to Britain in cans and fitted tanks: the first real tankers came in during the 1880s, and some of them were sailing ships. At first, the oil was refined at home in America before export, then later exported as crude for refinement at its destination. The crude carriers got bigger and bigger.

The idea of drilling for petroleum was prompted by the occasional contamination of wells that had been drilled for water with petroleum seepage. In Pennsylvania, an oil well was drilled in 1859 with the informed intention of finding the reservoir from which various seeps were thought to arise: the backers of this venture were rewarded with a source of readily flowing and easily distilled petroleum. Scientific assessment of oil formation and location was developed; the invention of the automobile and the growing demand for industrial and domestic energy spurred the science on. Surface seepage and the mapping of sedimentary rock outcrops offer clues to the subsurface presence of petroleum deposits, as does submarine seepage where it is detected. Drilling for rock samples and plotting of the seismic after-effects of artificial percussions (from an array of airguns) play their part, but in the end drilling a well is the only way to prove the presence or otherwise of the sought after petroleum. The pressure of the crude oil reservoir trapped below ground starts to bring the oil to the surface, and the gas in solution – liberated by the release of pressure at the well – furthers the propulsion of the oil up the well to the surface, until pumping takes over the process. Water injection and steam injection can enhance the recovery of the oil beyond what would be achieved by the gas expansion and pumping on their own, but at best only about a third of the oil in any given reservoir can be raised to the surface.

Oil beneath the sea

Some oilfields were soon recognised to extend out to sea beyond the dry land area where wells could readily be dug. After World War II, submarine recovery of oil supplies was tentatively initiated in the Gulf of Mexico, to help satisfy the USA's ever growing demand for both energy and, as time went by, also for such petrochemical products as detergents, fertilisers, synthetic materials like nylon and polyesters, and so forth. This bold enterprise in the Gulf of Mexico has led on to the prodigious engineering achievement of offshore drilling for oil in various places around the world, from platforms floating above or more usually planted in the seabed, in waters up to several hundred metres deep where the vagaries of winds and waves – and weather in general – must be continually met and matched.

At the end of the 1950s, Western Europe's largest known natural gas field was in the Dutch province of Groningen and it was obvious that it stretched out to sea. Where there was natural gas there was also going to be crude oil, and the world's growing demand for both resources soon drove on the exploration of the North Sea for these materials. Unlike some other oil and gas producing regions of the post-war world, Europe was politically stable and its markets for these energy supplies were guaranteed and close to hand, however expensive the means to recover the oil and gas were bound to be. The waters of the Norwegian Trench beckoned as a likely place to look, with American interest in this area in the early 1960s.

International agreements about territorial waters and the benefits of marine resources had not, of course, been constructed with the search for

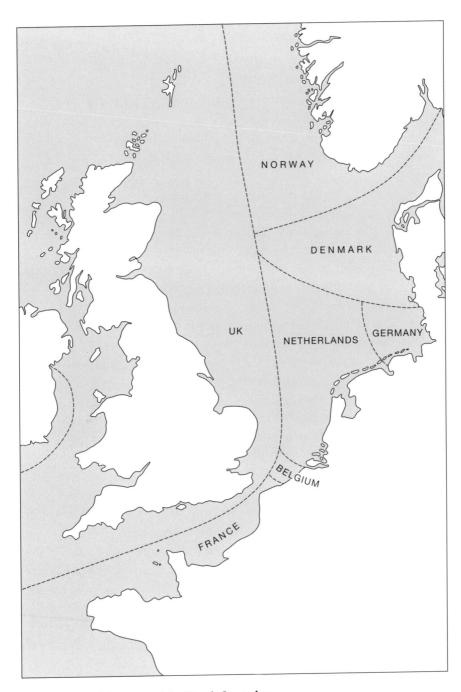

Map 6 Territorial waters of the North Sea today

oil and gas in mind. One provision only permitted the exploitation of the sea down to a depth of 200 m, and the Norwegian Trench was deeper than that: but Norway was able to argue successfully that the Trench was an accidental (glacially gouged) feature that should be open to that nation's attentions. The territorial waters had been shared out in a system of zones that, out of the 575,000 or so square kilometres of the North Sea (strictly defined), gave 244,000 to Britain, 131,000 to Norway, 62,000 to Holland, 56,000 to Denmark, 24,000 to Germany, 4000 to Belgium and 400 to France.

Norway's North Sea petroleum explorations began in 1965, with allocated blocks going to most of the world's large oil companies. Esso leased a drilling platform specially built in New Orleans for North Sea work, which was towed across the Atlantic in 1966. The North Sea is deeper and rougher, especially where the oil is to be found, than the Gulf of Mexico, so a ballasted semi-submersible rig is needed to do the drilling, after which the platform is brought out and settled over the capped pipe. The platform is then flooded to sink it and piled to secure it in place: it is hazardous, uncertain and expensive work. There was no early reward for the efforts undertaken by any of the companies: thirty-one dry holes were bored before any petroleum deposits were tapped. The first lucky strike came on Christmas Eve of 1969 with a Norwegian-built drilling platform; they had discovered what would come to be the complex of Ekofisk (about halfway across the North Sea on a line between the refineries at North Tees and Teesport in north-east England and the oil-revived Norwegian town of Stavanger). Ekofisk began production in 1971 and now sends gas and oil to Teeside and to Germany by pipeline: it has grown to be a whole town in its own right, just inside the Norwegian sector of the North Sea, and close to the British sector. Britain began to recover oil from the North Sea in 1975.

In 1974, the most extensive oil and gas discoveries were made in the North Sea at the Statfjord field, where production began in 1979. 1976 saw the decision to explore north of latitude 62°, outside the North Sea proper, and drilling began in 1980. 1977 marked the coming on-stream of the largest gas field at the Frigg location between the Shetlands and Norway; it was also the year of the first uncontrolled blow-out on a North Sea platform (Bravo) at Well 14 of the Ekofisk complex, when, for a week in April before it was stopped, 22,000 tonnes of petroleum were lost in a column of boiling oil and gas. There have been a number of losses over the years, to fires and capsizes, the worst ones being the overturning of an accommodation platform at Ekofisk in 1980 where 123 people were killed, and the fire on the Piper Alpha platform in 1988, with 185 dead.

Major discoveries continued throughout the 1980s and 1990s and output grew, reaching a peak in 2000 with oil production exceeding 6 million barrels per day, declining slightly to 5.9 million in 2001. From 2003 on, a long-run decline in North Sea production is predicted, as newer, smaller fields fail to quite make up for the expected reduction of output from the older, mature fields. High world prices favour the relatively high production costs of North Sea petroleum while low world prices or periods of extreme price volatility have negative implications for North Sea oil and gas production.

Oil and gas for now

Where oil is concerned, Britain and Norway are the largest producers by a long way. Norway has fewer fields than Britain but they are larger, while Britain's more numerous but smaller fields are often nearer to maturity, so that production faces a likely decline in the near future. Norway's small population (about 4.5 million) and relatively small demand for oil at home have allowed the country to stand as the world's third largest oil exporter for several years: it ranks fiftieth among the world's oil consumers but remains among the top ten producers, with recent discoveries adding to its reserves. It is not, of course, a member of the European Union being the only North Sea country to stand outside that growing association.

Britain is effectively the EU's only energy exporter, at the same time as being one of the world's greatest oil consumers. Nearly half of her remaining reserves are located in the central waters of the North Sea east of Scotland, with a further quarter to the north off Shetland. Annual depletion rates in the mature fields like Brent, Forties, Ninian and Beryl point to an early decline in overall output, but for all that new fields are still being started up and fresh discoveries being made. Among the smaller North Sea oil producers, Denmark is a net exporter but the Netherlands and Germany are both net importers.

Natural gas production from the North Sea continues to rise: demand for it grows in the countries around the North Sea and getting it to them by pipeline is cheaper than exporting it from elsewhere in the world. The

Netherlands with both offshore and onshore reserves is the EU's biggest net exporter of natural gas, though it is deliberately reducing reduction at its onshore field in Groningen so as to conserve supplies for future use. Britain, too, is now an exporter of gas: most of its production comes from North Sea sources, but it also has a certain amount of onshore production and several fields in the Irish Sea. Some of Britain's North Sea production comes from the southern area close to the Dutch allocation, but its three largest sources of natural gas are located off eastern Scotland and further north still. Norway is on the up as a gas supplier in Western Europe, second now only to Russia, with sources in both the North Sea and the Norwegian Sea to the north of it (also in the Barents Sea), some of them yet to come onstream.

It is by means of pipelines that most of the oil and gas found in the North Sea is transported to its various destinations in the bordering countries. Oil goes to Teeside in England via the Norpipe from Ekofisk and another major pipeline takes oil from the Forties field to Cruden Bay, north of Aberdeen. Production in the northern zone of the North Sea goes by one pipeline to Orkney and by two to the Shetlands. One of Norway's pipes runs from the Troll fields to Mongstad and the other from the Oseberg area to Kollesnes. Denmark has a pipeline from its Dan field to Kaergard and the Netherlands' two pipes run to the Hook and IJmuiden.

As for gas, Britain runs many pipes from its numerous sources in the southern part of its sector of the North Sea. These gas pipelines come ashore at places like Bacton, Theddlethorpe and Easington on the country's east coast, and at Teeside further north. Many lines from Britain's northern sector of the North Sea come onshore at St Fergus, north of Aberdeen. For its modest exports of natural gas Britain uses a pipeline to Belgium which can also be operated in reverse to draw supplies from Europe's main hub of natural gas trading at Zeebrugge. The Dutch sector feeds many pipelines to Den Helder in the Netherlands and also to connections in France and Belgium. Bunde-Oude on the Dutch-German border serves as another continental hub that links the Dutch system to German networks of gas distribution.

Norwegian gas travels into the EU via two pipelines into Germany, another to Zeebrugge and another to Dunkirk on France's short stretch of North Sea coastline. (France can pass gas on to Spain and Italy.) A new pipeline will make it possible for Britain to import Norwegian gas via the old Frigg field in the northern sector from newer Norwegian gas fields. Germany receives gas from Norwegian fields and Denmark has its own fields that connect to Kaergard in Jutland. The oil and gas of the North Sea will not last forever; indeed the recovery of these resources, with so much ingenuity and hazard involved, looks likely to prove a very short-lived episode in the history of human life around the North Sea and the exploitation of its various potentials – less than a century in all probability, though it may one day become possible to recover methane gas trapped in an ice-like form under the weight of the sea. Transport of goods across and around the North Sea and fishing in its waters will outlast the oil and gas era, when other sources of energy will have to be developed and demand perhaps curtailed.

The fate of the fishing industry

Cargo carrying – and travel for pleasure – seem to have a fairly straightforward future ahead of them, whatever the technological progress that may furnish marvels of propulsion and capacity. Of the prospects for fishing the same can hardly be said. The basic conditions for an abundance of marine life remain in place: the mingling of waters through the Channel in the south and down from the Atlantic and the Norwegian Sea in the north, together with the exchange with the Baltic and the input of many rivers, make for a rich supply of nutrients in the relatively shallow basin of the North Sea. The nutrients support an abundance of plant and animal planktons which in turn support a rich and varied supply of fish that can be commercially exploited. The main varieties fished include cod, haddock, herring and coley, with additionally some amounts of plaice, skate, sole and Norway pout, while mackerel and sprat can be taken for fishmeal. Norway and Denmark, Britain and the Netherlands have traditionally been the chief fishing nations.

After World War II, fish stocks in the North Sea were initially high, for the war was on the whole good for the fish and put an end for a time to pre-war fears of over-fishing. If such fears were raised before the war, they were soon to be heard again as postwar scientific and technological aids were brought to bear on the business of finding and taking fish. Fishing for herring, on an industrial scale (for reduction to meal and oil), was pursued by the Danes and Norwegians with the purse-seine net that can be closed by pulling on lines to form a great bowl of netting in the sea and so catch whole shoals of pelagic fish – from midwater and surface levels – like herring and also mackerel. The British fishermen adopted the purse-seine net in the 1960s. In 1977 a ban on North Sea herring fishing was imposed in an effort to try and save the industry. Meanwhile, fishing with seine nets on the Scottish and Scandinavian pattern, suitable for sandy seabeds, went on for haddock and other flatfish and the long-line method, with hundreds of baited hooks, was also employed. But mostly it has been the trawlers that have done the damage to North Sea fish stocks, oil-fired after World War II with stern trawlers since the 1950s. (Interestingly, the fishermen of the Thames Estuary petitioned the English king Edward III against the use of an early form of the trawl net as long ago as 1376, on the grounds that it caught immature as well as grown fish and disrupted breeding grounds – the trawl only became legal again in the seventeenth century.) It was the scientists, in fact, who first raised the spectre of diminishing fish stocks after World War II, only to be disdained by the fishing interests: like the coal miners, fishermen went into the post-war years in Britain as national heroes, both doing essential work in the toughest of circumstances. Unfortunately, benefiting from the scientists' know-how to catch more fish was not accompanied by harkening to their prognoses of declining resources. The British fishermen were content so long as foreigners could be kept out of their waters.

In the early years of the Common Market and then the EEC, fishing was a low priority. The British and Norwegians were not members and the original six countries, led by France and Germany, were taking fish from the two nations that really had fish to fish for in their own waters. The policy of the EEC was one of common fishing, so that when Britain joined up, EU members' fishing rights took them straight into erstwhile British waters. Fishing became a focus for internal EU disagreements, but the leadership of the government that took Britain into the Union was keen to compromise on new limits for inshore waters. Instead of immediately claiming twelve miles out to sea, the British negotiators settled for six (at least for a five-year period), hoping to make up for their EU partners' inroads into their fishing by being able to fish further into their fellow members' waters. The Norwegians would not make the compromise and kept out of the agreement, which meant the British could not operate in Norwegian waters. (Iceland, outside the EU, claimed 200 miles of territorial waters and countered British fishermen with gunboats.)

By the mid 1970s, British fishing boats were obliged to operate close to home and the shoals they fished were clearly dwindling through over-fishing. Lowestoft, for example, came down from eighty-five to fifty ships and distant water fishing ports like Hull declined. There was a tendency to blame the stern trawlers and factory ships from the Soviet bloc for Western Europe's fading fortunes in fishing and the EU took steps to keep them out with a 200-mile limit of its own, but in fact the East European ships were not doing as much over-fishing as the EU's own vessels. With all the latest scientific devices like sonar, and aided by Community grants, Western Europe's fishermen were trawling up everything in sight. Year by year catches fell, not so dramatically from year to year, but cumulatively the results were dire. Mackerel and herring catches fell badly in the 1960s and 70s: a shut-down of herring fishing from 1977 to 1981 led to something of a recovery, but the situation remained precarious.

Compromises

The Community's Common Fisheries' Policy of 1983 established yearly quotas, species by species, for fish caught outside the members' own terri-torial waters, with allocations of the total catch made by each member state. The system was open to abuse and so abused: fish that should have been officially thrown back were sometimes landed illegally (incurring no tax) while enforcement of the quotas was weakened by the exploitation of loop-holes and policing was really impossible with the very few inspectors avail-able, and the paltry fines at their disposal. A short-term bid for quick profits gripped the fishing boat owners and politicians preferred the easy way out of doing nothing about it, even though the very real prospect of there being no fish to catch had long since opened up. Meanwhile, the public (especially perhaps in Britain) stubbornly resisted the idea of eating anything but their old favourites like cod and haddock and turned up their noses at things like coley, which they would however on occasion permit to be fed to their cats.

At the start of the twenty-first century some fishing boats are idle, others are just landing sprats for a lot of their time, fishing becomes less profitable and fewer fishermen are employed; because of pollution and sea tempera-ture rise as well as over-fishing, skate, mackerel, plaice and cod remain vic-tims to decline, the latter pair in many fish populations by 90 per cent since 1970. Mature cod have become difficult to find and net sizes have made it possible to take fish too small and too young. Haddock and sole at last report (1997) appeared to be within safe limits. In the middle of 2002, the European Commission announced a long overdue break with the past by proposing changes that would give the responsibility for setting limits on catches to fisheries scientists and administrators rather than leaving it with the politicians. The scientists would like to see catches halved in some EU waters under the threat of a complete wipe-out of stock. Instead of spending money on a previously planned modernisation programme that would actually enhance the fishing industry's capacity to catch even more fish, the new proposals want to see the money spent on an aid package to wean fishermen off fishing. Spanish fishing interests oppose the plan but Britain's National Federation of Fishermen's Organisations in Grimsby recognises that fish stocks must be allowed to recover from the over-fishing of recent decades.

The quotas arranged as per the 1983 agreement have traditionally been subject to the final say of the various nations' agricultural and fisheries ministers, in all-night bouts of horse-trading in Brussels each December. The quotas arrived at in these sessions have almost always exceeded the recommendations of the biologists of the International Council for Exploration of the Sea (ICES, which first met in Denmark as long ago as 1902). The fact is that fish stocks are and always have been extremely difficult to assess and predict. It is a marine biologists' joke that fish are just like trees except that they move and they are invisible. All there is to go on amounts to the size of actual catches as a guide to total stock and the sizes of the fishes caught as a guide to age range and likely reproductive rate. It is generally agreed that the estimates arrived at by ICES tend to be overoptimistic in themselves, so the quotas that exceed them are doubly so. There has been a proposal that ministers be only allowed to set the quota limits for the first year of a ten-year plan for each fish stock, after which scientists and delegates from the national ministries will determine annual quotas on the basis of up-to-date scientific advice, in an unpoliticised spirit, or so the hope goes. One advertised benefit of the new arrangements would be to permit rapid adjustment of quotas if particular stocks collapse rapidly in any area. But EU ministers rejected this proposal at the end of 2002 and a related one intended to stop EU money being spent on improvements for fishing vessels. The British government wants the original proposals reinstated and contemplates the likely need for an outright ban on cod fishing if there is to be any hope of restoring stock, though haddock, sole and mackerel are acknowledged to be in relatively good shape.

A majority of Norwegians voted against Norway's membership of the EU in 1973, as much as anything, out of their passionate attachment to subsidised agriculture: since then, Norway (which is still a member of EFTA, along with Iceland, Liechtenstein and Switzerland) has negotiated comprehensive arrangements with the EU which take care of its participation in the single market, but exclude matters of agriculture and fishery. Norway is however a signatory to the 1995 UN Convention on Fishing on the High Seas, to which 112 countries and a consensus of the EU signed up.

Pollution

Over-fishing is almost certainly the North Sea fisheries' biggest problem, but global warming and pollution also modify the biological constitution of the sea. Marine life from warmer waters can spread into erstwhile colder areas as these warm up a little. Pollution, meanwhile, afflicts the North Sea both from the ships that sail over it and the lands that border it. Shipping volume has grown steadily with attendant navigational difficulties and accidents that spew sometimes toxic cargoes into the sea; without the accidents that make news, the routine operational discharges of more and more ships bring their own pollution, as does the incineration of wastes at sea and illegal cleaning out of tanks. (Ships' exhausts are reckoned to be a major source of atmospheric pollution, too.) From the land come the hazards of sewage, the dumping of industrial wastes into rivers and the drain-off of artificial fertilizers from farming, particularly around the southern part of the North Sea. (The Baltic has suffered worse pollution than the North Sea, with blooms of algae that threaten its marine ecology.) ICES has long records of both the fishing resources and pollution levels of the Baltic and the North Sea, and over the years numerous laboratories and research vessels have been commissioned in addition to the resources of ICES. In the winter of 1983, oiled seabirds were washed ashore in the German Bight and a plan was formulated for an International Conference on the Protection of the North Sea, which first met in Bremen in 1984, producing declarations on the need to monitor and regulate the impact of fishing and pollution (which latter includes the atmospheric pollution that can be generated in one place and damage vegetation in another). International agreements have been made to mitigate all these things, but enforcing them is often another matter and pollution remains a serious problem in parts of the North Sea. Meanwhile, the North Sea Commission, inaugurated in 1989, promotes the North Sea area as a major economic entity in Europe 'to facilitate partnerships between regions which manage the challenges and opportunities of the North Sea'. A Danish-led scheme to 'Save the North Sea' includes, as a British contribution, a 'Fishing for Litter' campaign, launched in Lerwick in the Shetlands in 2003. Ten fishing vessels, to begin with, are scheduled to bring back to port marine litter as well as fish; they hope to recover 50 tonnes in the first year.

It is not just the commercial exploitation of fish stocks that is at peril. Pollution and over-fishing are harming non-commercial aspects of marine life. The bottle-nosed dolphins of the Moray Firth in north-east Scotland, the last of their kind in the North Sea, are under threat both because of a decline as a result of pollution from sewage and because their food supply is being depleted by over-fishing. At a rate of loss to their population of about 6 per cent per year, the colony of just over a hundred animals could be lost in half a century. And what threatens them could threaten other sea animals too, including whales. In a mere ten thousand years or so, the North Sea area has gone from a postglacial paradise for hunters and fishermen and then a richly stocked body of water, to a fished-out and polluted sea in the midst of some of the world's richest and most industrialised nations. The change has overwhelmingly been brought about by the recent interventions of humanity, and it is a massive one. Nature, all the same, keeps her own ultimate powers undiminished and, in the memory of many of us alive today, has also made her interventions on the North Sea scene, with devastating effect on some of the human beings who have lived and died around the North Sea's coasts.

Chapter 11

Gains and losses

The Low Countries are known to have been subjected to episodes of flooding, called the Dunkirk Transgressions, from as early as the second century BC onwards. By way of getting their own back, the inhabitants of the Netherlands were embarked on the business of land reclamation by the middle of the eleventh century AD – and, no doubt, in a small way here and there, well before that. From about 1050 on, they proceeded to encroach on woodland and marshy areas to create more agricultural land to exploit: younger sons who would not inherit their fathers' farms and monks whose orders committed them to supporting themselves were at the forefront of the reclamation efforts. The monks were prominent in the process that led to land reclamation from the sea in the coastal regions of Flanders, Zeeland and Friesland. At first the intention was defensive, to build dykes against the sea, but when valuable land was seen to be liberated from the sea's encroachments, the deliberate business of reclamation was undertaken in earnest.

The Frisians were the eleventh-century pioneers of the reclamation work with the creation of the inland meadows they call Marschen today. They were soon to be followed by the Flemings, the Zeelanders and the Hollanders – efforts were made, too, in the plain of the Elbe. The system involved the building of banks and the digging of drainage ditches to lower the water-table and expose land that could be used at first for grazing cattle and subsequently perhaps for growing crops as well. Where reclaimed land was above sea level, drains could convey excess water via opened sluices into the sea at low tide (the sluices were shut at high tide).

Later on, when reclaimed land was below sea level, pumps, notably wind-driven, would be employed to take the water over a sea wall and so away. The drainage went on widely in the Low Countries, not just coastally but also in marshy inland regions. The feudal landowners encouraged the development, but were keen to take a cut from the profits of their tenants. Particularly in the coastal zones, the organisation of intensive labour and the high degree of planning and administration of the works and their maintenance called into being tiers of water authorities with great powers. The agricultural wealth generated by the new land prompted the growth of towns in which non-agricultural pursuits of industry and trade could be elaborated. The middle classes who emerged in the towns gradually freed themselves from the constraints of the waning feudal organisation of European society.

It is reckoned that between 1540 and 1715 the people of Friesland, Zeeland and Holland wrested some 145,000 hectares of land from the waters around them, mainly in the areas of the river estuaries, but also to a lesser extent around lakes. It was a business requiring intensive capital investment, which was the forte of this part of Europe in early modern times, and a sophisticated technology of pumps and windmills. The expertise generated in the Netherlands was to be brought to bear in other places, like France and Germany, but mostly notably in the fenland region of England south and west of the Wash. This area of England and the Netherlands as a whole, both located on the margins of the southern part of the North Sea and quite different in physical character from the more rugged northern coasts on both sides of the water, are the two places around the North Sea where large-scale human alteration of the landscape has been achieved. They are also two regions vulnerable to the retaliation of Nature in her more violent moods, bordering on the shallow southern part of the North Sea where adverse conditions of tide and tempest can pile up water in a very dangerous way, as we shall see.

Keeping out the sea

If not protected by dunes and dykes, the most heavily populated parts of the Netherlands would routinely be inundated by, mainly, the sea and also, to some extent, by rivers. More than half the country is accounted for by land at only 1 m above sea level; another quarter by land actually below sea level (by up to 6 or 7 m in places), These areas constitute the Low Netherlands that concern our North Sea story. (The southern and eastern region constitutes the High Netherlands.) In the low, flat landscape of the Low Netherlands, much land has been reclaimed from the waters and building can only be done on the basis of extensive piling with concrete, maybe 20 m deep into the sand.

The Zuider Zee of fading memory was originally an estuarine lake of the Rhine which became an inland sea ('Southern Sea') as a result of the action of tides and winds that turned it into an expansive and almost circular body of water behind the West Frisian island chain in the early Middle Ages. In 1920 work began on the Zuider Zee project that was, in effect, to put an end to this more or less inland sea's existence, in the aftermath of serious floods in 1916. The Afsluitdijk, over whose 30 km length you can now drive from Noord-Holland to Friesland or back, was begun in 1927 to seal off what would be left of the old Zuider Zee from the Waddenzee immediately behind the Frisian islands and the North Sea outside them. The shallow Waddenzee stretches to the base of Jutland and is called the Wattenmeer in its German stretch and the Vadehavet along the Danish coast. Its Dutch waters conceal a reservoir of natural gas that is increasingly becoming a bone of contention between nature conservationists and industry. When the Afsluitdijk was completed in 1932, the Zuider Zee was renamed the IJsselmeer (Lake IJssel) and the dyke itself is alternatively known as the IJsselmeer Dam. It is provided with sluices and locks to control the exchange of the Waddenzee and IJsselmeer, which is fed by the IJssel river and several other streams out of the inland Netherlands.

Four large polders were developed around the new freshwater lake of the IJsselmeer (polder is the Dutch word for a tract of lowland reclaimed from the waters). Naturally, soil in newly forming polders is so salty that most plants will not grow in it, and a sequence of operations is necessary to arrive first at grazeable and later arable land. The first two of the four polders of the IJsselmeer, drained before and during World War II, were dedicated to agriculture, but the two drained in the fifties and sixties were given over to residential, recreational and industrial use, with cities like Lelystad (capital of the new province of Flevoland) and Almere created upon them. The whole area has for its modern inhabitants, and for visitors especially perhaps, an extraordinarily clean and pristine character, like the new-made world that it is.

The gales and spring tide early in the year 1953, whose dire effects on the North Norfolk coast of England we shall look at presently, were even more devastating in the Netherlands. More than 160 hectares were flooded in the south-west and 1,800 people were killed. The tragedy speeded up the already existing Delta Plan with the aim of closing many of the sea inlets of the south-west delta of the Rhine and associated rivers, mostly in the province of Zeeland. Ten dams and two bridges were constructed between 1960 and 1987, the largest of the dams being built across the East Schelde Estuary for 8 km in length to act as a storm surge barrier: its sixty-one openings are normally open to let salt water into the estuary at about 75 per cent of its previous capacity but can be closed in time of flood. In order to keep shipping access open to Rotterdam there are no dams on the New Waterway which connects that giant port to the North Sea, nor is there one across the approach to the West Schelde which leads to Antwerp. Along these waterways the old dykes have been strengthened to keep the sea out of their surrounding lands at all times.

Draining the fens

In the fen country of eastern England, west and especially south of the Wash, a similar situation obtained to that exploited by the Dutch from the eleventh century onwards. The low-lying Wash fens formed in postglacial times as an area subject to salt-water flooding by the sea and freshwater flooding from the rivers running through them out to the North Sea. The sea brought silts to the fenland and the rivers built up peats on the margins of the sea's reach. In prehistoric times, as we saw, there were villages on the edge of the flood-prone fens and in the Roman period there was some settlement in areas of natural drainage round the Wash by people bent on extracting salt. The Romans cut many canals, with river linkage, in East Anglia and Lincolnshire, both for transport purposes and for drainage – you could go from Fenland to York by inland waterways, as grain supplies for the military evidently did. There was also a ferry across the Wash, with its southern terminal at Holme-next-the-Sea. The fens always offered, in general, rich possibilities for grazing animals, haymaking, fishing and wildfowling. It seems the Anglo-Saxons made some beginnings of modest drainage on the edge of the fens and the practice was carried on in medieval times, as it was north of the Wash, too, between Boston and Wainfleet. But nothing like the steady progress of the Low Countries in substantial land reclamation occurred until the seventeenth century and then it was done very much on the basis of Dutch example and expertise.

Cornelius Vermuyden is the best-known of the Dutch engineers who worked in the English fens, in the interests of English gentlemen willing to venture capital in schemes that re-routed rivers to stop them feeding so much water into fenland, dug networks of drainage channels and installed first handpumps and then wind pumps to take the excess water away. The fenland locals who had perfected a way of life to exploit the natural resources of their environment were not pleased with the results of the rich men's interference and riots and murders were not unknown as the business was prosecuted throughout the seventeenth century, with only a lull during the English Civil War: the Stuart kings and Oliver Cromwell (at least when he was in power) were all keen on fen drainage. Drainage continued into the eighteenth century with wind pumps, then in the nineteenth century with steam-powered pumps, and in the twentieth century with diesel and electric. It continues still as a necessity to keep the reclaimed land dry and safe to live in and to farm. After the major schemes of the seventeenth century, reclamation was reduced in scale but went on modifying the southern coastline of the Wash and here and there the northern coast of Norfolk through the eighteenth and nineteenth centuries, with fresh fields brought into use for farming purposes.

In the peaty heartlands of the fens, the English approach to drainage has brought severe problems. The dried-out peat oxidises to a point where it cannot be rehydrated and crumbles into dust that the wind blows away, sometimes to fill up the very dykes that do the draining, so that the dykes and ditches have to be dredged and indeed dug deeper to keep them effective in a generally lowering landscape. The trend was not helped in the period of World War II. The Dutch flooded areas of their lowlands to impede the German invaders, which at least had the merit of topping up their water levels, but the English 'dug for victory' and worked their fenland for all it was worth in the quest for food. The Dutch have traditionally maintained the water-table of their reclaimed land as high as possible while the English have too often treated their fenland as though it was for agricultural purposes the equivalent of chalk lowlands. Intensive agriculture and deep drainage threaten the whole terrain of English fenland around the Wash, and not least the rich archaeological heritage it contains – rich so long as it remains wet! The opinion has been mooted that some of fenland, at least, should be allowed to pass out of unnecessary agricultural usage and revert to semi-wetland, as nature you might say intended.

Phenomena of nature

The gains that human intervention has secured in some parts of the littoral zones, on both sides of the North Sea, have occurred alongside gains and losses delivered by natural processes. The rugged coastlines of more northerly regions like Scotland and Norway are not subject to the workings of the sea in the same way as the southerly and less rocky stretches of eastern England and the Low Countries. In the north the after-effects of the ice do have an impact, as land depressed under the weight of the last ice age's glaciers has slowly risen since the melting of the glaciation, and sea level has, with some fluctuations, risen too. But in the south, the chalk cliffs, shingle beaches and widespread lowlands have always been, and remain, very vulnerable to the force of the sea.

The relatively benign phenomenon known as longshore drift is constantly shifting shingle, clay and sandbanks along the East Anglian coast of England. These materials are the products of the periods of glaciation that have gripped the North Sea zone (along with the entire regions of the north and south poles of our planet) in the Pleistocene epoch. The deposits left by the trundling glaciers, scouring the landscape beneath them and pushing rubble ahead of them as they advanced (to leave it behind when they melted and withdrew), make up an unconsolidated mass of gravel, sand and clay that is easily moved around by tide and storm at sea. Some of the shingle, indeed, comes from the bed of the North Sea, where it was left by the glaciers before the sea level rose again after their retreat: the sea's tidal movements bring it to the shore. Longshore drift is the process whereby shingle and sand are pushed along a shoreline as incoming tides drive on to beaches at an oblique angle and outgoing tides withdraw straight out to sea. With each tide cycle, an amount of material is zigzagged along the beach, sometimes with gigantic effects in the long run.

Blakeney Point on the North Norfolk coast, for example, has been made from westward-travelling shingle driven along from Weybourne and Happisburgh. It has kept its general shape for several centuries now, but moved progressively westward – with interruptions, even perhaps reversal for a time – until it has quite altered the outflow of the river behind it to the sea, and played its part in the alteration of the fortunes of the medieval ports of Cley, Wiveton and Blakeney on the River Glaven. Just inland from Lowestoft, in Suffolk, the River Waveney has been partially dammed by shingle to produce Oulton Broad. The River Alde once entered the sea near Aldeburgh south of Lowestoft but was diverted southwards by an ever-extending stretch of shingle till it passed Orford 8 km further down the coast: so that it now flows parallel to the seashore for 16 km before it can reach the sea. Similarly, Spurn Head south of Hull is gradually extending south-eastwards into the North Sea. At the very southernmost corner of the North Sea, at the 'Isle' of Thanet in Kent, material dropped by the sea has clogged the channel between the former islet and mainland, converting the former into part of the latter.

A dramatic alteration to the previous coastline and hinterland in the region of Great Yarmouth in Norfolk occurred after Roman times. When the Romans and Romano-British people were trading with the European continent, their ships were able to sail into a broad estuary that opened between Caister to the north and Gorleston to the south of present-day Yarmouth, which simply wasn't there at all. The estuary stayed wide and easy to navigate round the headland where Reedham stands today, all the way up to the Roman town of Venta Icenorum which is now marked by a few short stretches of low wall in fields with a stream of no consequence trickling through them. Around AD 1000 a sand spit started to develop across the estuary mouth, frequented at first by fishermen who beached their boats on it and probably built a few huts to shelter in during fishing operations. The spit eventually closed with the mainland on the north side and the huts grew into the town of Yarmouth, joined by more building on the banks of the river that was now forced to flow south behind the spit until it could veer east and get out into the sea. The story was not over when this stage was reached for there have been a succession of harbour mouths artificially cut across from the river to the sea, at various points up and down the spit, to try and keep pace with nature's ongoing rearrangements of access to the open sea.

Coastal losses

A gain like the creation of Great Yarmouth is more than countered by the topographical losses of the East Anglian coast, which have involved the depletions of whole communities in places like Dunwich and Shipden. At Dunwich, thanks to the erosion of the sea at work on very sandy cliffs, the sites of three historical communities have been worn away and submerged: the Roman settlement, the Saxon town and the nationally significant medieval port. The medieval port was helped on its way by the growth of a sand and shingle spit across the previously wide estuary that temporarily benefited the town with a sheltered harbour and then, overnight in a storm in 1286, sealed its fate by starting to choke off its access to the sea. By 1328, after another disastrous storm with terminal blockage to the harbour, the port was to all intents and purposes defunct and little incentive remained to locally rehouse the inhabitants whose dwellings were steadily and some-times cataclysmically going over the crumbling cliffs: four hundred were lost in one night in 1347. The period from about 1200 to 1300 saw par-ticularly violent seas around North Sea coasts, with no great let-up until the seventeenth century: things have not always been so good, since, for that matter. Cuts were made in an attempt to keep Dunwich's maritime trade, but the decline was irreversible, dwindling in the seventeenth and eigh-teenth centuries to a certain part in the Iceland herring fishery and a little export trade in corn and dairy produce. The loss of the coastline was also irreversible and there is very little left of any of the previously existing town of Dunwich today – every visit confronts one with further losses.

Similar but smaller-scaled losses have occurred round the coast of East Anglia north to the Wash. Smaller-scaled because the settlements involved were not on a par with Dunwich in its medieval heyday. The candle-powered lighthouses of Winterton Ness have gone, Little Waxham's church and houses are submerged and Great Waxham's fine barn which was built some 22 km from the sea now stands close to the coastal sand dunes. Flint-constructed blocks that were once the church of Eccles, a parish of some eighty householders, can sometimes still be seen in the sea when the tides and the state of the beach reveal them. Whimpwell church or the town's old harbour walls have been identified 3 km to sea off Happisburgh. The town of Shipden once thrived 3 km north-east of Cromer, with two churches and the homes of many merchants, weekly markets and an annual fair. In 1888 a pleasure boat ran aground on the submerged tower of Shipden's seaward church, to become for a while a tourist attraction in its own right, until it could be removed and the tower blown up as a hazard to shipping. These various places disappeared at different times over a long span – Shipden's troubles began in the fourteenth century, whereas Little Waxham only went under in the eighteenth century. There is constantly a complex interplay of global, regional and local factors, involving world sea level fluctuations, changes in land levels around the recently glaciated North Sea basin and details of currents, tides and the physical composition of the shoreline in particular places. And there is the weather.

The weather can do sudden, drastic and sometimes irreparable damage, as it did in Dunwich more than once. The North Sea lies in the northern hemisphere's zone of prevailingly westerly winds that are part of the global weather system, driven by the sun and the rotation of the earth. The heat of the sun at the equator causes air to rise and head off towards the poles, sinking as it cools to be drawn back to the equator by the low pressure there under the ascending air. That, at least, is what would happen without the rotation of the earth with its uneven surface distribution of seas, lowlands and highlands to drag the air along, in eddies and vortices and currents that distort the circulation from equator to poles and back. Prevailing winds, changes in wind direction and gales with storms of rain and snow (when the winds get to work on precipitation in different air temperatures) are the products of the global weather system that we experience on a daily and seasonal basis. There are longer-term processes, too.

Storm and flood

The storm path of the northern hemisphere's prevailing westerlies runs west to east along the northern edge of the North Sea region today, but there have been times since the last ice age when it has crossed our sea further to the south, and times when the usual westerly winds have given way to more north-westerly ones. Such north-westerlies, running over a greater stretch of open ocean to reach the North Sea, bring rougher seas and bigger swells. When they prevail, the level of water in the shallower, narrower southern reaches of the North Sea can be pushed up 3 or 4 m higher than usual. Moreover, the depressions which bring these winds permit the sea to rise up even higher under the low pressure over them, perhaps by as much as half a metre more. And this piling up of water can be increased or reduced by the state of the tide, with potentially catastrophic results at spring tides when the moon's pull on the earth's waters is augmented by the sun's in alignment. The tides of the North Sea are, in any case, highly irregular as a result of two tidal systems entering into the North Sea basin, from the north and from the south. There have been occasions when just such a conspiracy of circumstances has led to the direst disaster for people living on the southern margins of the North Sea, when the sea has flooded over low-lying land and broken down all defences against it – most recently in 1953. In fact, there have been whole centuries in the past when the incidence of flooding has been much more marked than in others.

A patchy record, getting more detailed and reliable through the years, can be put together to indicate the century-by-century frequency of severe sea-flooding disasters, with notable loss of life, since Roman times in the southern part of the North Sea. There seems to have been markedly less in the way of North Sea flooding right up until about AD 1000, with only one or two severe floods per century. After that came a steep rise, with more like seven such floods in the eleventh century, dropping back to three in the twelfth. The thirteenth century saw a dramatic increase to double the eleventh century's bad record: it was towards the end of this century that a severe storm heralded the doom of Dunwich, but most of the worst flooding incidents of this century, and into the next, were experienced along the German and Danish coasts. A storm turned the hitherto inland town of Husum on the German North Sea coast into a coastal location in 1362, with a natural harbour conveniently adjacent. At about the same time the previously Marschen farmsteads of Halligen were left perched as islands in the Wattenmeer. These great storms raged against a background of high sea level as a result of several preceding centuries of rather warm weather that had made inroads into the northern glaciers. The melt water had added perhaps 0.5 m to the level of the sea. This was the era of medieval vineyards in England and on the continent well to the north, suggesting an absence of late spring frosts: the latter-day Vikings could sail from Norway to Iceland and Greenland without ever encountering much in the way of sea ice.

After the thirteenth century, the general incidence of severe floods around the North Sea gradually fell back to around three per one hundred years until the seventeenth century, but during that century there was a lot of flooding along the coasts of England and the Netherlands – at a time when the onset of the 'Little Ice Age' had lowered sea level again. This cold episode probably resulted from a spell of low sunspot activity. For these inundations to have occurred without the raised sea level of earlier times it can only be concluded that the world's weather system was delivering exceptionally severe storms in the North Sea region at this time. Certainly, the Spanish Armada appears to have encountered stronger winds in 1588 than we would expect to see today, perhaps as a result of the steeper temperature gradient between the cold Norwegian Sea and the warmer North Sea. From the sixteenth century to the eighteenth there was more ice in the North Atlantic than before or since, with expansion of glaciers in Iceland and Norway and permanent snow on some Scottish peaks and permanent ice in some of the lochs. During these years polar waters spread down into the Norwegian Sea, which has usually benefited from the warmer surface flow of the North Atlantic Drift extending the reach of the Gulf Stream in the north since the last ice age ended: on occasions, here and there, the North Sea itself might freeze up.

In recent memory

With the end of the seventeenth century, frequency of flooding around the North Sea declined for a while, but started to rise again from the mid twentieth century on, to something like the level obtaining between the fourteenth and seventeenth centuries; and the second half of the last century was scarcely under way before the appalling floods of early 1953 occurred, killing more than 300 people in Britain and 1,800 in the Netherlands, which also suffered the inundation of hundreds of square kilometres of fertile land. It is worth noting that the floods of medieval times were evidently much more destructive of human life at a time when the European population was generally much smaller than it is today. The last year of the eleventh century saw big losses of life on the coasts of England and the Netherlands and in a storm in Holland in 1421 thousands of people are claimed to have been lost overnight. It was the old story all over again in 1953 of freak winds piling up water in the southern half of the North Sea in concert with a spring tide. Hundreds of people, thousands of animals died; thousands of people lost their homes while gasworks, power stations and industrial premises were wrecked. Canvey Island in Essex went wholly under water and had to be completely evacuated. The monetary cost of the disaster in England in 1953 has been put at £50 million.

Fifty years ago, there were few telephones, few television sets and much less sophisticated provision for warning people of imminent danger by radio or other means of telecommunication. People got ready for bed in eastern England on the night of 31 January 1953 with no inkling of the colossal threat already manifest out in the North Sea. To the extent that weather monitoring and forecasting, broadcasting of information and deployment of emergency services are now all so much more developed than they were, to that extent the coastal inhabitants of eastern England and the Netherlands are much safer today than fifty years ago. Whether the weather prospects they face are any kinder now is very uncertain: probably the reverse is the case, since global warming is raising sea level while the land continues to settle down after its rise in the wake of the last ice age. In another hundred years many a part of England's east coast, as well as its fen-land and the Low Countries themselves, will be well below sea level. Meanwhile some computer models of the potential impact of further climate change predict that storm surges will become more frequent.

Though much can be done to improve coastal defences against the sea and to maintain the ones in place, there is a growing body of opinion that would set a limit to how far we go in trying to defend each and every inch of the eastern English coast. In some places, to do so must be a losing battle in any case; in others it may often produce unlooked-for side effects when somewhere down the coast suffers as the result of measures taken some-where further up, with unwanted loss or gain of sand and shingle. There is often, moreover, an ecological argument for reinstating old salt marshes that have been precariously reclaimed from the sea. One thing is certain: the eastern coast of England – away at least from rugged northern parts – has never remotely been a fixed and permanent thing, and will always be sub-ject to quite drastic change.

One prospect is very drastic, indeed, and not perhaps as remote as might be hoped. Global warming promises a rising sea level that will mostly take place at a pretty steady rate, easily accommodated in any given decade. But eight to eleven thousand years ago something happened off the west coast of Norway that has made some people think about the possibility of its hap-pening again and what its effects would be. Previously frozen gas below the bed of the Norwegian Sea thawed with the postglacial warming of the northern world and escaped violently enough to trigger the 'Storegga slides' which brought about large-scale disruptions of the seabed. These in turn sent out tsunami waves that, if duplicated today, would very likely inundate the whole British coastline from the Shetlands down to Norfolk, together with most of the Netherlands. Higher temperatures in northern waters, if global warming continues, could bring about the release of further gases from beneath the seabed and do dramatic damage to North Sea coastlines rather sooner than any slow rise in global sea levels will do. Short of such a catastrophe, we may expect the global warming that seems under way in our own times to bring rising sea levels to the North Sea over the next centuries: of course, any ultimate return to ice age conditions may very well abolish the North Sea all over again.

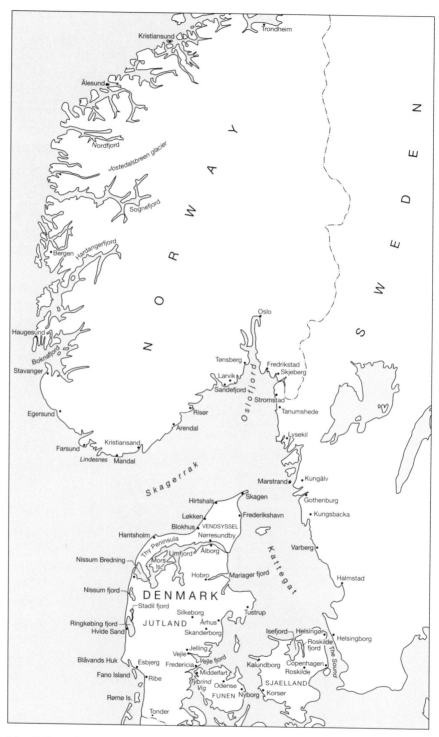

Map 7 From Norway to Denmark

Chapter 12

A North Sea journey: from Norway to Denmark

Modern means of travel, by ship and by road, have made it possible to envisage a leisure tour round the entire coastline of the North Sea that could scarcely have been contemplated a century ago. Indeed, a project boosted by European funds was launched in 2001 to establish a North Sea Cycle Route that will allow ambitious cyclists to do the whole journey on their bikes – though not necessarily all in one go! Of course, ferries are required to make the crossing from southern England to the continent and also to return from Norway to Shetland across the open sea in the north.

On a map the North Sea looks like a vertical rectangle that has been allowed to drop its left-hand side and turn into a rhomboid: its top edge is delineated by the relatively shallow water across from the Shetlands to the point where Norway's coast turns north-east on the Norwegian Sea. Only along this northern boundary is the North Sea wide open to other seas and oceans.

It is at that corner of Norway that an armchair tour of the North Sea as it is today may very well begin, in a landscape far removed from the low-lands we shall come to further south before going north again, up the east coast of Britain, to end in Shetland at the top left of the rhomboid, oppo-site our starting point. On the whole we will stick to the coastal zone, except where places too important to omit are to be found not so far inland, and we shall favour the locations that have significance for our North Sea history, particularly where they involve long-distance human interactions around and across the North Sea.

Norway saw human occupation after the last ice age at a surprisingly early date for somewhere so northerly – what is more, some of the earliest evidence of human activity comes from places well north of our North Sea starting point, in the form of those rock drawings from the Komsa region inside the Arctic Circle that we mentioned at the start of this book. Norway is, in fact, the only country directly on the North Sea today that still retains, in the north and in the mountains, something of the character of the ice age world, with glaciers and snow-capped mountains, reindeer and polar bears. The great city of Trondheim is really a little north of the North Sea, and some way inland at the end of an inlet of the Norwegian Sea. But it merits its position at the start of our tour on the grounds of its historic import-ance: it was once the capital of Norway with the name of Nidaros, founded by Olav Tryggvasson in 997. The Nidarosdomen (cathedral) houses the bones of his successor, Olav Haraldson, whose cult became a first focus of Christianity in Norway (it was abolished with the Reformation in 1537). One of the first monasteries in Norway was set up in the early eleventh cen-tury on the island of Munkholmen out in the fjord. Although only of eighteenth-century date, the wharves and narrow streets lined with wooden buildings in the old part of the town convey a vivid impression of Trondheim's important past history: the real medieval city was destroyed in 1681 by fire, always a hazard in the wood-built towns of cold northern Europe. The harbour structure built on iron stilts is a rather late feature of the city's history – it was constructed by the Germans during World War II for U-boat operations.

To the south-west of Trondheim, as the coast bulges out towards that corner where the Norwegian Sea gives way to the North Sea, we may note in passing such exotica as the hunting lodge at Alfheim built in 1876 in Scottish Highland style by Lady Arbuthnot, who farmed and generally lairded it nearby (about 600 km further north than the Scottish Highlands); and the gardens run by Trondheim University which are filled with, among other things, thousands of colourful rhododendrons. We are in a land of fjords backed by high mountains, the 'Home of the Trolls'. Kristiansund on the coast was once known as Fosna and as such has given its name to that other early occupation of the north in southern Norway and western Sweden we call the Fosna Culture: the Kristiansund Museum exhibits finds associated with these summertime reindeer hunters who shifted to the coast in winter to tap the marine resources there, well before farming arrived in this part of the world. Kristiansund has long been a focus of Norwegian dried cod exports: the stockfish of the medieval trade.

Just north of Kristiansund, there is a tiny island called Kuli where stands a stone from the early years of Christianity in these parts with the first mention of the name of Norway, which means quite literally 'The Northern Way': the sea way to the north, so called at a time before the emergence of the separate Scandinavian nationalities. The island of Grip, not far from Kristiansund, has a long history of storm and flood which saw the destruction of a hundred houses in 1796 and the same number washed away again in 1803, reminding us that not all the seaside disasters of the North Sea zone have been confined to low-lying southern regions. Ålesund to the south is still Norway's largest fishing town, though not going so strong today as it was in the 1950s. The nearby chain of islands is now linked with undersea tunnels and the many shipwrecks of the area include a Dutch ship found to have been carrying gold. The modern equivalents of gold, in the shape of oil and gas and related industries, are to the fore now.

In North Sea waters

With the Nordfjord, at the eastern end opposite the Shetland Islands at the top of the North Sea rhomboid, we start to arrive in true North Sea waters. This fjord leads inland to the Briksdalsbreen glacier with its ice cascade over the floating ice floes of a glacial lake of green water. The glacier connects southwards with the great Jostedalsbreen glacier, and the islands off the coast between the Nordfjord and the Sognefjord feature rock carvings of the late palaeolithic hunters who had chased the reindeer north as the glaciers retreated to these northern mountain strongholds at the end of the last ice age. All down the coast here there are islands after islands, and lakes after lakes inland. It's an area of those distinctive early wooden stave churches of Scandinavia, that may well echo the boat-building techniques of the time and undoubtedly follow something of the pagan temple pattern that preceded them: Lustev, inland on a branch fjord of the great Sognefjord, has Norway's oldest stave church, from the earliest years of Christianity in this region.

The Sognefjord is 200 km long and 1300 m deep, leading into the mountainous interior, where so much power is generated hydroelectrically at the many great falls that descend from the mountains. South of the fjord is sited the key oil terminal and refinery at Mongstad, with the island of Fedje offshore: this island was always important as a navigation point and now marks the place where tankers pick up their pilotage into Mongstad. The area is a major scene of fish farming, for salmon and trout and also for experiments in the farming of cod and halibut as North Sea stocks fade with overfishing.

With Bergen, we have really arrived at the North Sea proper, and at one of the most historically important towns of the medieval trading world. Like Rome, Bergen is a city built on seven hills – it is spread around a harbour that connects with bridges to various islands and headlands in the vicinity. It was founded in 1070 and served as Norway's capital in the thirteenth century, but lost that status to Oslo in the late Middle Ages (though it remained Norway's largest city until 1830). This city of churches, chapels, monasteries and hospitals for the poor owed its pre-eminence to its association with the Hanseatic League, from which it had to break away in the end. It still has its fine Hanse houses and warehouses along its quay, but they postdate the great fire of 1702 and so, also, the formal wind-up of the grand League. There is a Hanseatic Museum to show what life in these fine wooden buildings was like in the early eighteenth century, which must have been grim in winter since heating was never installed in them for fear of further conflagration. The Hanse focus was the quay called the Tyskebryggen ('German Bridge' or 'Pier') until after World War II, when it became just the Bryggen. Naturally, the town's oldest surviving buildings are made of stone, like the Hakonshallen (the largest secular medieval construction in Norway) of 1247–61. It was on an English ship, incidentally, that the Plague came to Norway at Bergen in 1349.

The next major fjord south of Bergen is Hardangerfjord, its mouth full of islands – and oil platforms. There are Bronze Age rock carvings at Herand on the south side of the fjord, while the inland ends of the fjord and its branches feature wonderful waterfalls including the 300 m high Skykkjedalsfossen. On the promontory that forms the southern edge of the mouth of Hardangerfjord stands the fishing, shipping and farming town of Haugesund – off that lies an island famous for its part in the roll-call of shipping forecasts, the most westerly place in Norway – Utsira. On the large island of Karmøy close to Haugesund, there are Bronze Age barrows and standing stones of Iron Age date: beside one of them a Roman bowl of about AD 350 was dug up, a long way from home and traded (or more likely looted) from the fading Roman Empire of the time.

Across the wide mouth of the Boknafjord to the south, with more islands and many lighthouses on the way, is Stavanger – Norway's oil capital today, its profusion of oil rigs and associated installations satisfactorily dwarfed in its fjord setting among the mountains. Nearly a tenth part of Stavanger's inhabitants are of foreign extraction, thanks not just to oil but to the town's long history of seafaring, fishing and trading. In the nineteenth and early twentieth centuries it was a port of emigration to the United States of America, sending more Norwegians than there were foreigners coming in. The town prospered on fishing and trade, and in the 1870s the curing and canning of the small herrings known as Norwegian sardines saw the sale of this product all over the world. Demand declined after World War II and so did Stavanger's fortunes, until the arrival of the oil industry in the 1960s. Across the harbour from the town's Maritime Museum stands the tower built in the ninth century as a lookout for outbreaks of fire, always threatening disaster for these originally wooden townships. South of the city lies the site of an Iron Age farmstead of AD 350–550, at Ullandhaug, where three houses, a cattle track and encircling stone wall have been reconstructed. Also to the south of Stavanger is the battlefield of Hafrsfjord where Harald Fairhair won a decisive fight in his struggle to unite Norway as far back as AD 872.

Into the Skagerrak

Between Stavanger and Egersund, the flat and fertile country constitutes Norway's main area for dairy produce, meat, poultry and eggs – Egersund itself is the country's largest fishing harbour. On the Lista peninsula south of Egersund, with the coast now curving round at the entry to the Skagerrak, the vicinity of Vanse features some 350 burial mounds of the Iron Age with archaeological remains of houses of that period, too. Further along comes Farsund, in the early nineteenth century a base for pirates and privateers. Soon afterwards we reach the southernmost part of the Norwegian mainland with its lighthouse at Lindesnes: the Norse Sagas mention this promontory as a sheltering place for Viking ships waiting to turn the corner in or out of the Skagerrak. Some of the North Sea's deepest waters roll to the south in the Norwegian Trench that follows the entire

North Sea coast of Norway round into the Skagerrak. Mandal to the east was once home to Dutch and Scottish merchants; it's on about the same latitude as Inverness. With Kristiansand, founded by King Christian IV of Denmark–Norway in 1639, we are certainly on the Skagerrak, at an ideal point to control the coming and going of both North Sea and Baltic traffic. Arendal further along was the port from which much of the timber to rebuild London after the fire of 1666 was exported: Arendal's own town hall is one of the largest wooden buildings in Norway. Risør was visited in 1795 by Mary Wollstonecraft, mother of the authoress of *Frankenstein*, who commented on the men's habit of smoking incessantly in homes where the windows were never opened: a detail that testifies to the influence of the Dutch at a time when Holland was Norway's chief trading partner. Nearby Ullefoss was traditionally the scene of ice production from which ice was sent into the interior via a system of canalised inland waterways including the 110 km long Telemark Canal. It was within inland Telemark that the age-old practice of walking on snow on wooden boards (something like it is depicted in the prehistoric rock drawings) was elaborated into the sport of skiing. The Telemark interior was also the scene of the Anglo-Norwegian sabotage of the Germans' nuclear aspirations at Rjukan in 1943.

Past the coastal Iron Age cemetery at Mølen, with its boat-shaped cairns among so many other graves, we have almost arrived at Oslofjord. On the western side of the wide opening of the fjord stand Larvik and the old whaling town of Sandefjord, close to which is the 1889 find site of the Gokstad Viking ship now in the Vikingskiphuset (Viking Ship House) in Oslo. Tønsberg's main street is flanked by Viking graves and 2 km away lie the remains of the ninth-century town of Kaupang ('The Market'), the Nordic world's oldest town of 872. The archaeological excavations of this town are preserved under glass on the ground floor of the local library. Just north into the great fjord is the site of the finding of the Oseberg ship, which is also housed in the Viking Ship House in Oslo together with the spectacular grave goods found in it, but the mound of the original burial place remains at Oseberg. There are a great many Viking grave mounds and also burial sites of the preceding Iron Age era in the Borre National Park.

Oslo and on to Sweden

At the head of the fjord, surrounded by wooded hills, stands Norway's capital, Oslo. Old Oslo, having become Norway's first city in the later Middle Ages, burned down in 1624: the rebuilt city was named Christiania after the energetic King Christian IV who founded so many new towns. Christiania it remained until the twentieth century, when the old name was revived to encompass a much larger municipality that took in surrounding districts. From the historical and archaeological point of view the museums on the Bygdøy Peninsula, across from the harbour under the Akershus Slott (castle), are of tremendous interest. There is a general Museum of Seafaring (the Sjøfartsmuseum) and the Viking Ship House with its wonderful halls showing off, at right angles to each other, the Oseberg and Gokstad ships and their associated finds. Also on display in their own houses are Nansen's polar exploration vessel, the *Fram* (designed by a Scotsman living in Larvik), and the *Kon-Tiki* boat of Thor Heyerdahl, who also came from Larvik. There is also the Norsk Folkemuseum with its reconstructions of Norwegian village life that include an entire stave church.

Human occupation around Oslo goes back a long way – near the city is Nøstret which has given its name to an archaeological culture of mesolithic hunting and fishing folk who made a distinctive sort of stone axe. Today both sides of the 100 km long Oslofjord carry a heavy concentration of industry, with roads and waterways busy with commercial traffic. Down the eastern side of the fjord, we come to Son which started life as Zoon, a Dutch free port. Between Fredrikstad, a fortress town from 1567, and Skjeberg to the east along the Oldtidsveien (Highway of Old Times) there are some of the most accessible and vivid of the prehistoric rock carvings, showing skin boats among other scenes. About 15 km after Skjeberg, the coastal road crosses the border into Sweden.

Unlike Oslo, Sweden's capital of Stockholm on the Baltic is a long way from the North Sea. It demands a little of our time, nonetheless, for the bearing some of its features and treasures have on the North Sea network of international relations throughout history. The world's most spectacular shipwreck, the ill-fated *Vasa*, is precariously preserved there in all its seventeenth-century splendour: under threat of biologically caused decay. The open-air museum at Skansen, with its streets, houses, churches, farms and windmills offers a vivid picture of life in Sweden in past times. Vendel and Valsgärde, of the pre-Viking ship burials that relate to East Anglia's Sutton Hoo, are not far away to the north. Nor is Old Uppsala, where pagan kings were buried under three super-barrows that once led to a temple in a grove sacred to Odin, but now to a church built on the site of an earlier wooden one that replaced the pagan temple in the twelfth century. Outside the church is a stone with runic inscription set up to his father's memory by a 'man who travelled to England'.

Sweden's North Sea coast is not as long as Norway's, nor that of Denmark and the Netherlands, but it is longer than Germany's and much longer than Belgium's or France's. Coming south from the Norwegian border, we encounter first the faded grandeur of the eighteenth-century spa town of Strömstad; soon after that, an altogether older cultural landscape appears with the rock drawings of the Tanumshede. These pictures, some of them easily accessible from the road, constitute the greatest concentration of Bronze Age drawings in Scandinavia, with four major sites whose designs run from cup marks hollowed in the rock to large and elaborate depictions of boats, people, animals. There are 204 sq m of them at Vitlycke, with a museum and reconstruction of a Bronze Age village. Some idea of Scandinavia's natural history and that of the North Sea itself is provided by the Norden's Ark wildlife sanctuary, with – among much else – lynxes and arctic foxes living in a dense forest habitat, while Lysekil has a Marine Life Museum with an underwater tunnel from which to observe the fish.

With the island town of Marstrand, we are leaving the Skagerrak and, strictly speaking, the North Sea too. The Kattegat is neither North Sea nor Baltic, but its historical importance and the importance of many places around it make its coastal exploration essential for our North Sea story. (The waters south of the main Danish islands, including the Bight of Kiel are westward extensions of the Baltic and we will not venture into them here.) Marstrand was founded by the Norwegians in the thirteenth century and enjoyed great prosperity as a herring fishing town in the fourteenth. After that, in one of their periodic shifts, the herring deserted these waters until the late eighteenth century, only to disappear again in the 1820s – since when they have not returned to date. Marstrand recreated itself as a fashionable bathing place. Kungälv has its fortress of Bohus, originally built by the Norwegians as a wooden fort on what was then the southern border of Norway. The stone castle which replaced the wooden one repelled six

Plate 26 The large Martello tower by the sea at Aldeburgh in Suffolk.

Plate 27 The Irrawaddy, a late nineteenth-century steam trawler out of Hull.

Source: Hull Maritime Museum.

Plate 28 Cranes and containers at the modern port of Felixstowe.

Plate 29 A North Sea oil installation nearing completion at Lowestoft.

Plate 30 Flooding at Yarmouth station after the terrible North Sea storm of 1953.

Plate 31 A wooden 'stave church' in Norway.

Source: Photo by David Collison.

Plate 32 The replica Viking ship house at Moesgaard in Jutland.

Plate 33 Viking houses reconstructed at Hedeby near Schleswig.

Source: Photo by David Collison.

Plate 34 The preserved treadmill crane of Stade, west of Hamburg.

Plate 35 Windmill and barge in the centre of Leiden in Holland.

Source: Courtesy of the Netherlands Tourist Board.

Plate 36 Dover Castle and its Norman keep.

Plate 37 Henry VIII's castle at Deal.

Plate 38 The towers of Reculver's ruined church on the Kent coast.

Plate 39 Kit's Coty House megalithic tomb by the Medway.

Source: Midnight Blue, © 2003 JTH Consulting.

Plate 40 Upnor Castle, which failed to stop the Dutch in the Medway in 1667.

Source: Midnight Blue, © 2003 JTH Consulting.

Plate 41 Part of the medieval town wall of Yarmouth.

Plate 42 Low tide reveals a submerged forest at Sea Palling on the Norfolk coast.

Plate 43 Erosion eats away the cliffs at Happisburgh.

Plate 44 Crab boats are still launched into the North Sea at places like Cromer.

Plate 45 Bones of an extinct elephant were dug up at West Runton on the North Norfolk coast.

Source: © Norfolk Museums & Archaeology Service. Photo by David Wicks.

Plate 46 The undercroft of a medieval merchant's house at Blakeney in Norfolk.

Plate 47 The Bronze Age timbers of Seahenge at Holme-next-the-Sea by the Wash.

Source: Photo by John Sayer.

Plate 48 Former properties of the Hanseatic League at King's Lynn.

Plate 49 The memorial to his Romano-British wife set up at South Shields by a man from Syria.

Source: Courtesy of Tyne & Wear District Museums.

Plate 50 Bamburgh Castle on Northumbria's North Sea coast.

Source: Photo by David Collison.

Plate 51 Dunnottar Castle on its dramatic North Sea promontory.

Source: Photo by Jim Henderson AMPA ARPS.

Plate 52 One of the neolithic houses excavated at Skara Brae on Orkney.

Plate 53 Ruins of many periods cluster at Jarlshof at the southern tip of Shetland.

Plate 54 Treasure hidden from the Vikings on St Ninian's Isle off Shetland Mainland.

Source: Photo by David Collison.

Plate 55 Shetlanders celebrate their North Sea heritage with the winter fire festival of Up-Helly-Aa.

Swedish attacks in the 1560s; and then went on after passing into Swedish hands to withstand no fewer than fourteen Danish sieges in the seventeenth century.

Sweden on the Kattegat

Gothenburg on the Kattegat is Sweden's second city, its modern siting owed to the Swedish king Gustavus Adolphus in the seventeenth century. The Swedes were keen to establish a trading port of their own that would be free of Danish influence, so long exercised in south-west Sweden in the form of extortionate tolls on all sea traffic into Sweden. In the eighteenth and nineteenth centuries many British and Dutch traders settled in Gothenburg which consequently displays a rather Dutch appearance in its gridded avenues and squares, its canals and its tramways. Its city museum displays the timbers of a Viking merchant ship from the River Göta. The town once enjoyed a great trade with the East Indies, but its shipyards are pretty quiet now. It marks the North Sea end of the Göta Canal to Stockholm, linking the Baltic and the North Seas without the need for passage through the Kattegat and the Sound, built partly for commercial and partly for strategic reasons in the post-Napoleonic era. South of Gothenburg there stretch flatlands with fishing ports along the coast in an area constantly swapped between Denmark and Sweden from the fourteenth to the seventeenth centuries. Indeed the region of Skäne (Scania) across the Sound from the large Danish island of Sjaelland (Zealand) still wears a rather Danish look in places, for it was only ceded to Sweden in the seventeenth century. It sounds rather Danish too, with its Scanian accent that other Swedes can find hard to follow. It's good farming land, rather flattish in a way reminiscent of East Anglia in England: we have well and truly left behind the mountainous country of parts of the Norwegian coast and will not see anything like it again until we travel north up the British coast to Scotland. South of the Kullen Peninsula, the Sound communicates through to the Baltic and the North Sea is definitely left behind.

Immediately south of Gothenburg, before we leave Sweden and cross over to Denmark, is Kungsbacka which once traded with the Hanseatic League but was burned down in 1846. Ten kilometres inland runs a glacially-formed ridge with Bronze Age barrows and Iron Age standing stones on it. South again, and just to further demonstrate the continuity of

North Sea interchanges, is the grand manor house of Tjolöholm built at the end of the nineteenth century for a Scottish merchant and horse breeder named James Dickson. Varberg is a nineteenth-century bathing resort with a moated thirteenth-century castle; its museum houses a rather unusual bog-body find in the shape of the Bocksten man, not of Iron Age vintage like so many of these rather gruesome bodies preserved in acid bogs, but from the fifteenth century. This garrotted, drowned and impaled man of the Middle Ages was kitted-out in cloak, hood, shoes and stockings that now constitute the best preserved set of medieval clothes in Europe. Whatever the motives for his despatch, the Bocksten man, with those ritualistic hints of death and disposal, looks very like a proper Iron Age effort.

Halmstad was once a heavily defended Danish stronghold, but most of its walls were thrown down when the final defeat of the Danes saw it pass to the Swedes in 1645. On the attractive peninsula of Bjäre there is a cemetery of British sailors who were killed here in 1809, having been sent to bombard Copenhagen during the Napoleonic Wars. Swedish Helsingborg faces Danish Helsingør across 4 km of the Sound: this was a much contested spot in medieval and early modern times, with Helsingborg only passing finally to the Swedes in 1710.

Across the Sound to Denmark

Helsingør in Denmark features the magnificent Kronborg Slot, built to enforce Danish dues on shipping through the Sound: we may imagine Shakespeare's Hamlet musing on its battlements, for Helsingør is the original of Elsinore. It stands on the largest of the Danish islands, of which there are in fact a great many including Bornholm to the east in the Baltic. Passage between islands and mainland was formerly a matter of ferries (some of them carrying railway carriages) but the main islands and Jutland are now linked by bridges and tunnels. Nowhere is very far from the sea in Denmark, which possesses entirely coastal borders apart from the 65 km frontier with Germany across the southern part of Jutland. A drive from Helsingør to Copenhagen will take us along the 'Danish Riviera', past Lyngby with its museum of restored seventeenth- to nineteenth-century buildings from all over Denmark: it is also the type site for a mesolithic group who developed a particular sort of stone axe before the first farmers came to Denmark. Copenhagen itself lost many of its own old buildings in great fires that raged in 1728 and 1795. Nelson's bombardment of the town in 1807 destroyed, among much else, the old cathedral – it was history's first modern assault on a civilian population, predating the bombardment of Charleston in Virginia by half-a-century. The result of all this is that Copenhagen is now a city whose core is baroque and neoclassical in style, but the town started life simply as the Havn, fortified in 1167 against the threat of Wendish (Slav) pirates from the Baltic.

The town came on as København (the Merchants' Harbour) during the long reign (1588–1648) of King Christian II. The Swedes came close to taking it in 1658 but could not prevail against the determined resistance of its townsfolk. (But the Danes had to cede Scania, with adjoining regions, to the Swedes in the peace deal of 1660.) Though not exactly of archaeo-logical or profound historical interest, the Tivoli Gardens of Copenhagen – a very superior sort of funfair – are not to be missed; nor is the National Museum, with its wonderful archaeological collections housing many of the finds mentioned in this book, including the Hjortspring boat. Due west of Copenhagen lies Roskilde, burial place of the kings of Denmark. Roskilde fjord opens into Isefjord, a large gap in the north Sjaelland coast, and so into the Kattegat and the North Sea. The Viking Ship Museum at Roskilde houses all those wrecks of various sorts of Viking vessel that were sunk to block the fjord in the eleventh century. West of Roskilde, the lavishly recon-structed Iron Age village of Lejre presents houses, barns, streets, lakes, dugout canoes and even a sacrificial horse offering on a long pole out over a boggy mere.

Keeping on west across Sjaelland brings us either to Kalundborg where the ferries leave for Jutland or, past Trelleborg's vividly reconstructed Viking barracks, to Korsør for the crossing to the island of Funen (Fyn) which lies between Sjaelland to the east and Jutland or Jylland to the west. It also stands between the Kattegat in the north and the Bight of Kiel in the south. Funen's farms and manors, even its chief town of Odense, make for a small-scale and picturesque atmosphere. Nyborg is the point of arrival from Korsør, with a slot dating back to 1170 that was again built against the Wends. North of Nyborg is the little village of Ladby where, close to a local farm, the mound that covers the Ladby Viking ship can be found: the mound has been opened up inside so that visitors can see the 22 m Ladby ship in situ, preserved in a humid haze. Weapons, hunting dogs and eleven horses were found in association with the ship.

The Hindsholm peninsula forms one side of the entrance to the Odense fjord, with barrows dotted in its rather dramatic landscape: Odense itself, at the bottom of the fjord, is first mentioned in a document signed and sealed by the German emperor Otto in 988 granting tax privileges to the Church, but as the town's name means 'Odin's Sanctuary' we may assume it to go back further than that. The king the English call Canute died here in 1015, on the site of the Skt Knuds Kirke. The city is now Denmark's third largest. West of Odense, the way leads to the road and rail crossing to Jutland at Middelfart. But travel a little further south of there and you come to the important mesolithic site of Tybrind Vig: a fishing village of 4000 BC which, although predating the arrival of farming in the area, was a settled place with a stone roadway to the sea where mooring posts were installed, to go with the dugout boats and paddles found nearby; its cemetery is one of the few of mesolithic times in Europe.

East Jutland

Crossing to Jutland and setting off up the east coast, we soon arrive at the interesting town of Fredericia, founded by Frederik III in 1650 as a place offering religious asylum to foreigners like Jews and Huguenots, with consequent economic advantages. To the north is Vejle fjord and the town of Vejle at its head. Close by is the very attractive little town of Jelling where the arrival of Christianity in Denmark is vividly recalled at the white church between two pagan mounds. The large stone outside the church carries Denmark's first piece of Christian iconography, while two runestones memorialise King Gorm and his queen. They were set up by their son, the first Christian king Harald Bluetooth, who built the earliest church on the site at Jelling in 960. The mounds covered the pagan burials of the old king and queen, before their (possible) reburial under the church.

North of Vejle fjord is Skanderborg at the eastern end of Jutland's Lake District, with its twelfth-century royal palace about 15 km from the waters of the Kattegat. At the western end of the Lake District, rather inland from the sea is the small and relatively recent town of Silkeborg which is remarkable for one particular exhibit in its museum: the most famous of the Iron Age bog-bodies, that of the Tollund man. His serenely smiling face consorts rather oddly with the circumstances of his death by being hanged and thrown in a bog in around 200 BC. He was one of those victims, either of a sacrificial religious cult or a criminal trial, that vividly bring back the customs of the Germanic tribes outside the Roman Empire.

Denmark's second city is Århus, on the east coast of Jutland, started as a Viking settlement around AD 948. Viking times are recalled 3 m under the pavement outside the Andelsbank in town, where a section of rampart is preserved and a small Viking house has been reconstructed. To the north-west of the city centre stands the astoundingly well-realised reconstruction of an earlier sort of Danish town called Den Gamle By ('The Old Town') with seventy renovated old buildings from mainly Jutland but also Funen and Sjaelland. Den Gamle By truly amounts to a place in its own right, in which the visitor can become lost in a veritable time warp. Near to Århus is the Museum of Prehistory at Moesgaard, which has among so much archaeology of all periods another famous bog-body, the Grauballe man. There is also an outdoors reconstruction of a Viking settlement with, on the sea, a very evocative reconstruction of a ship house complete with Viking ship. To the north-east of Århus, the Djursland peninsula ('Land of Beasts') presents a very prehistoric picture in places: its heathland and woods shelter the rich megalithic site of Tustrup in a landscape of tombs and other mortuary constructions of large boulders and standing stones. To the north-west of Århus, the museum at Hobro (at the head of Mariagerfjord) houses finds from the nearby Viking site of Fyrkat where in the time of Harald Bluetooth earthen fortifications enclosed four sets of four longhouses, one of which has been reconstructed. Also near to Hobro, to the west, can be found the very well-preserved neolithic passage graves at Snaebum, five thousand years old.

Ålborg is situated on the south shore of the Limfjord that cuts across the entire Jutland peninsula at this point from east to south-west and renders the area to its north, called Vendsyssel, in effect an island. Ålborg is Denmark's fourth largest town – a Viking settlement once and then a great merchant town of the Middle Ages. Its fifteenth-century cathedral is dedicated to that patron saint of seafarers, St Botolph, like Boston's great church across the North Sea in Lincolnshire. The museum holds many finds from Scandinavia's largest cemetery of the Germanic Iron Age (600 graves) at Lindholm Høje, across the Limfjord to the north-west of Nørresundby, where there are also many Viking graves with ship-like settings of stones. To the west along the Limfjord is the largest of those great circular Viking fortresses, at Aggersborg.

Back to the North Sea

On the island of Vendsyssel, heading north for Jutland's tip at Skagen, we can visit one of the longest passage graves at Blakshøj, before reaching Frederikshavn which formerly grew from a fishing village into a fortified town and is now North Jutland's main port for Sweden and Norway (and for the holiday island of Laeso out in the Kattegat). At the top of the peninsula on which Skagen is situated, you can stand – they say – with one foot in the Skagerrak and the other in the Kattegat. Skagen is a fishing port which became popular with artists in search of the 'Nordic Light' – a wreck from off the peninsula has its place in the history of the Hanse cogs. Just west of Skagen, Den Tilsandede Kirke is, indeed, a sanded-up church whose steeple alone is still visible above the sands, having been reluctantly abandoned as long ago as 1795. A little further south-west down the North Sea coast, the location of Råbjerg Mile shows the workings of the migrating sand dunes, moving a bit further east each year under the force of wind and sea.

To the south is Hirtshals, a fishing and ferry town (to Norway) which features a North Sea Museum dedicated to the marine life of the whole North Sea zone. Its oceanarium sports the largest fish tank in Europe with a surface area 22 m by 33 m and a depth of 8 m. All the fish of the North Sea are in there, especially herring and mackerel. There's also a sealarium and a variety of specialised habitat tanks showing everything from the open North Sea to the muddy bed of the Skagerrak.

On the way south again come seaside towns like Løkken and Blokhus, in an area of great sand drifts and cliffs as high as 74 m. The disused lighthouse at Ruberg Knude serves as the Sand Drift Museum. The Hanstholm region was heavily fortified by the Germans in World War II with long-range guns. There are wonderful sandy beaches to the south of the town, too, backed with inland reaches of heath, forest and lakes. Behind that region lies the estuary-like expanse of the western part of Limfjord with the large island of Mors within it, popular now with sailors but once a centre of the herring fishery, till the herring went away. The whole area is one of islands, spits, bridges, ferries, villages. On the North Sea beaches, fishermen still draw up their boats on the sands, as they do across the North Sea at places from Kent to Scotland – the Danish beaches are on a latitude with Aberdeen. At Ydby Heath at the bottom of the Thy peninsula, where the narrow mouth of the Nissum Bredning (in effect the western end of the Limfjord) opens to the North Sea through the Thyborøn Canal, there are fifty Bronze Age mounds. It is in this region that gas from the Danish fields arrives at Kaergard.

South of the Nissum Bredning lies flatter land than in the north, with the great forest plantation of the Klosterhede. The smaller Nissum and Stadil fjords follow to the south along a coastline of sand dunes on long and narrow spits, especially where they separate the large expanse of shallow water called the Ringkøbing Fjord (nothing like the popular idea of a fjord) from the North Sea of which it was once a part. It is now a salt water lake cut off from the sea by drifting sands except for the narrow channel at the fishing village of Hvide Sand (White Sand) which is just wide enough for small boats to pass through. To the south, the pattern of shifting sands continues to the lighthouse at Blåvands Huk, which is the most westerly point of Denmark. The spit at Skallingen points south-east to the picturesque island of Fanø guarding the entrance to Esbjerg harbour: Fanø was once the private property of the Danish kings, but was sold at public auction in 1741. The locals were able to buy it and started building ships there – by 1900 they had built a thousand sailing ships and its church is full of ship models.

Esbjerg itself is a result of the circumstances in which Denmark lost southern Jutland to Germany in 1864 (though North Slesvig voted to return to Denmark in 1920). To make up for its losses, Denmark promoted the erstwhile fishing village at Esbjerg to be a major port (it's the destination of ferries from Harwich in eastern England) which has become the fifth largest Danish town and remains the country's biggest fishing harbour. It, too, has an important Maritime Museum. South of the relatively new-made town of Esbjerg, we reach Denmark's oldest town of Ribe which started with the Vikings in the ninth century and was an important place in the Middle Ages: it is still full of antique charm. The flatlands around it, heath and forest and marshlands with dunes on the coast, were prone to flooding in earlier times and Ribe itself, its harbour now silted up beyond the reach of any but small craft, was once a port. The town sports a Viking Museum with extensively reconstructed farmstead and market place. To the south of Ribe the town of Tønder was also once a port, but is now well inland. Offshore lies the large island of Rømø, once the home of whaling men, which has a ferry to the nearby island of Sylt – but Sylt is in Germany.

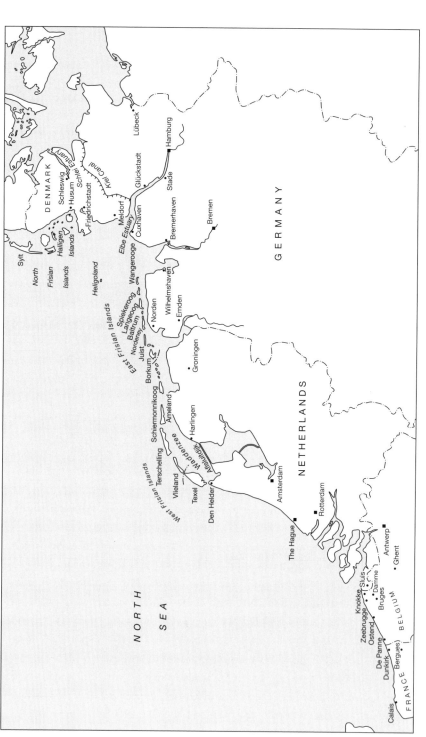

Map 8 From Germany to France

Map 9 The Netherlands

Chapter 13

From Germany to France

In the course of our tour of the North Sea coastline as it is today, with particular interest in the historical and archaeological associations that relate to the long North Sea saga that we have sketched in the rest of this book, we have arrived at the present-day border between Denmark and Germany.

The German island of Sylt stretches north of the German-Danish land border. It can be reached from the German mainland by a car-carrying train that travels over a long mole called the Hindenburg Causeway: since one stays in one's car for the trip, there is the odd impression of being in a car, on a train, at sea! Sylt is a holiday playground, with the major seaside town of Westerland, but it also has its picturesque villages and some megalithic tombs of the first farmers in these parts that are now flooded by the North Sea tides on the foreshore. Sylt is one of the North Frisian Islands, settled since at least the sixth century AD by the Frisians. Islands and coast in this region have been pretty changeable over the years – Amrum Island has a northern sandspit that gets longer and longer every year because of the action of wind and waves. The Halligen Islands, as we saw in our chapter on gains and losses around the North Sea, were part of the mainland till 1360 and their farms are now perched on earth banks that keep them out of the sea. The port of Husum, a little further south on the mainland, was an inland town till a storm in 1362.

Due east of Husum, on the other side of the Jutland peninsula (here at its narrowest point) is Hedeby, the Viking town the Germans call Haithabu. Its quiet location today ringed, except on its waterside, by a

D-shaped earthen embankment, gives little impression of its bustle in Viking times – and its squalor, according to the report of an Arab traveller who visited it in its heyday. The museum in the Schloss at nearby Schleswig has evocative reconstructions of Haithabu, together with the Nydam Boat and a striking collection of bog-bodies including the blindfolded Windeby girl, and the man with his hair in the Swabian side-knot style mentioned by Tacitus. The Schlei estuary opens into the Kiel Bight and the south-west reaches of the Baltic, but portage across the neck of Jutland allowed the Vikings to communicate between the North Sea and the Baltic at this point, without going all the way up and down Jutland. The Kiel Canal (Nord-Ostsee Kanal) of the late nineteenth century made the passage of large ships between the two seas fully practicable. South of Husum, inland from the pretty Eiderstedt peninsula is Friedrichstadt whose gabled houses and canals recall its building in the early seventeenth century by Dutch emigrés.

Between Friedrichstadt and the northern bank of the Elbe estuary to the south lies the region known as Dithmarschen with its cathedral city at Meldorf. From the end of the eleventh century, Dithmarschen was for several centuries a wealthy farming region that dealt with the Hanse towns: the region is backed by moorland and protected by dykes on its seaward side, generating the security and independence that gave it a ruling council of its own and made it, in all but name, an autonomous republic within the loosely administered Holy Roman Empire. In 1500 Dithmarschen saw off a twelve-thousand strong Danish army by opening its sea defences and flooding the Danes out. It had to accept Danish rule by the end of the decade, but remained a pretty independent region until 1860 when along with Schleswig-Holstein it was incorporated into the Prussian empire. There is a museum of Dithmarschen prehistory at Heide that includes a reconstructed farmhouse of the first century AD.

Hamburg

Brunsbüttel on the northern side of the Elbe estuary is the western end of the Kiel Canal and has been an important oil terminal since 1959. Further along the northern bank of the Elbe, Glückstadt is another Dutch-looking town, founded in 1617 by the Danish king Christian IV to rival the German Free City of Hamburg as a commercial port. Dutch Protestants and Jews enjoyed its religious freedoms along with its freedom from taxes.

Hamburg is the great city halfway across the base of Jutland that communicates with the North Sea via the long wide course of the Elbe and yet is not far overland from the Baltic port of Lübeck with which it was closely associated in Hanseatic times. It is Germany's biggest port and second largest city. Its history goes back a long way to the time when a son of Charlemagne, Louis or Ludwig the Pious, promoted the old town of Hammaburg to an archbishopric in 831 and built a great fortress to awe the local Saxons, fend off the nearby Slavs and generally safeguard trade. In 1189, the emperor Frederick Barbarossa granted it special trading and navigational rights together with tax exemptions. It was in effect Lübeck's North Sea port from the thirteenth century. It became an autonomous Free City in 1510, and went on to trade with – and see people off to – the New World in the seventeenth century. In 1814, after Napoleon, it joined the confederation of German states and towns as the 'Free and Hanseatic City of Hamburg', a situation still celebrated in the number plates of its vehicles. By 1913, it was the world's third largest port after London and New York. After World War II, it became a Federal Land in its own right. It is interesting to recall that one of northern Europe's earliest archaeological cultures, of the late glacial period, is named after the City of Hamburg: the hamburgian, with its main sites at Meiendorf and at Stellmoor close to the city. A later phase of the same culture is called ahrensburgian, after a town just along the way towards Lübeck. The ahrensburgian people appear to have pioneered the practice of lake sacrifice (of animals in their case) that was to have such a long future ahead of it in north-west Europe – and at Stellmoor, as we saw in our first chapter, they appear to have set up a sort of totem-pole and mounted it with the skull of a reindeer buck with a splendid set of antlers. It is salutary to think that there were totem-poles by the North Sea a mere twelve thousand years ago.

To the south-east of Hamburg is Lüneburg, the centre of a salt-mining industry after the tenth century that worked in conjunction with Lübeck and the Hanseatic League. About halfway back along the southern bank of the Elbe, a little inland, stands the picturesque town of Stade in its half-timbered splendour where one can inspect an impressive treadmill crane. On the promontory to the west that forms the southern opening of the Elbe estuary is the port of Cuxhaven, on the North Sea. From there you can go out into the North Sea some 70 km to the tiny island of Helgoland (Heligoland), a natural haunt of pirates in the thirteenth century, which belonged first to the Danes and then to the British who, as we saw, exchanged it with the Germans in 1890 for the African island of Zanzibar.

Bremerhaven and the East Frisian Islands

South of Cuxhaven at the bottom of the southern extension of the German Bight, stands Bremerhaven, the port of Bremen (to its south) on the River Weser. Still a fishing port and nowadays a great container terminal too, Bremerhaven was the port of emigration for ten million people from Germany and eastern Europe on their way to the New World in the nineteenth century: its 'Pier of Tears' bears witness to this poignant history. Bremerhaven's Seafaring Museum displays, among much else, the preserved Hanse cog that has told us so much about the design and construction of the League's typical vessel of the Middle Ages; there are also submarines from World War II. From marshland by the Weser estuary north of Bremen, at a place called Fallward near Wremen, come the recently discovered little boats of the fourth or fifth century AD that make a companion piece to the larger Nydam Boat in Schleswig; while the site of Feddersen Wierde – that elaborate Germanic Iron Age settlement of the first few centuries AD on its protective mound (Wierde) – lies beside the Weser just to the south of Bremerhaven.

Bremen itself is well worth seeing for its picturesque old quarter called the Schnoor and its magnificently restored and developed (after bombing in the 1940s) Böttcherstrasse, and there is a full-scale replica of the Bremen cog in the Old Town. Across the waters of the southern reach of the German Bight is Wilhelmshaven, only started in 1854 by Kaiser Wilhelm I as a North Sea naval base for the German Empire. Thanks to the oil trade, it is now a highly successful commercial port. A little inland of Wilhelmshaven to the north-east, Jever is noteworthy for the fact that it came under the rule of the German-born Russian empress Catherine the Great in 1793 and remained Russian until 1818, along with the island of Wangerooge – a remarkable situation even by the standards of North Sea comings and goings. Wangerooge is the most easterly of the East Frisian Islands (there are a few other stray islands in the German Bight between the East Frisians and the North Frisians). The East Frisian Islands continue west from Wangerooge with Spiekeroog, Langeoog, Baltrum, Nordeney and Juist to Borkum – the latter pair across the wide estuary of the Ems. All of these islands are prone to flooding and all of them are attractive for their fishing. Between them and the mainland are the shallow, tidal waters of the Wattenmeer, rarely more than 3 m deep, more often only 1 m, which results in mudflats at low tide. They are intriguing places to visit and only Nordeney and Borkum permit cars: this is the setting English readers know from *The Riddle of the Sands* as the conjectured source of a North Sea invasion of Britain by barges before World War I. The towns on the mainland, only a few kilometres across the Wattenmeer, include Bensersiel, Norden with its seventeenth-century houses called the Drei Schwestern (Three Sisters) in the Marktplatz and Greetsiel with its two great windmills.

Inland in this region of East Friesland lies a landscape of canals, locks, bridges and windmills where peat was cut on a grand scale to be sold for heating fuel. Grossefehn was the site of the first occupation of the fenland here and there is a Fen Museum at Westgrossefehn and an open-air museum at Moordorf. At Emden on the estuary of the Ems there is an East Frisian Museum and a Shipping Museum on a lightship – and at Emden, we are by the border with the Netherlands.

Into the Netherlands

In Dutch waters now, the Frisian island chain continues as the West Frisian or Wadden Islands – and the Wattenmeer is now the Waddenzee (watt means muddy shallow). The first island of any size is Schiermonnikoog, only reachable from the tiny port of Lauwersoog on the mainland opposite. It is a nature reserve with no cars allowed and a rather bleakly antique air about it: from the high point called the Wasserman, a panorama is afforded that takes in the turbulent North Sea on one side and the still waters of the Waddenzee on the other. The next island is Ameland, a bit busier than Schiermonnikoog, with skippers' houses of the seventeenth and eighteenth centuries. The island of Terschelling was important for its whaling port from the sixteenth to eighteenth centuries and its main harbour has a sixteenth-century lighthouse: its North Sea beaches are backed by shifting dunes, driven by wind and waves. Vlieland permits cars only to its own small population. With Terschelling to its north and Texel to its south, Vlieland forms part of a line of islands that curves across the old mouth of the former Zuider Zee. Its eastern side faces the shoals of the Waddenzee, its western side is an 8 km stretch of sandy beach on the North Sea. Among the wrecks off Vlieland is the famous one belonging to the *Lutine*, whose bell is now an ornament of Lloyds of London: she went down in 1799. Texel, completing the line of the West Frisians by nosing close to Den Helder across a narrow channel, is the largest of the chain and allows cars, while its lamb is renowned for a sweet and, perhaps not unexpectedly, briny flavour.

Inland in the north-east corner of the Netherlands, the first major town is Groningen, in the province of the same name. It's a region of terps, those mounds like the one at Feddersen Wierde in Germany, that protected ancient communities from flooding before they started building banks – dykes – to keep out the sea (and reclaim the land behind them at the same time). There are still terps to be seen under some of the churches in the Netherlands, even under whole villages. The main industry around Groningen today is focussed on sugar beet, in which pursuit the area parallels certain parts of East Anglia. Groningen's former days are recalled in the shipping and tobacco museums of the town, whose university is world-renowned. The Netherlands' next province along to the west is Friesland, well-settled in Roman Iron Age times but rather given up on by the Romans, after having a hard time capturing it, as too difficult to keep under control: the Frisians in the Netherlands as well as in Germany have always been an independent-minded people. Their language, still favoured at home, is more like English than Dutch and the following doggerel is reckoned to be as easily understood in Friesland as in England: 'Good butter and good cheese is good English and good Fries.' The Friesland capital is inland at Leeuwarden, on the way from Groningen to Harlingen on the coast, which is an old and still active fishing town and commercial port with fine sixteenth- and seventeenth-century houses and warehouses of the East Indies Company.

Just down the coast from Harlingen, we arrive at the eastern end of the remarkable Afsluitdijk, the barrier (with a road on it) that closes the great inland lake called the IJsselmeer off from the Waddenzee and so from the North Sea, too. Its completion in 1932 turned the Zuider Zee, a salt water inlet of the North Sea, into this inland lake. The Zuider Zee itself was, as we have seen, a comparatively recent feature of the local topography, having been formed only in the early Middle Ages when flooding made the former Lake Flevo into an extension of the North Sea. Stavoren, on a promontory just down the eastern side of the IJsselmeer, was once an important town of the Hanseatic League on the Zuider Zee.

Around the IJsselmeer

Land reclamation on the Zuider Zee's margins began as early as the thirteenth century, particularly close to Amsterdam where commercial interest could be aroused. At an early stage, the process saw some fishing towns turned into market towns. The creation of the IJsselmeer led to further polder-making, and the post-World War II creation of that still pristine new world of Flevoland at the bottom of the inland lake. After that, the threat of turning yet more ports into inland towns provoked the curtailment of well-advanced plans for fresh phases of reclamation. The citizens of Hoorn in particular, at the base of the bulge into the Meer on its western side north of Amsterdam, objected to the prospect that their home – one of the old Dutch Republic's greatest seafaring towns, birthplace of Tasman of Tasmania and Schonten who named Cape Horn – would become another inland locality. Enkhuizen on the promontory north of Hoorn has a museum that tells the whole story of reclamation in the Zuider Zee region: it was a top herring fishing town in the seventeenth century and, like Yarmouth on pretty much the same latitude on the other side of the North Sea, it features three herrings in its coat of arms. From immediately south of Enkhuizen a new barrier with a road on top runs across the IJsselmeer to Lelystad on the shore of reclaimed Flevoland, from where a road will take you north-east to Noordoostpolder. There the town of Blokzijl has a diving museum that also records the changing configuration through the ages of the Zuider Zee-cum-IJsselmeer. South of Blokzijl stands Kampen, which reached its mercantile peak in the sixteenth century (when it was exporting wool to England) and is full to this day of late medieval towers, gateways and gabled façades: it offers one of the vividest available impressions in Europe of what a fine medieval town looked like at its best. The distant view is especially evocative, though Kampen no longer faces towards the sea as it did before the creation of Flevoland. Further down the road to the east is Zwolle which was a Hanse town in the fifteenth century and retains its medieval gatehouse of 1409 among many well-restored old buildings. North of Zwolle and east of the Noordoostpolder (and so once nearer to the sea than it is now), Havelte is one of the megalithic sites of the Netherlands: in the Netherlands the huge boulder-constructed tombs of the first farmers are often known as 'Huns' Beds'.

Flevoland may have removed towns like Kampen and Zwolle from the vicinity of the sea, and it may itself be an all-new world, but at its Batavia Werf (wharf) near Lelystad authentic sailing replicas have been constructed of the Dutch East Indies Company merchantman the *Batavia* and of de Ruyter's seventeenth-century warship *De Zeven Provincien*, reminding us that the Dutch Republic's fortunes were founded on trade and the ability of their naval forces to protect it. Flevoland's south-west corner comes up close to Amsterdam, the centre of the Republic's trade and wealth, once upon the Zuider Zee and open to North Sea access. Since 1855, the old inner harbour's wharves and quays have been blocked by the building of the Central (Railway) Station on an island in its waters. Polder-making both before and after the station's construction has helped to remove the city further from what is left of its former Zuider Zee access. Though the 1876 Noordzeekanaal leads west (some 25 km) to the North Sea, Amsterdam has rather turned inland, away from all ready familiarity with the sea. Like London when we come to it, Amsterdam is neither directly on the North Sea nor modest enough to deserve skimpy description here: but we may briefly note this pre-eminent mercantile city's Historical Museum, which very vividly tells the town's story since its thirteenth-century beginning as Amstelledamme, and also the Jewish Historical Museum which reminds us of Amsterdam's, Holland's and Europe's long interaction with its Jewish people. By the seventeenth century, up to 10 per cent of the Amsterdam population were Jews from Spain and Portugal; from the 1620s, poorer Jews arrived from Poland and Germany, whence came Anne Frank's family to live in hiding in the Anne Frank House in World War II, which is now a museum, too.

Holland's North Sea Coast

If we go back now to the start of the road that runs across the Afsluitdijk, we can travel over the barrier at the top of the IJsselmeer to Den Helder on the promontory that almost touches the most westerly of the West Frisian Islands, Texel. Den Helder is the terminal of the Dutch gas pipeline from the North Sea. Just offshore here was the scene of the Dutch Fleet's defeat, under de Ruyter and Tromp, of an Anglo-French fleet in 1673 in what the English call the Third Dutch War. Den Helder was a fishing village before Napoleon fortified it in 1811, now it is the main Dutch naval base. Further south is Alkmaar, an inland market town that successfully withstood a Spanish siege in 1573 (the year before the Spaniards had murdered almost all the inhabitants of Naarden at the southern end of the Zuider Zee). After that, we reach IJmuiden, the 'Mouth of the Ij' that leads by way of the North Sea Canal into the heart of Amsterdam. On its way, the North Sea Canal goes by Zaandam where Peter the Great of Russia went, incognito, to study Dutch shipbuilding in 1697. (He went to Greenwich and Chatham in England, too, in the same spirit.)

Katwijk aan Zee is the place where the Oude Rijn (the Old Rhine River) finally makes its way out into the North Sea, in canalised guise today. Katwijk is a seaside resort with a seventeenth-century lighthouse and some Roman remains of the first century AD, reminding us that we have now arrived in the southern zone of the North Sea region in which the Romans were at home. The Franks who came after the Romans are also represented here with seventh-century archaeological finds. Twenty kilometres inland from Katwijk stands Leiden, with the oldest university in the Netherlands, founded in 1575 by William of Orange in the aftermath of the town's heroic 131-day resistance of a Spanish siege when Leiden was rescued by the opening of the sea dykes so that Dutch ships could come in right up to its walls. Leiden's Roman name was Lugdunum and the Rijksmuseum has archaeological exhibits from the Netherlands, from the classical world and from Egypt: the complete little Egyptian temple in the spacious entrance hall of the museum has come a long way from home to take its place so close to the North Sea; presented by the Egyptian Government in recognition of Dutch help in rescuing monuments threatened by the construction of the Aswan High Dam.

South-east of Leiden, The Hague is rather closer to the North Sea, with the seaside resort of Scheveningen to its immediate north where there is a Sea Life Centre with a glass tunnel on the seabed that permits inspection of North Sea marine life at close quarters. The Hague is not, however, in essence a sea-trading town but rather the political capital of the Netherlands and the seat of the country's administration. Den Haag grew out of 's Gravenhage, the 'Count's Hedge', as the little village around a hunting lodge of the Counts of Holland was called in the thirteenth century. The place came to importance in 1586 when the States General of the Dutch Republic met there. Not far inland, on the River Vliet, stands Delft which was the military headquarters of William of Orange (called 'the Silent') in the struggle against Spanish control of the Netherlands. It was the main arsenal of the Republic: in 1654 a gunpowder store exploded, killing two hundred people and destroying one-third of the houses of Delft, which was one of the chief cities of the Dutch East Indies Company.

South of Delft, the extended port of Rotterdam stretches on both banks of the Nieuwe Maas from Rotterdam itself to the Hook of Holland, opposite the gigantic part of the port complex called Europoort. Rotterdam came up with the Dutch East Indies trade but declined in the eighteenth and early nineteenth centuries, until the construction of the Nieuwe Waterweg (1866–90) vastly improved its access to the North Sea which had previously to be gained through a network of difficult waterways. Rotterdam was extensively rebuilt and developed after World War II, and its older character is better reflected in Delfshaven, founded in the fourteenth century as the port of Delft but now part of Rotterdam. The design of the Maritime Museum is appropriately based around the image of a ship's interior. Today the port handles some 250 million tonnes of goods a year, including about half the tea drunk in Britain. It lies on a main branch of the Rhine river called the Lek – in the Netherlands, the great river out of Central Europe breaks up into a number of wide branches including the Rijn, the Lek, and the Waal (called the Merwede downstream), of which the Lek is the main waterway coming out into the North Sea past Rotterdam at the Hook. The Frankish town of Dorestad lay at the confluence of the Lek with the Rhine. (The Maas connects this part of the Netherlands to Belgium and northern France, and the Scheldt – called the Schelde in its estuarine reaches in the Netherlands – also flows down from Belgium via Antwerp.) Europoort on the North Sea handles the ships that are too big to get to Rotterdam along the Nieuwe Waterweg, whose entire run from Rotterdam to the sea constitutes – with its container parks, oil depots, storage tanks, refineries, glimpses of wide water and big ships – an eerie landscape through which to drive, if you care to. It's better to see it by means of a boat tour.

The Delta world

Dordrecht lies to the south of Rotterdam, having grown up around an eleventh-century castle sited to control shipping in and out of southern Holland. It is the oldest town of the province of Holland and was one of the first to side with the Protestant rebels. It shows a very picturesque, if decaying and far from active, waterfront, though it is still a busy river junction where perhaps 1500 vessels of one sort or another pass per day. Although Dordrecht seems a long way from the sea, it stands in fact only a few kilometres north of one of the great estuarine arms that reach into the interior of the Low Countries from the North Sea: in this case, the arm that starts south-west of Dordrecht as the Hollands Diep (into which the Waal and the Maas flow) and becomes the Haringvliet as it approaches the North Sea past Hellevoetsluis, under a road-carrying dyke. The Hollands Diep runs also through the Krammer into the Grevelingemeer and the Oosterschelde, with many a barrage and highway along the way.

South of this first channel system, we are in the province of Zeeland and, as its name makes clear, in a North Sea world almost cut off by wide water from the rest of the Netherlands. In the past it was more isolated than today, when all those dykes, bridges and roads have joined the parts of Zeeland together and linked them as a whole to the rest of the country. Zeeland is a region of big and little islands, prone in the past to flooding, and its only substantial land-bridge to the mainland runs east from the island-peninsula of Walcheren and Zuid-Beveland – and that is only a few kilometres wide. This region was the scene of the terrible loss of life and destruction of property that struck on 1 February 1953, simultaneous with (but even worse than) the tragedy that afflicted East Anglia. It was the Delta Plan, boosted by the disaster, that put in place all the dams and dykes and barrages which now carry the roads that have integrated the islands of Zeeland with the mainland. The line of roads that connect the mainland south of Europoort to the islands of Overflakkee, then Schouwen-Duiveland, then Noord-Beveland and then the peninsula of Walcheren and Zuid-Beveland has technically shortened the North Sea coastline of the Netherlands by 700 km. Not altogether so 'technically' in fact, since the salt waters of the North Sea can now be shut out in stormy weather and former inlets of the sea transformed into sheltered lakes.

This region has much of historical interest: Schouwen-Duiveland has its thirteenth-century Slot Haamstede and Zierikzee of the early ninth century with its medieval harbour; Noord-Beveland has Colijnsplaat with its Roman-period remains that linked the trading of the day with eastern Britain; in Walcheren, there is the medieval town of Veere with its fortified harbour tower and sixteenth-century Schotse Huizen, once a depot of

Scottish wool merchants, while the museum in the Old Abbey in Middelburg displays Roman finds including an altar to the goddess Nehalennia favoured by seafaring merchants. The Romans had a naval base in this area, like the ones they maintained across the North Sea in association with the Forts of the Saxon Shore.

Vlissingen (which has featured sufficiently in English dealings with the Dutch to get its own English name of Flushing) is on the sea south of Middelburg and serves as a ferry port across the open mouth, without barrage and road, of the Westerschelde. Most of the southern bank of this estuary and its hinterland is also a part of the Dutch province of Zeeland but at its eastern end lies the great city of Antwerp, on the Scheldt in Belgium.

With the Low Countries our North Sea tour has reached the narrow and shallow southern funnel of the North Sea basin. The estuarine landscape of the Dutch province of Zeeland resembles (except in the greater degree of its topographical complexity) the estuary region of the Medway, Thames and Essex rivers, on about the same latitude across the North Sea to the west. The North Sea coastline of Belgium and France south to Calais is a straighter run altogether.

Antwerp and the Belgian Coast

The Scheldt river rises in northern France (where it is called L'Escaut) and flows north-east across Belgium to Antwerp, after which it flows out into the Westerschelde in Dutch territory. It keeps a course pretty parallel with the North Sea coastline as it goes from France to Antwerp, up to 100 km inland. Frisians settled along the Scheldt in the region of Antwerp in the first few centuries AD, to be joined by the Franks in the seventh century: they built a fortress here to assert their control, which was destroyed by Vikings in the ninth century. Antwerp was Frankish and French to start with, going to Lorraine in 843 and to the German Empire a century later in 963; from the twelfth century it came under the Dukes of Brabant, to be subsequently annexed to Flanders in 1357. It is worth recalling that by this time Antwerp was growing rich on English wool imports and trade with Genoa and Venice. In 1406 it was reunited with Brabant under the powerful and glorious Dukes of Burgundy. Bruges, to which we shall come, was losing its mercantile pre-eminence at this time as its river silted up and Antwerp grew in its place into a city that was huge by the standards of its time in the mid sixteenth century – of perhaps a hundred thousand people with a thousand foreign merchants living in the town and a hundred foreign ships coming and going a day. The city's stock exchange was instituted in 1532, which made it the most modern commercial city in the world.

With this background, Antwerp under William the Silent was at the forefront of the revolt against Spain whose rulers had inherited the Low Countries, and against the Catholic religion they sought so cruelly to impose. Philip II of Spain sacked the city in 1576 but was expelled the next year. The Spanish forces took it again in 1585 after a long siege. Spanish excesses, and the situation that navigation of the lower reaches of the Scheldt came into Dutch Republican hands by the late sixteenth century, led to a decline in the city's population to a half of what it had been and to the loss of its central financial role in the Europe of the day. The Scheldt was in effect closed to traffic in the seventeenth century and it was only opened up again at the end of the eighteenth, when Napoleon established a naval base there. The Dutch revived Antwerp with their East Indies trade in the post-Napoleonic settlement, but the Belgian separation of 1830 left the mouth of the Scheldt under Dutch control: their taxation of the Scheldt passage was only lifted in 1863. Port expansion ensued and Antwerp was transformed, a process accelerated in the boom after World War II. Antwerp is now Belgium's second city and its port stretches to the Dutch border with shipbuilding, chemical plants, refineries, car factories. The National Maritime Museum in the twelfth-century Steen Castle overlooking the harbour has marvellous displays of the city's seafaring history, including a very evocative large-scale model of the late medieval quayside with a treadmill crane and the Engelse Kaai that reminds us of the long commerce of Antwerp with England. It is worth noting, too, that Antwerp has been a diamond-dealing town since the fifteenth century – a role it took over from Bruges, to which the Venetians started taking precious stones in the thirteenth century that they had traded from India. (Amsterdam took to this business, too, and the two cities have vied in it ever since, Antwerp on top from the 1950s with a large Jewish community involved.)

Medieval Bruges

Belgium's capital of Brussels lies south of Antwerp and a long way from the North Sea, as is much of the rest of the country. Ghent, south-west of

Antwerp, is nearer to the sea on the River Leje, a tributary of the Scheldt, and has a connection via a canal to Bruges with the North Sea. Ghent is remarkable for, among other treasures, its exceptionally fine buildings from the twelfth century onwards, of astounding scale and ornament, especially along the river. Bruges, however, is the place in all Europe that presents the most vivid picture of a wealthy medieval town – albeit that, thanks to the superimposition of modern amenities, it inevitably looks too neat and clean (and free of everyday barbarities) to pass as a real medieval European city. Bruges owes its survival in such grandeur to its commercial decline after the Zwin estuary silted up in the fifteenth century and restricted its access to the North Sea, and to the ending of the line of the Dukes of Burgundy in 1482 and with them the end of their ambition to rule royally as a third great European power between France and the German Empire. In that situation the citizens of Bruges took their opportunity to extract rights from the Empire that were not honoured and Bruges's trading privileges passed to Antwerp, from which blow the town never recovered until the last century. Instead it stayed frozen in its fifteenth-century magnificence because its townspeople could not afford to spoil it, which is our good fortune today, since Bruges remains the most magical of all northern European towns. Bruges, incidentally, is the French name for this city, which has stuck with English-speaking people despite the modern insistence in Belgium on the Flemish version, Brugge. Belgium is less a nation than an administrative federation of two nations, Flanders (Vlaanderen) in the north and west with its Flemish language (a variety of Dutch) and Wallonia in the south and east with its French. Historically Flanders, which is the region with the North Sea coastline, also took in what is now the French département of Nord and the Dutch province of Zeeland. The name Vlaanderen is thought to have meant 'flooded land', appropriately enough.

Along the coast to Calais

Damme, just to the north-east, was one of Bruge's out-ports in the Middle Ages at the end of an inlet of the North Sea that was formed in the fifth century AD and then very gradually got silted up with sand pushed in by the sea: again, commercial decline has preserved it as an image of late medieval life. It is interesting to note that England's King John sent his ships there to disarm a French fleet threatening to invade England and that it was at another of Bruges' out-ports, Sluis (now in the Netherlands), that the English cog *Christopher* was captured in the course of an English victory in 1340 with the first recorded provision of guns on an English vessel. North of Bruges, the landscape is only about a thousand years old, having been sea in earlier times. The whole coast from the Dutch to the French borders remains a holiday zone with seaside towns developed since the early nineteenth century. Knokke is the best of them, though Blankenberge has a fine pier. Zeebrugge between them is really Bruges on Sea, the harbour of Bruges by courtesy of a canal, from which ferries come and go to Hull, Dover and Folkestone in England; gas is piped in from the North Sea to this important distribution point. Ostend, along the coast to the southwest, is another old town that stood out against the Spanish and suffered grievously for it at their hands: it came up again after Belgian Independence in 1830 as a bathing place with railway connections to the rest of the country. Its National Fishing Museum tells the story of fishing on the North Sea coast from prehistory to today. After Ostend, an area of sand dunes runs on past De Panne to the French border: and behind this region of Flanders, 30 km or so inland – and in pretty much the same way as in northern France – lies the sad landscape of the horrors of World War I.

This is a mixed French and Flemish world. Bergues, some 10 km from the sea, sits in a land of windmills, looking very Flemish. Dunkirk on the coast to the north (at various times under English and Spanish control) was once a great port and haunt of troublesome pirates. It was also the scene of the evacuation of British and French forces in the face of the Germans' advance in 1940, when the old town was all but totally destroyed by bombardment. A pipeline from the Norwegian gas fields comes in now. As with Sweden, Germany and Belgium, France's capital city is too far from the North Sea to visit it here and, while Lille is France's fourth largest city and the capital of French Flanders, at 60 km or so from Dunkirk it is hardly a North Sea feature, either. It was an ornament of the Burgundian empire, later of the Spanish Netherlands, and French from 1667. Meanwhile, Bergues might look Flemish, but Calais, where our exploration of the eastern coast of the North Sea ends, still looks pretty English at times (they lost it in 1558) thanks to the lure of sensibly taxed supplies of alcohol and tobacco. It was wrecked in World War II and remains nowadays, alas, not so much a place for history as for supermarket shopping. Let us note, however, that in the immediate aftermath of the death of King John of England a French fleet sailed from Calais in 1217 to attack England (probably London) but was defeated by an English fleet out of Sandwich either in the Downs or further north off Ramsgate. With mention of Ramsgate and the British shopping in Calais, we have come to our Channel crossing.

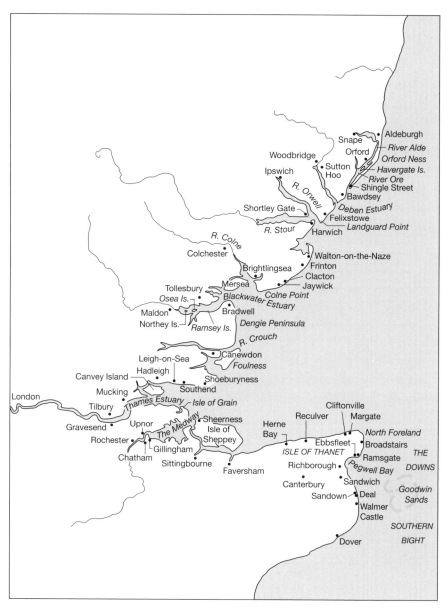

Map 10 From Dover to Aldeburgh

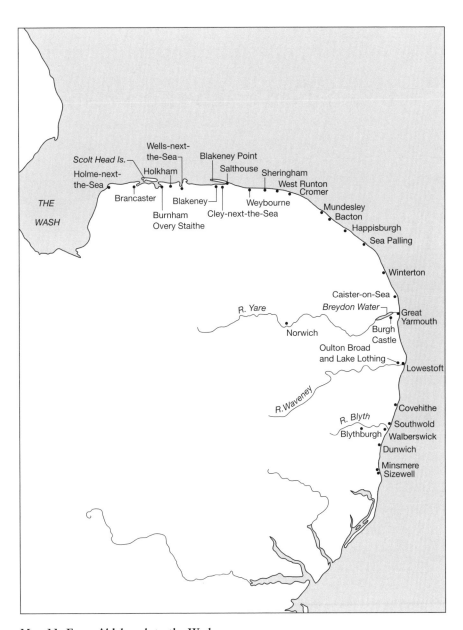

THE

WASH

Scolt Head Is. ─
Holme-next-
the-Sea
Brancaster
Wells-next-
the-Sea ┐
Holkham
Burnham
Overy Staithe
Blakeney
Blakeney Point
Salthouse
Cley-next-the-Sea
Weybourne
Sheringham
West Runton
Cromer
Mundesley
Bacton
Happisburgh
Sea Palling
Winterton
Caister-on-Sea
Breydon Water ┐
R. Yare
Norwich
Great
Yarmouth
Burgh
Castle
Oulton Broad
and Lake Lothing
Lowestoft
R.Waveney
Covehithe
R. Blyth
Blythburgh
Southwold
Walberswick
Dunwich
Minsmere
Sizewell

Map 11 From Aldeburgh to the Wash

Chapter 14

From Dover to the Wash

When we cross from Calais to Dover we are not quite in the North Sea, but rather in the Dover Strait – the spout, as it were, of the funnel at the bottom of the North Sea, with the hazardous Goodwin Sands coming down the middle of the funnel. Dover was the base of the Romans' Classis Britannica, their fleet for the protection of the Strait and the southern part of the North Sea. (There was another fleet across the Channel at Boulogne.) There is the extensive ruin of a Roman lighthouse within the complex of Dover Castle today, while the town has seen considerable excavation of Roman remains which include a house with well-preserved wall paintings. The Bronze Age Dover Boat comes from the town, too. It is, naturally enough from its position, a very old centre of human occupation and defence: the town and its surroundings to this day incorporate a complex range of fortifications from Roman through Norman and medieval to nine-teenth century and modern times. In the Middle Ages, Dover was one of the Cinque Ports and always the gateway to England with a busy harbour for both commercial and naval purposes: it was enlarged in the twentieth cen-tury to accommodate the Grand Fleet's battleships and cruisers; nowadays, the harbour is more of a leisure scene alongside the cross-Channel ferries. The Channel Tunnel, mooted since the nineteenth century, has brought a new dimension to Britain's relations with Continental Europe, already trans-formed by air travel – Blériot's first flight from France to England is still com-memorated at his landing place behind Dover Castle, which among its many attractions includes a great gun given to Queen Elizabeth by the Dutch for her help against the Spaniards, 'Queen Elizabeth's pocket pistol'.

Up the coast to the north from Dover are three of the castles built by Henry VIII to counter the threat of his several enemies in the sixteenth century: Walmer Castle was once on the sea but is now at the back of a stretch of shingle and trees: Walmer shades into Deal with the best preserved and most impressive of these castles right on the shore; while Sandown's at the north end of Deal is a ruin. Deal is also more or less the place where Julius Caesar's forces came ashore in the summer of 55 BC, though the coastline has inevitably changed hereabouts since then. Off Deal are the Downs, where sailing ships used to wait in the safe channel behind the shifting Goodwin Sands for a fair wind to take them north to the Thames and North Sea or south to the Channel.

Sandwich, 3 km or so inland, is the northernmost of the Cinque Ports, an important port on the winding Stour in the Middle Ages with a surviving medieval street plan and an old gateway still in place. But, in a pattern duplicated widely around the North Sea, the river got silted up as ships got bigger and Sandwich lost its standing as a port. The Cinque Ports were a confederacy of shipbuilding and ship-owning towns formed in the eleventh century to furnish ships and men for service as required against the enemies of the kingdom. The original five towns were Hastings, New Romney, Hythe, Dover and Sandwich, of which only the last could be said to be really on the North Sea. Winchelsea and Rye were added as 'head ports', and thirty other places – called 'limbs' – were associated with the Cinque Ports structure. From just before the Norman Conquest till the fourteenth century the Cinque Ports provided what was in effect a prototype of the Royal Navy of England: in return for putting their ships at the State's disposal when required, these trading towns received commercial and tax-related privileges. In time, alterations to their coastlines reduced all but Dover to the status of minor ports and the need for a more formally instituted and permanent navy, especially in Tudor times, helped see an end to their importance.

The one-time isle

North up the coast, on a channel that leads to Pegwell Bay and the North Sea, stands Richborough where the Romans began their invasion of Britain in earnest in AD 43. As their conquest progressed, they turned Richborough into the grand ceremonial gateway to the province, with a huge triumphal arch whose base survives. Rutupiae, as the Romans called Richborough, shared with Regulbium to the north-west (Reculver now) the guarding of the ends of the channel that in those days made the Isle of Thanet truly an island: Richborough is several kilometres inland now, overlooking the Stour and marshy ground to the sea. It was revived as a fortress in AD 285 as one of the Forts of the Saxon Shore against North Sea marauders – lengths of its turreted walls in this guise remain very impressive.

In 1949 a Danish crew sailed a replica of a Viking-style boat called the *Hugin* across from Jutland to Pegwell Bay, to celebrate not Viking predations but the landing of Hengist and Horsa at the start of Anglo-Saxon settlement in England, fifteen hundred years before. Ebbsfleet is the traditional spot where they and, later on in 597, St Augustine arrived here. The seaside resort of Ramsgate, where many of the evacuees from Dunkirk were brought across in 1940 (there is an excellent Maritime Museum), merges into Broadstairs going north round the bulge of the Isle of Thanet. On the bulge, North Foreland, facing due east, has had a beacon light of some sort since 1505 to warn ships of the Goodwin Sands. Cliftonville and Margate continue the seaside theme: before the railways, Londoners came to these resorts by sea. Chalk cliffs extend along the northern coast of Thanet, with the very necessary protection of a massive sea wall. Reculver is marked by the now spireless towers of a twelfth-century church in ruins on the cliff. In 669 King Egbert of Kent founded a monastery and church inside the Roman fort here on a pattern we shall see elsewhere up the east coast, using the old Roman forts as bases for the spread of the newly-adopted religion of Christianity. Half the Roman fort of Regulbium is lost to the sea now.

Next to the west is the early Victorian seaside town of Herne Bay: it lost its pier to storm damage in 1979, before which it was the country's second largest after Southend's. Some 8 km inland to the south is Canterbury, at the old mouth of the Stour at the time when Thanet was an island: this was a Roman town on the road from Dover to London and the north called Watling Street, and it still shows parts of its Roman walls and a large Roman theatre. In the sixth century, it was the chief town of Kent under a Saxon king who married a Frankish Christian princess, bringing in Augustine and a monastery that went on to be England's first cathedral. The Danes raided it savagely in 851 (when they overwintered at Thanet) and especially in 1011; it later became the focus of a pilgrim cult of St Thomas à Becket, till the Reformation and an influx of Protestant refugees from the continent, mostly weavers, put an end to that. It was badly bombed in World War II. To the west lies Faversham, a Saxon town that much later came to the fore as a place of gunpowder manufacture, particularly for the Napoleonic and Crimean wars. Sittingbourne on the coast, like so many other North Sea locations, was once a busy port.

The Medway

Across the Swale, the Isle of Sheppey is still an island (on which the Danes overwintered in 855): on its northern shore stands Warden Point, where vessels coming into the Thames Estuary and the Medway could always be usefully observed. Like many an area we shall come to right up the east coast of England, this is a scene of coastal landslips and endangered properties on the cliffs.

West is Sheerness, on its triangular promontory pointing into the mouth of the Medway (with the Swale coming up round the south to complete the isolation of Sheppey). The Sheerness dockyard was started in the time of Charles II, under Pepys during the Second Dutch War. It's now the site of a container and car ferry port. With Sheerness, we are coming into an area with a hint of the topographical complexity of the Dutch coast in the region of the great river estuaries: channels, creeks, islands and the estuaries of two major rivers with long-term commercial and naval associations make up this part of the world. At the bottom of the Medway complex of creeks and islands is Gillingham, running into Chatham on the Medway proper, with Rochester across the wide river at this point. Chatham was, until the 1980s, a naval dockyard since 1547 when Henry VIII felt impelled to build up his defences against the array of enemies his policies had generated. The old dockyard and its environs have been turned into an extensive complex of historical attractions and museums. These include some of the largest nineteenth-century ship houses over dry docks ever built for the construction and maintenance of warships: when people came to want to build grand railway stations in the course of railway expansion it was to these ship houses they resorted in search of inspiration for design and building techniques. Above and behind Chatham's great dockyard area rise the eighteenth- and nineteenth-century fortifications called the 'Great Line' that were built to defend it from any attack that might come not directly from the river. These include the great fortress of the Napoleonic Wars, Fort Amherst.

Rochester is an old settlement, always a point at which to cross the Medway: there was pre-Roman occupation, a Roman army compound, a Roman bridge to carry Watling Street over. The Norman cathedral and the still imposing castle (its keep is 30 m high) stand side by side overlooking the river. Eight kilometres south of Rochester near Aylesford – inland but still on the Medway river – is the Kit's Coty House megalithic tomb: the nearest such stone monument of the early farmers to the North Sea on the southern English side. North-east along the north bank of the Medway from Rochester, and opposite the northern end of the long run of Chatham Dockyard, is Upnor, with its compact and impressive little Elizabethan castle sticking out its wedge-shaped bastion on the waterside. It saw no action until 1667 when the Dutch attacked and burned Sheerness, sailed up the Medway and set fire to several of Charles II's ships, towing his flagship back to Holland as a trophy. Upnor's guns achieved little or nothing against the Dutch as they passed it.

The estuary of the Thames

Further to the north-east lies the almost-an-island Isle of Grain, from which you can look north across the wide mouth of the Thames Estuary to Essex. West across the peninsula that backs the Isle of Grain stretch the tidal reaches of the Thames Estuary, leading to London. Where the estuary narrows and turns west again towards the capital, the approach was guarded in the nineteenth century by the grim stone-built forts at Shornmead and Cliffe on the south bank and Coalhouse on the north. Developed in the 1860s, and armed with some very big guns in enclosed emplacements, they could have withered any invading vessels with murderous crossfire. Coalhouse in particular is well-preserved and gives off a menacing air to this day, especially inside. Further up the Thames on the south bank is Gravesend, now a container port, where Pocahontas died and was buried on her way back to America in 1617: she had come to England as something of a sensation the year before after saving Captain Smith and marrying Mr Rolfe back home in Virginia. Opposite Gravesend on the north bank Queen Elizabeth memorably rallied her troops on the eve of the Armada struggle in 1588 – Tilbury is now a great container port; just downstream is Tilbury Fort, built in 1682 against the threat from the French and Dutch, with a moat on its inland side and an ornate arched entrance on its water side.

West of Gravesend, Swanscombe is the site of the discovery of the skull bones and tools of a remote ancestor of ours, of many hundreds of thousands of years ago, predating our North Sea story altogether. Of times much closer to our own are the Anglo-Saxon remains – including many graves and those sunken-floored houses called Grubenhäuser – at Mucking, north of Tilbury. Inland, of course, is London which goes back beyond the Saxons to Roman times, when it was called Londinium, and to pre-Roman days as a settlement of Celtic-speaking people from whom the Romans derived their name for the place. By the seventh century, it was an important enough international market to be mentioned as such by Bede, whom we shall encounter again much further up England's North Sea coast. Alfred the Great took the city in his struggles against the Danes. The Normans signalled their control of London with their intimidating White Tower just outside its old city walls. By the end of the twelfth century, there were merchants from Italy, Gascony, Flanders, Denmark and, above all, from Germany in London – the Germans in their Steelyard compound that was one of the great Kontore of the Hanseatic League. In the late nineteenth and early twentieth centuries London could boast the world's largest docklands.

Going east again, out of London and past Tilbury along the north bank of the Thames Estuary, we reach Canvey Island, which really is just about an island, thanks to the creeks that surround it. Here fifty-eight people drowned on the night of 31 January 1953 despite the flood walls and drainage measures in place since the seventeenth century: a massive concrete sea wall with steel floodgates now protects this very vulnerable place's bungalows and chalets. Upstream the Thames Barrier of the 1980s is designed to safeguard London itself.

The constant need to monitor and defend the approaches to London is exemplified in the two great round towers of Hadleigh Castle across the Benfleet Creek from Canvey Island, built by Edward III against the French threat of the thirteenth century. Over the sands stands the rather old-world resort of Leigh-on-Sea and then the not altogether old-world Southend, with its famously long pier, not quite what it was. Southend runs on east to Shoeburyness, whose long history as an artillery range began in 1858, testing guns against the new ironclad warships of the time. There's more Ministry of Defence terrain up the coast to the north-east on Foulness Island, which remains an avian paradise (ness, or promontory, of fowl) because of its closure. Inland along the River Crouch from Foulness is Canewdon, where Knut (Canute) defeated Edmund Ironside in 1016. On the way back to the sea along the north bank, Creeksea is one of two places (the other is at Bosham in Sussex) where Knut is supposed to have demonstrated his incapacity to turn back the tide by royal command.

From Foulness to the Naze

North up the coast of the Dengie peninsula, there points out into the North Sea the little promontory of Bradwell Shell Bank, a spit of sand and shingle with broken and compressed sea shells. Immediately inland stands St Peter's Chapel: St Peter's-on-the-Wall, built out of bricks and stones from the Romans' old Saxon Shore Fort of Othona, on the site of the fort's main gateway. This little chapel dates back to 654 when St Cedd arrived here from Northumbria as missionary to the East Anglians. Just round the northern bulge of the peninsula, the Bradwell nuclear power station makes a striking contrast. Going south-west into the Blackwater Estuary, we encounter Ramsey Island which isn't an island, Osea Island which is and then, at the end of the estuary just before we get to Maldon, Northey Island which is and isn't according to the tide, for its causeway to the mainland is flooded (very quickly) when the tide comes in. This island played an important part in the Battle of Maldon in 991 when marauding Danes crossed from their temporary base there to fight the Saxons in a bloody struggle that ended with all the outnumbered Saxons killed – though the Danes were exhausted by the fight themselves, with only the inevitable Danegeld to console them. A famous Anglo-Saxon poem celebrates the Saxons' bravery.

On the north shore of the Blackwater Estuary, past Tollesbury whose wooden sail lofts testify to its erstwhile fishing fleet of a hundred smacks at the turn of the last century, and past the large island of Mersea with its occasionally flooded causeway to the mainland, we may head up the River Colne towards Colchester. Colchester is famously the oldest recorded town in Britain and the first major Roman settlement of the British Isles. Its Roman fortress was established in the year when the conquest began, AD

43, close to the British township of Camulodunum. Roman Camulodunum survives well above ground in walls and gateway as well as in archaeological excavations. The Norman castle of the town today was built on the foundations of a Roman temple slighted in the general sack of Colchester by British natives under Boudicca in AD 61. The Norman keep closely resembles, but is bigger than, the White Tower of the Tower of London: it houses a wonderful collection of Roman exhibits and excellent models of its history. The Roman town, rebuilt and elaborated after the Boudiccan revolt, was inherited and robbed (and also partly inhabited) by the Anglo-Saxons between the Romans and the Normans. The town went on to suffer a terrible siege in 1648 during the English Civil War and the Siege House carries the visible scars of it in its bullet-holed timbers. The part of the town called the Hythe, on the Colne, was the port area of medieval times when there was a thriving local cloth industry.

Brightlingsea, on the eastern bank of the Colne estuary towards its mouth, was also a medieval port and the only 'limb' of the Cinque Ports outside Sussex and Kent. South of Brightlingsea across Flag Creek, Colne Point is a place of shingle and saltings where the coastline turns sharp east towards first the seaside haunts of Seawick and Jaywick and then the more aspiringly refined nineteenth-century resorts of Clacton and Frinton. Spear fragments of yew wood, some 450,000 years old, were found at Clacton: older by far than the North Sea as we know it. This is a coastline of Martello towers, those defensive lookouts against the Napoleonic threat with flat roofs for their swinging gun mounts. There's one between Seawick and Jaywick and three at Clacton. There's another at Walton-on-the-Naze that isn't on the sea but rather at the end of the Walton channel that comes in behind the town. To the east of Walton-on-the-Naze, what is left of the Saxon Shore Fort that goes by that name lies some 3 km out to sea from the present shoreline.

On the Stour and the Orwell

The opening of the estuaries of the Stour and Orwell faces south to the Naze from about 6 km to the north. The western side of the opening is the site of Harwich, with its own bay facing north, while on the eastern side is Felixstowe. From Harwich's nineteenth-century Parkeston Quay go the ferries to the Hook of Holland, Cuxhaven, Hamburg, Esbjerg, Gothenburg,

Kristiansand. The combined estuaries of the two rivers and the bay at Harwich constitute the finest natural harbour between the Thames and the Humber. In 1340 Harwich was the assembly point for Edward III's fleet to cross the North Sea and defeat the French and Genoese at Sluis where the French lost 190 ships and the English cog *Christopher*, armed with guns, was captured. Among its other claims to fame, Harwich was the home of the master of the Pilgrim Fathers' *Mayflower*, and it has a treadmill crane of 1667. It was a Norman town, vital for east coast defences and the place of embarkation from the thirteenth century of emissaries from England to the states of northern Europe, indeed of passenger embarkation in general. Harwich is the only East Anglian port to have been also a naval base. It was a Royal Naval Dockyard from 1674, but leased to private shipbuilders from 1730. Its first light-tower was installed in 1543 and it became a Trinity House depot in 1669. The country's first true mail packets operated to Hellevoetsluis from 1661. With the railways came freight traffic and the running of steamers to Rotterdam and Antwerp as we saw in an earlier chapter. But its old quays were not up to the demands of big ships and Parkeston Quay was constructed from the 1880s for the passage to Esbjerg, the Hook and Hamburg.

On the north bank of the Stour estuary, the promontory of Shotley Gate marks the turning point north into the Orwell estuary with Ipswich at the top of it, nearly 20 km from the sea and just beyond the graceful and imposing Orwell Bridge of the 1980s. Ipswich was a very important focus of Anglo-Saxon trade and England's largest port at the time, which made the kings of the East Angles rich. Wool was already being exported from its sheep-rearing hinterland to Flanders, and Ipswich went on in the wool trade into medieval times, becoming in 1404 a Staple Port for the legal export of what was really England's only trade resource. Later on, it was a base of the Iceland Fishery too – many east of England ports were, making the North Sea a major factor in this business though it was conducted in distant waters. Ipswich peaked as a shipbuilding town at around 1500 and it is interesting to note that its twelfth-century town seal is one of the earliest, if not the earliest, to show a ship with a stern rudder instead of a side steering oar. But, squeezed between London and Yarmouth and with the attentions of the Dunkirk pirates coming as no help to its fortunes, Ipswich declined as a shipbuilding port and by 1800 its harbour had almost silted up. In the nineteenth century, dredging over a long period and the building of new docks saw the port's renewal: it thrives today with pallets, containers and bulk oil alongside old favourites like timber, grain, some coal and even wine as in the Middle Ages.

Back down the estuary on its eastern side, we arrive at Felixstowe, extending now almost but not quite to Landguard Point across the estuary mouth from Harwich. Felixstowe really had no history as a port till the late nineteenth century, but it is now the last word in modern container ports, with huge cranes lining the shore on the estuarine side. Modernisation began in 1956 after the floods of 1953 damaged the nineteenth-century harbour. In 1964 came the oil terminal jetty, next year roll-on roll-off ferries and a container area, followed in 1968 by the Transatlantic Container Terminal dealing mainly with traffic to and from the USA but also with Scandinavia, Germany, Holland, Spain and Portugal. The seaside town of Felixstowe, which grew south from a fishing village to the north, is on the other side of the promontory from the port, facing the open North Sea but sufficiently to the south and east to sport fine seafront gardens. South of town and port is Landguard, whose first fort was built in the 1540s, to oversee the entrance to Harwich harbour. The very elaborate complex of the fort we see now was mainly built after the early eighteenth century. (The Saxon Shore Fort of Roman times known as Walton-next-Felixstowe has, like its twin at Walton-on-the-Naze, gone under the sea.)

From the Deben to Dunwich

A Martello tower stands at the point of the ferry crossing north of Old Felixstowe for foot passengers (in the summer) to cross to Bawdsey Quay on the northern side of the Deben estuary, with its RAF station where radar was developed in World War II. At the end of the estuary, the picturesque town of Woodbridge recalls its Saxon origins in its name, which means 'Odin's Borough'. Across the Deben and a bit uphill inland is the site of Sutton Hoo, under one of whose mounds was discovered the Sutton Hoo ship and its fabulous Anglo-Saxon treasure in 1939: the pagan ship burial of King Raedwald who died in about AD 625 and who perhaps believed in Odin as much as he believed in the new religion the missionaries were promoting. (His body, missing from the ship, may have received a Christian burial.)

Back down the Deben on the coast, a run of Martello towers takes us from Bawdsey to Shingle Street, aptly named in its lonely – even bleak –

sort of natural beauty. From just north of Shingle Street, the channel of the River Ore opens up and runs parallel to the shore behind the long spit of Orford Beach for a good 20 km including the Alde with which it is continuous. The spit is the result of wave action along this coast, extending the sandbank south and creating Havergate Island behind it, leaving Orford and its great castle nowadays a long way from easy access to the sea. The castle was built in 1165 to command its maritime approaches: its keep stands 30 m high, made all the more imposing by the total robbing away of all the other buildings and wall that once surrounded it. There is still an Orford quayside, but it is 10 km from the opening to the south instead of straight on the North Sea: the town is now in consequence a quiet, but delightful, place. Orford Ness across the channel of the Ore is marked by its red-and-white lighthouse and various Ministry of Defence structures. North of Orford, the river channel is known as the Alde: it takes a sharp turn to the west just south of Aldeburgh with another Martello tower – the most northerly – on the very narrow spit at this point. Aldeburgh was a medieval port and fishing town which became a seaside resort in the nineteenth century. Its Moot Hall of the early sixteenth century now stands all by itself virtually on the beach, backed by Georgian houses at the foot of quite a hill for this part of the world, but when it was built there were three roads between it and the sea. Inland at the end of the Alde estuary, Snape was the site of another shadowy Anglo-Saxon ship burial.

North along the coast looms the nuclear power station by the small village of Sizewell, south of Minsmere Bird Reserve with an old landscape of heathland still surviving inland to its north. Then comes the ever-intriguing lost (or almost entirely lost) town of Dunwich. This was a major port of Anglo-Saxon times and a great Norman town thereafter with a bishop and a grammar school and perhaps as many as five thousand inhabitants. The coast here has always been at risk from stormy seas, but until late in the thirteenth century the people of Dunwich had evidently managed their problem by putting down brushwood, weighted with stones, to control the erosion of the beach over winter. But the particularly bad storm of January 1328 brought thousands and thousands of tonnes of sand and shingle across the harbour mouth in a single night, diverting the river north and killing off the town's trade in short order. There followed decline and neglect but not the total eclipse of the town – that was achieved slowly over many years as more and more of the streets and buildings were undermined by the sea's assault on their cliff-top perch. By 1677 the encroachment had reached the old market place and now only the ruin of the once well-inland leper chapel and a Victorian church survive, along with a pub, a museum and a fish-and-chip restaurant, all worth a visit. There used to be a last gravestone on the cliff edge but that has gone now, too. Today the most prosperous town of Norman Suffolk lies jumbled under the sea, and most of the later versions of Dunwich lie with it.

Wool country and herring ports

The coastal hinterland hereabouts was the scene of a constant influx of Flemish weavers from Norman times onwards, from the first truly industrialised part of Europe – driven out by guild restrictions and religious differences, to settle places like Blythburgh, Sudbury, Lavenham, Long Melford, Southwold, Norwich, Worstead. In time, growing restrictions in England drove some of them further to places like Sheffield, Leeds and Manchester. On the next great river and estuary going north stands Blythburgh, about 5 km inland: the size of its church, rather out of keeping with the small-scale (and very charming) character of the village today, bears witness to the wool-derived wealth of these parts in former times. Once there was a busy quay here – it was the old story of bigger ships and silting waterway to the sea. Walberswick, on the southern side of the estuary mouth, was also once a flourishing port. Across the mouth is Southwold, a prosperous fishing town in the eleventh century, which retains a long run of landing stages on the Blyth, busy with leisure sailors and some fishermen. The town is to the north of this river mouth, with six guns pointing out to sea at its southern end on Gun Hill: guns were first installed here by courtesy of Charles I for protection against the visitations of the Dunkirk pirates. In 1672 the Battle of Sole Bay was fought offshore to the north between the English and the Dutch. Southwold is itself almost an island, cut off from its hinterland by the river to the south and Buss Creek to the north and west, named after the herring busses that used to operate in the North Sea out of Southwold. Covehithe to the north demonstrates even more dramatically than Dunwich the dire effects of coastal erosion: twenty years ago quite a stretch of road ran past the church to the cliff-top, ending in a jagged edge of broken tarmac even then, and today that stretch of road is very much further truncated.

Lowestoft sits astride the North Sea mouth of a series of bodies of water made up of the River Waveney inland, a connecting channel to Oulton Broad, then Oulton Broad itself and Lake Lothing coming into the town from the west, which occupies a bulge in the coast marking the easternmost point of Britain at Lowestoft Ness. The town grew up on the herring business from the mid nineteenth century with a trawler basin by the end of it. More than seven hundred steam drifters were based in Lowestoft just before the First World War. Along with the fishing went the traditional trade of wool to the Low Countries and grain to the Baltic, with timber and pitch coming in from Scandinavia and the Baltic, iron ore from Sweden and Russia. A Maritime Museum tells the story and it was until recently an evocative experience to spot the consular badges of various North Sea countries on the buildings around the port, which in its modern form is a creation of the railway age. Fishing is not eclipsed in Lowestoft, which has seen heavy investment in high-powered fishing vessels. The first lighthouse in Britain was built down on the beach in 1609, and a high twin was added on the cliff in 1670.

Around Yarmouth

Lowestoft and Yarmouth to its north shared the fishing business in its heyday, with the inevitable rivalries it brought. Yarmouth's topography, of relatively recent genesis as we have seen, allows it to maintain a seaside resort on its North Sea side and a commercial port on the river that runs more or less parallel with the coast, north-south from Breydon Water inland to the present harbour mouth at Gorleston. Before the seaside era, the town had always rather turned its back on the sea, with a defensive wall (some of which survives from the time of Henry VIII) including an arrow-shaped bastion that goes almost unnoticed in the town today. It is odd to think that the whole place and the ground on which it stands did not exist in Roman times, when there was a broad estuary with a wide opening through which ships could pass all the way up to the inland town of Venta Icenorum. After Roman times, a sandbank grew across the estuary mouth and fishermen started to use it on a temporary basis: it grew bigger and the settlement on it became more permanent until by the eleventh century the foundations of Yarmouth were laid, with a mention in Domesday. There followed shipbuilding and the herring trade, which brought conflict with the Cinque

Ports who claimed control of all North Sea fishing rights. Fifty-nine ships from Yarmouth joined seventy-three from the Cinque Ports against the French invasion of Flanders at the start of the fourteenth century: seventeen or more of the Yarmouth ships were lost.

The herring fishery was so important to Yarmouth that the medieval town's seal shows a ship with three herrings below it (like Hoorn's on the Zuider Zee). The business declined after 1500 in a period of Dutch supremacy and the seventeenth century saw a dearth of herring in the southern part of the North Sea, but the trade was revived in the late eighteenth century and prospered in the nineteenth. In the year before the First World War Yarmouth and Lowestoft between them landed 2000 million fish and 1100 steam drifters operated out of Yarmouth alone. Now they are gone: changes in the herring pattern in the North Sea and overfishing have put paid to the business. A whole world has been lost in the process, which once saw the Yarmouth river jammed with boats from all around Britain, especially from Scotland whence came the Scottish fish girls, cleaning and packing the fish, that were a noted feature of the season. The town is on the up again, though, as a base for oil and gas exploration and a marina is being added to its leisure features. The fishing years are memorialised in the town by the smoke-houses and the thatched ice-house associated with the keeping and preserving of the catch. The procurement and hoarding of ice was very important in the fish trade from the eighteenth century on. There are also Hanse warehouses in Yarmouth for the trade in Worstead cloth. The Norfolk Pillar, with a statue of Britannia on top, is a memorial to Nelson, who landed at Yarmouth after his exploits across the North Sea at Copenhagen. The Maritime Museum in the seaside part of the town has housed an excellent record of the town's dealing with the sea, while the Tolhouse Museum, in one of England's oldest municipal buildings (thirteenth century), tells the story of Yarmouth's strange topographical development, including the wanderings up and down the coast of its harbour mouth as a result of blockages and human interventions.

Five kilometres inland at the western end of Breydon Water, but once on the open waters of the old estuary, stands the Saxon Shore Fort of Gariannonum, which is now known as Burgh Castle. Its massive brick-banded flint walls and tottering towers remind us again of the late third-century threat to Roman Britain from across the North Sea and down from Pictland in the north. In the seventh century, Christian missionaries propagandised out of the fort's ruin along the lines we have seen elsewhere with these old Roman bases; later on, the Normans piled up a mound inside it as the base for a no doubt wooden keep. Norwich, founded in Saxon times but only coming to prominence with the Vikings, was also furnished with a wooden Norman keep before the building of its great stone castle. It, too, was a major port until about 1300 when the Yare silted up and Yarmouth came to function as the port of Norwich, which was not to see a ship from the North Sea again until 1833. Near to Norwich, but only visible in aerial photographs, is the site at Arminghall of a neolithic wooden henge monument of about 2500 BC.

The Norfolk coast

Back on the coast to the north of Yarmouth there's another Roman settlement at Caister-on-Sea with walls, foundations, and a stretch of road surface that can still be seen on site. Winterton, north again, has a 40 m tall church that must have been a welcome marker to sailors of all sorts in days gone by and a 'Fishermen's Corner' inside it serves as a memorial to the many people who have lost their lives at sea around here – fragments of wrecks used often to be turned up on the beach from the many wrecked ships. Horsey just inland was a hot-spot of smuggling in the eighteenth and early nineteenth centuries, reminding us of the constant appeal of dealing in contraband along these eastern coasts of England in those days. This is also a coastline that has taken great losses from the action of the sea, especially in the storm tide of January 1953 but also on a continuing basis, as at Happisburgh where the cliff and its appointments, including houses, face destruction currently. Off Happisburgh lie the dangerous Hazeborough Sands (the pronunciation is the same!) where HMS *Invincible* was lost in 1801 on her way to join Nelson's fleet at Copenhagen. The lighthouse of 1791 is unmissable with its bold red-and-white banding. Sea Palling to the east is one of those places that reveal forest beds at low tides as indicators of previously low sea levels after the last ice age. At Bacton to the west the high-fenced installation of gasholders and massive piping is even more unmissable than the Happisburgh light – the site of the Bacton Natural Gas Terminal. A run of seaside towns follows: Mundesley with its Georgian beginnings (and a fine windmill with its sails in place, just outside it), Cromer which, in the form of the lost village of Shipden, once stood much further out to sea, and Sheringham which was formerly just a depot on the shore for fishermen living up the hill in the old village. Along this stretch, crab boats still go out from places where they can be got down to the beach: close to one such place, at West Runton, the fossilised bones of an early species of elephant were discovered in 1990, standing over 4 m tall in life and 650,000 years old.

At Weybourne, the steeply-shelving shingle beach of Weybourne Hope has historically been an anxiety to England's rulers as an obvious place for a foreign invader's big ships to come in close to shore and discharge men and material. It seemed especially vulnerable at the time of the Armada and big plans were made for an extensive complex of defences there, though it isn't clear now how much of it was actually constructed. It is certain it was dropped the moment the threat was over. On a more or less dead straight line running due west from Weybourne, we pass Salthouse which was the scene of pioneer land reclamation in the 1630s under the Dutchman van Hasendunck, on our way to Blakeney Point. The Point is a creation of wave action out of shingle that has, with some fluctuations, extended so far to the west and spread its claw-like end as to block the access of the formerly important Glaven Ports, like Cley and Blakeney, on the River Glaven. Saltmarsh reclamation had played its part, too, in the demise of these ports: Cley has an eighteenth-century Customs House it doesn't need today and Blakeney an undercrofted medieval merchant's house facing a quay whose access dries up almost completely at low tide.

To the west of Blakeney spreads England's largest coastal nature reserve of dunes, beaches and salt marshes, with Wells-next-the-Sea at its south-west corner. Wells is actually at the end of a long channel leading north to the sea (where the beach is) and its present quay is not where the town's medieval port was until the 1720s. That site is now a grassy hollow backing on to old houses that with a bit of imagination can still be conjured as a quayside. The church has a lectern from the Low Countries. South-west of Wells is Holkham Hall and its estate, where 'Coke of Norfolk' revolutionised English farming in the first half of the nineteenth century. South-east lies the multi-walled Iron Age fort of Warham Camp.

The cluster of villages called the Burnhams, west from Wells and Holkham, has its waterside constituency at Burnham Overy Staithe and its maritime claim to fame at Burnham Thorpe, 3 km inland, where Nelson was born. The coast to the west is marshland with inlets of the sea and Scolt

Head Island, a nature reserve. Past the almost landlocked small harbour of Brancaster Staithe, we reach Brancaster itself, which once had another of those Forts of the Saxon Shore, called Branodunum. Titchwell marsh below Brancaster Bay was an area of reclamation from the 1780s, until the floods of 1953 smashed through its defences and it reverted to marsh ground. We have now arrived at the Wash, and Holme-next-the-Sea, where a striking piece of archaeology was discovered only a few years ago.

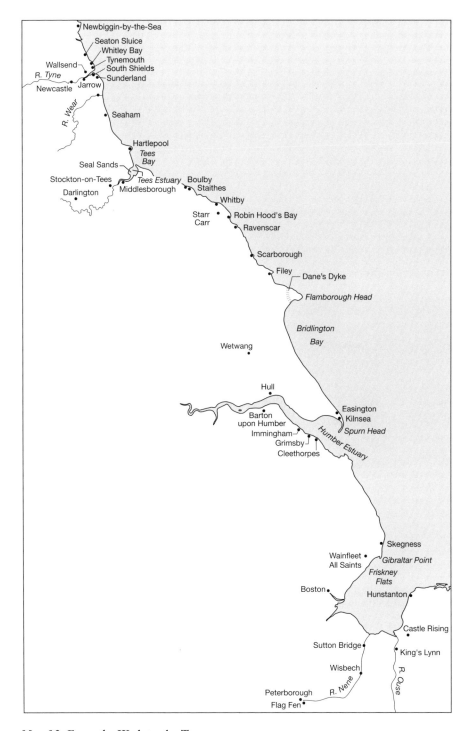

Map 12 From the Wash to the Tyne

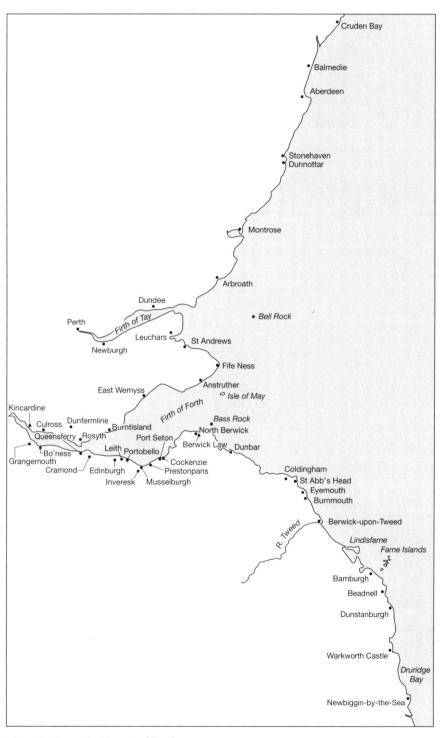

Map 13 From the Tyne to Aberdeen

Chapter 15

From the Wash to John o' Groats

Seahenge is the name that has been given to the circle of fifty-five posts, with an inverted oak tree-trunk in the middle, discovered at the end of the last century at Holme-next-the-Sea on the North Norfolk coast. Dendrochronology (counting annual tree rings to arrive at a date for the end of a tree's life) has assigned a date of 2050 BC for the felling of the central oak and the surrounding posts are thought to have been cut down the next year. Cut marks on the timbers reveal that metal axes were used in the work, only about a century after the introduction of metal tools into Britain in the Bronze Age. The circle was clearly a ritual construction, to do with the religious beliefs of those far off days, and a second and larger feature which may represent a Bronze Age barrow has since been discovered close by on the foreshore of Holme-next-the-Sea: when they were made, these structures stood well inland on marshy ground. Holme-next-the-Sea also marks the end of the Peddar's Way, a perhaps pre-Roman trackway running inland for 80 km. Hereabouts, too, there was a Roman ferry across the Wash.

Hunstanton, as we go south along the eastern side of the Wash, has the distinction of being the only seaside location on the east coast of England that faces west, so one can see the sun set over the sea all the year round (if one can see the sun). It was into the waters of the Wash that William the Conqueror brought his fleet after the Battle of Hastings as part of a land and sea blockade to harry Hereward the Wake hiding in the Ely marshes to the south. Betrayed by monks, Hereward fled to Lincolnshire to continue his resistance to the Normans for a few years, till he made his peace and kept his estates. The Wash has a long history of topographical alteration: it came much further inland in the Bronze Age – as far as Flag Fen near Peterborough, for example, where there was the important site of ritual deposition we looked at in Chapter 2. In Roman times, the Wash's waters still came much further in than they do today, especially into what are now the prime market-gardening areas to its south and west. Reclamation has reduced the Wash and so have natural processes: Castle Rising, for example, was once a port to rival Lynn to its south, with a great Norman castle to go with it, but it is very hard now to stand in meadows by its little stream and imagine it as the busy port it was till the familiar combination of bigger ships and a silting river put an end to it.

King's Lynn, at the bottom south-east corner of the Wash, is mentioned as a salt-making area in the Domesday Book. It received a charter from King John early in the thirteenth century, when it is interestingly characterised as:

> *much haunted of long time with Hollanders, Flemings and other Nations of the East Country.*

Lynn came up in the aftermath of a tidal surge in 1260 that killed off Wisbech, to the south-west on the Nene, as a port (it ceased to be one for 250 years). Lynn exported wool and salt from nearby salt workings, and imported coal and wine. It was also a fishing port: bench ends from a chapel in the town show English boats fishing for cod; later on it was an important base of the Iceland Fishery. In 1347 it was contributing nineteen ships to the English fleet at a time when London was only sending five more.

Sutton Bridge is interesting for its swing-bridge to allow ships up the Nene river and for the curious history of its nineteenth-century port, which opened in 1881 and closed almost the same day as a result of irreparable leakage. Its site is now a golf course and traditionally the spot where King John lost his treasure, in what was then marshland, on his way north after Magna Carta. But Sutton Bridge now has a new port, built a hundred years after the failure of the first.

From Boston to Hull

The northern side of the Wash, over the River Welland, brings us to Boston whose 85 m high landmark church tower – called The Stump – is said to have been modelled on one in Bruges or Antwerp: it was once a valued beacon for navigation in the Wash. Boston was reckoned the second port of England in the early thirteenth century and by the end of it, the first. The memorial slab in the church floor of one Wisselus from Munster in Germany points up the commercial relations of the Middle Ages, when Boston was also trading with Norway and Denmark, the Low Countries and France, and with Mediterranean countries, too, in wool, grain, hides, fish, and lead from mines in Derbyshire that roofed castles and cathedrals in southern England and northern France. Flooding and silting of the River Witham induced a long decline in Boston's fortunes from the fifteenth century, which is one reason why there is a Boston, Massachusetts; but trade revived with the opening of the Grand Sluice in 1766 and deepening of the river. It was further revived by the coming of the railways, with new docks in 1882 and the cutting of a straight channel through to the Wash: Boston is a thriving port today.

From Boston north to Skegness, the road runs 2 to 3 km inland in a landscape so flat that, despite its proximity, you can't see the sea over the marshes: the coastal waters of the Wash are dangerous here in the region of the Wrangle and Friskney Flats with Wainfleet Sand at the end of them, where the Wash meets the North Sea at Gibraltar Point. The farmland around Friskney village has largely been reclaimed, by the progressive advance of dykes and sea-banks since the early nineteenth century. In the area north of Wainfleet All Saints, the Romans extracted salt: a network of inland waterways was maintained by them from the Wash through Lincolnshire to Yorkshire. Skegness stands on the sea, if sometimes rather a long way from it at low tide, to the north of the nature reserve on the spit of Gibraltar Point: the town went like so many others from fishing village to holiday resort in the nineteenth century. A run of seaside towns follows to the north and the coastline here is often one of constantly changing sandbanks under the impact of sea and wind, rather like its counterparts across the North Sea to the north-east on the coast of Jutland. Out to sea to the east of Cleethorpes stands Bull Sand Fort, and nearer in is Haile Sand Fort – submarines patrolled between them in

World War II to guard the entrance to the Humber, which we are now approaching.

Cleethorpes merges into Grimsby, whose raison d'être was always fishing – on a grand scale once – but which has also been a commercial port with links to Denmark for the import of dairy produce and bacon. Along the south bank of the Humber Estuary is Immingham from which the Pilgrim Fathers set off to Holland in 1608 on their way to America: it is now a huge commercial port and industrial complex handling oil, chemicals, fertiliser, and iron ore. Just south-west of Barrow upon Humber (which has the mound of a Norman castle), the road approaches the wide-spanning Humber suspension bridge of 1981: in the midst of all the modernity Barton upon Humber has one of the best preserved Saxon churches in the country. After the Norman Conquest, the Northumbrian Saxons were aided in their opposition to William the Conqueror's rule by the Danes, who brought 240 ships into the Humber in 1069 under Svein. The Humber Bridge leads, like the Humber Estuary, to Hull: named for the River Hull which comes into the Humber Estuary through the town via a defensive moat of 1321. The Hull still affords a harbour for barges and coasters, with a surge barrier at its mouth to prevent flooding of the town. The associated docks of the late eighteenth and nineteenth centuries have been filled in and superseded by the 10 km waterfront of the modern docks (with ferry terminal for the Low Countries) which constitute the world's largest fishing port now working. Hull also features the comprehensive aquarium called The Deep.

North-west to the Tees

East from Hull to Spurn Head, the village of Kilnsea has one side on the wild North Sea and the other on the sheltered Humber Estuary. Erosion operates on the sea side, as part of the process that maintains the narrow spit of sand called Spurn Head, curving 5 km like a hook into the mouth of the Humber opposite Cleethorpes. It is built of sand fetched down the coast from the north and silt from the Humber – only 50 m or so wide in places and sometimes breached by the sea, only to be built up again.

The coastal zone of the North Sea, so far on our way up the eastern side of Britain, is lowland backed by no great elevation of ground except for the Lincolnshire Wolds. The lowlands continue north, inland from the Humber

Estuary up into the Vale of York, but between them and the sea the terrain becomes more hilly now with the Yorkshire Wolds and then the Yorkshire Moors. From there on, we are back in a highland zone of the sort we have not seen since we reached southern Scandinavia on our way down the eastern coasts of the North Sea. Along the coast north from Spurn Head, the Easington Gas Terminal is the place where North Sea gas was first piped ashore in 1967. The coast continues north in a smooth sweep to Bridlington Bay with constant erosional losses of the mud cliffs along the way. To the west, further inland than we usually venture on this tour, is Wetwang, worth notice for its Iron Age chariot burial (with a skeleton between two large wheels, looking for all the world like a man on a bicycle) which is one of several from the distinctive pre-Roman Iron Age of this eastern part of Yorkshire.

Sticking out into the North Sea north of Bridlington is Flamborough Head, a turf-covered plateau some 45 m high with the sea on three sides of it. The Dane's Dyke runs north-south across it, defending it from the mainland side. The Danes were here from the ninth century, but they didn't dig this dyke: flint arrowheads show it to be of Bronze Age date or earlier. There are stone-built burial monuments of the Neolithic Period inland, reflecting our arrival in a more highland zone capable of supplying the stone for such constructions. Thornwick Bay with its sea caves and the bird-haunted Bempton cliffs follow along the coast. There are seaside resorts at Filey and, famously, at Scarborough, which also has a medieval castle and the foundations of a Roman signal station on the crag that divides its two bays. Scarborough was a Viking stronghold, too; it was a wealthy merchant town in the eighteenth century and still thrives as an inshore fishing port. There was another Roman signal station on the Old Peak headland at Ravenscar to the north, at the southern end of Robin Hood's Bay. Any association with Robin Hood is doubtful, but the village of Robin Hood's Bay was a notable eighteenth-century smuggling centre, with secret doors and tunnels interconnecting its houses.

Whitby was a whaling town in the eighteenth and nineteenth centuries, and Captain Cook's three ships were built in its harbour which is overlooked by the impressive ruins of the Abbey. Whitby jet was used to make ornaments from Bronze Age through Roman to Victorian times, and prized as a charm against witchcraft in the Middle Ages: this 'jet' is fossilised wood, chemically altered in stagnant water and then subjected to pressure, a sort of equivalent of the amber from the Jutland coast. Inland to the south of Whitby is the site of Star Carr, of the Mesolithic Period when the pre-farming hunter-fishers of ten thousand years ago could still follow the coastline of their day all the way across the North Sea to the base of Jutland. Nearby Seamer Carr has even older archaeological material going back to a late phase of the Palaeolithic or Old Stone Age. On the present-day coast, picturesque villages and little harbours take us north to the most picturesque of them all at Staithes with its houses on the steep sides of its gorge. Boulby to the north has the highest cliffs of England's east coast, up to 200 m high, while Hummersea Scar's cliffs are broken by a man-made harbour channel for the trade in alum which was mined from them from the seventeenth to the late eighteenth centuries, for dying wool (blue), tanning leather and sizing paper. Iron ore was also mined along this coast. There are more fishing villages on the way to Tees Bay and the estuary of the Tees, where boats are beached with rusting tractors just as they are along the North Norfolk coast.

Tees, Tyne, Tweed

In the mouth of the estuary of the Tees, Seal Sands is an area of land reclaimed from the waters where a vast industrial area of oil refineries and chemical storage tanks sits. Middlesborough is some way inland on the southern bank of the upper reaches of the estuary, with Stockton-on-Tees and Darlington further west, where the world's first railway was run. Hartlepool, at the northern end of its bay, retains a stretch of its medieval wall with an archway leading to the beach: Crusader knights set out from here to harry the eastern Mediterranean. A 20 km stretch of coastal coal mines around Seaham runs north from here, recalling the old coaster coal trade down the eastern side of England. Sunderland stands on the mouth of the Wear, a port for a thousand years and long-time centre of shipbuilding – its St Peter's Church of 674 has a Saxon wall and tower. South Shields goes back further still, with its Roman granaries to supply the Empire's forces in the north: a memorial to his British wife was set up here by a Roman merchant all the way from Palmyra in Syria. Oil tanks overlook the little church at Jarrow that stands beside the monastic ruins where Bede wrote his *Ecclesiastical History of the English People* in 685: this is the written source for the story of the Anglo-Saxon peopling of Britain; there is a very good museum.

Shipbuilding is on the up again on the Tyne, where once two-thirds of the world's shipping was constructed. Inland on the Tyne is Newcastle, prodigious for its bridges across the river and one of Britain's top ports for industrial exports in the past, when its surrounding countryside was full of the coal, iron and steel works whose products it handled. Newcastle's shipbuilding achievements include the construction of the world's first steam turbine ship, *Turbinia*, in the early twentieth century. Steep flights of steps lead between timbered warehouses of the seventeenth century to the enclosure of the twelfth-century castle, with its 25 m high keep, while the Victorian town centre is one of England's finest: the old Baltic trade complex has recently been converted into a grand art gallery. Surviving lengths of Hadrian's Wall, built across the country by the Romans to control the northern frontier zone of their empire, begin in the outskirts of Newcastle to the west, though the wall reached further east to Wallsend on the Tyne Estuary. Back on the North Sea coast at Tynemouth, the remains of an eleventh-century priory mark the site of an Anglo-Saxon monastery abandoned under Viking threat in the mid ninth century. Past Whitley Bay, Seaton Sluice had a seventeenth-century harbour for the export of coal and salt. Newbiggin-by-the-Sea resembles Dunwich on the Suffolk coast in showing the coastal erosion of a cemetery, only here the bones have been powdered into a coarse white sand among the rocks. Northwards brings more evidence of coal mining and its waste tips, and then the extensive sands of Druridge Bay. To the north again and about 1 km inland stands Warkworth Castle, where Harry Hotspur was born, and there is a fourteenth-century castle at Dunstanburgh, on the coast. What looks with its round towers like yet another fortress by the sea, at Beadnell further up the coast, is not a castle but actually eighteenth-century limekilns.

Bamburgh has one of England's most striking castles, towering over the community: its origins go back to the Anglo-Saxon kings of Northumbria and it was assaulted by the Danish Vikings; what we see now is its twelfth-century keep and a lot of late nineteenth- and early twentieth-century rebuilding. Off Bamburgh by between 2 and 7 km lie the Farne Islands, about twenty-eight of them in all and half of them submerged at high tide. The largest and closest to shore is Farne Island itself, associated with St Cuthbert, who was Prior of Lindisfarne to the north. He retired to Farne Island isolation in 676 and eventually died there in 687, but his body was taken to Durham during Viking disturbances. Lindisfarne is Holy Island, cut off for up to half of each day from the mainland and becoming for the other half the tip of a wide peninsula. Aidan, from Iona off the west coast of Scotland, founded a monastery on Holy Island in 634 at the request of King Oswald of Northumbria – it was destroyed by the Vikings in the ninth century, but the seventh-century illuminated *Lindisfarne Gospels* survived and are now in the British Museum in London.

Berwick-upon-Tweed stands on the south-pointing peninsula between the North Sea and the River Tweed: in the Middle Ages it passed continually between England and Scotland and has ended up as an English town north of the river that forms a natural border between the two countries. It became English for good in 1482, but only 4 or 5 km to the north, with Marshall Meadows Bay, we are in Scotland.

From the border to the capital

Burnmouth and Eyemouth lost fishing boats and men in a great storm that came out of a clear sky one October day in 1881. Eyemouth in particular was the place the Scottish fisher lasses came from – so well-known in Yarmouth in the nineteenth and early twentieth centuries – who followed the herring between May and November from the Shetlands to Norfolk, cleaning and barrelling the fish. Going north, the coast turns west after St Abb's Head to reach Coldingham Loch at whose northern tip there was an Iron Age settlement. The priory in Coldingham is a good indicator of the changing fortunes of this border area – sacked, burned down and blown up at various times by one side or the other. At Dunbar, some 30 km along, Edward I of England defeated John Baliol of Scotland in 1292 and Cromwell got the better of a Royalist force in 1650: it's very much on the invasion route from England to Scotland. The Ironsides took Tantallon Castle to the north of Dunbar in 1651 and the castle makes a magnificent ruin on its 30 m high promontory over the sea; 3 km offshore rises the 100 m tall Bass Rock, a sheer-sided volcanic core with lighthouse and seabirds. Another volcanic hill, Berwick Law, looms nearly 200 m high behind the town of North Berwick, on the south side of the wide opening to the Firth of Forth: this law makes an ideal lookout to survey the Firth and was used as such during the Napoleonic Wars.

Westward along the southern side of the Firth of Forth takes us past fishing ports like Port Seton and Cockenzie, with Prestonpans close by where

Prince Edward Stuart enjoyed his one victory of the Jacobean uprising of 1745. The name of the place comes from the exploitation of salt pans in the region from the twelfth century – later on, it was a coal mining area. Musselburgh was a Roman port with a fort at Inveresk to its south, in the days when the Romans maintained their more northerly frontier on the Antonine Wall across from the Firth of Forth to the Firth of Clyde. The sandy coast at Portobello to the west is Edinburgh's seaside, as Leith further along is Edinburgh's port and a part of the city since the 1920s. In keeping with its long history of commerce with the Low Countries, Leith's buildings sometimes recall Antwerp and Bruges. The city of Edinburgh lies inland to the south, long the capital of Scotland (if not always in name in the past) and now with its own seat of government again for the first time since the Union with England of 1707. To the west of Edinburgh, Cramond on the estuary of the Almond was the site of a Roman harbour and supply base for the Antonine Wall.

Historical detour

The Romans retreated south to Hadrian's Wall from the end of the second century AD and the various northern tribes, particularly the Picts, went on to cause them increasing trouble in the following two centuries. The Picts were themselves supplanted after the Romans left Britain by the Scotti from the region around the northern end of the Irish Sea. The later Anglo-Saxon kings of England had enjoyed a degree of loose overlordship all over the British Isles (in which their naval fleet played an important role), but their Norman successors rather lost that in their inevitable concentration on their relations with northern France. After the Norman Conquest of England, the Norwegians were still in possession of the Western Isles of Scotland and the Northern Isles, to which we shall come at the end of this tour of North Sea coastlines. Indeed, if Denmark and Norway had not been reduced to civil wars in the late eleventh century, the Normans' grip on their new kingdom would have been a good deal less secure. (As it was, the Danes were in the Thames in 1070 and William was, in fact, the last English king to pay the Danegeld.) The Norwegians interfered in the Irish Sea in the thirteenth century with some very big ships, but were defeated by the Scots who took the Isle of Man and the Hebrides from them into their own, now well-established, kingdom of Scotland. The Scots allied themselves with France,

England's enemy, which led to an English attack on Scotland in 1304 with the aid of ships brought up the east coast of England into what the English at the time were calling the 'Scottish Sea'. (The ships carried prefabricated bridges with which to cross the River Forth, sent up from Lynn on the Wash.)

A subsequent treaty between England and France drove the Scots into alliance with England's erstwhile allies in Flanders and Flemish ships harassed English shipping and fishing off East Anglia. The English lost ground in Scotland and were defeated at Bannockburn in 1314, after which a Scottish naval blockade took Berwick-upon-Tweed in 1318. The English were back on the attack in 1333 and took over the Lowlands as far as the Clyde-Forth line (more or less where the Romans had tried to maintain their border), though without Galloway. There was a plan in the 1380s for the French to land a force in Scotland to help the Scots attack England (while the main French force would land in Kent): more than a thousand ships were assembled at Sluis, of which no less than seventy-two were required for the transport of a prefabricated fortress; but there were problems in Flanders and it all came to nothing, without resolving the trouble between Scotland and England. The Scots meanwhile brought the Lords of the Isles to heel in the north, building some big ships to fire on their coastal fortifications. In the time of Henry VIII of England, the Scots were allied with the Danes whose growing fleet was bigger than the English navy of the day. The Danes were currently in league with the Hanse, who controlled the Baltic trade. The Scots were counted among Henry's potential enemies and they did side with the French against him, though the death of James IV of Scotland at Flodden in 1512 reduced the threat. In 1522 during war between France and England, the Scots weighed in with some action down the east coast of England, but the French were defeated by the Holy Roman Empire with no great thanks to its ally, England.

Henry went on harassing Scotland and trying to keep its east coast ports isolated from French dealings. In 1544 the English attacked Scotland in force with ships chartered from Dutch and German ports, burning Edinburgh, but they were obliged to go home when the foreign crews wouldn't hazard their ships any further. Henry died three years later, leaving unsettled conflict with the Scots behind him. The English attacked again with naval support, but were forced back to Berwick with supply difficulties. In 1549, they withdrew from Scotland altogether and came to a peace in 1550. Scotland ran into its own internal troubles, which saw the Catholic Mary Queen of Scots fleeing to the tender mercies of Elizabeth I in England. On Elizabeth's death, the English kingdom went to Mary's Protestant son, James VI of Scotland and James I of England, who brought his country's Danish alliance with him to the benefit of England's Baltic trade upon which so many of the country's shipbuilding raw materials depended. It is interesting to note that it was at about this time that the Scots were noted for their pioneering concept of territorial waters, having long taxed foreign fishermen in their firths and sea lochs. The Hanse were treating the access to the Baltic in the same way, but more on the basis of power than any legal concept of territoriality. The English would get into trouble with the Dutch in Stuart and Cromwellian times for doing the same in the Channel.

From Firth of Forth to Firth of Tay

The Firth of Forth is really a great inlet of the North Sea that narrows to the west of Edinburgh where the promontory of North Queensferry faces Queensferry on the southern side. Hereabouts the striking red-painted Forth Railway Bridge of the 1890s crosses the Firth of Forth, with the also spectacular Forth Road Bridge of 1964 to its west. Bo'ness further inland up the firth was a coal mining town and also a seaport and whaling base. In the early 1770s, James Watt built his first full-size steam pumping engine there, marking his eminent participation in the inauguration of the Steam Age, which was to have such an effect on the North Sea and its environs (as elsewhere round the globe) with steamers, steam fishing boats, railways, steam-driven factories, and steam warships. Further along to the west is Grangemouth, its great oil refinery signalling the replacement of steam power by a later technology. Upriver on the Forth by Stirling, nineteenth-century discoveries of the bones of marine life – including whale vertebrae – well away from the sea and well above sea level help to prove the phenom-enon of rising land levels in Scotland since the melting of the heavy ice cover of the last glaciation. Coming back along the Firth of Forth to the east on the northern side, we pass the coal mining area of Kincardine to reach Culross, a very picturesque seventeenth-century port town that once traded with the Low Countries and shows it in its red-pantiled buildings. Inland to the north-east is Dunfermline, which was the Scottish capital for six centuries: Robert Bruce, the victor of Bannockburn who made the English recognise him as king of Scotland in 1328, is buried in the Abbey. It was founded on the inspiration of an English princess who married Malcolm Canmore of Scotland in 1070. South of Dunfermline on the coast is the site of one of the greatest British naval bases, at Rosyth.

Back out on the wide open part of the Firth of Forth, Burntisland marks the place where the Roman general Agricola landed troops as part of his empire's conquest of Britain in the first century AD, and where naval convoys mustered in World War II. Further along at East Wemyss, caves in the rocky shoreline provide evidence of human presence from the Bronze Age to the Middle Ages. There are Pictish carvings and a rough-and-ready Viking representation of Thor with his hammer. Right out of the Firth of Forth and back on the North Sea proper, we pass along an occasionally sandy but mostly rocky coastline with old fishing villages and ports. Anstruther has its Scottish Fisheries Museum. Seven kilometres offshore lies the Isle of May with its cliff-top lighthouses and its priory over the grave of a saint murdered by the Vikings in 870. Fife Ness marks the coast's turn to the north-west towards St Andrews, of the famous university and golf courses. It is still an essentially medieval city, scene of religious strife that involved the robbery of the fabric of both its cathedral and castle in the past. North past Leuchars and its RAF base, the Firth of Tay opens up, with Perth well away from the North Sea to the west and Dundee on its northern side. Dundee is an old royal burgh and whaling town with docks on a grand scale, the whole place centred round the volcanic rock called Dundee Law in its midst. From its top, wide views take in the Tay Railway Bridge that replaced its predecessor after the disaster of 1879: the centre span went down with engine, six coaches and seventy-five people. Newburgh towards the western end of the Firth of Tay, having been founded by the English king Edward III in 1266, distinguished itself as the headquarters of the Inquisition in Scotland.

Towards the Moray Firth

Out of the Firth of Tay to the north, we are headed only a little to the east of north along a coast of rocks, cliffs and seabirds, sandy bays and fishing harbours. Arbroath is famous for its 'Smokies', haddock cured over a hardwood chip fire. It was the scene in 1320 of an assembly of Scottish nobles under Bruce, to assert the independence of Scotland from all English interference: the Declaration of Arbroath. Eighteen kilometres offshore, the Bell Rock lighthouse warns of the Inchcape Reef, where so many ships have been lost. At the mouth of the South Esk, with a large tidal basin behind it, Montrose is a port and oil industry service centre. Past the fourteenth-century Dunnottar Castle, dramatic on its promontory where there are also Pictish remains, lies the seaside town of Stonehaven. Fishing villages and former fishing villages continue up the coast to Aberdeen: the granite-built seaside and fishing town that has played such a huge part in the oil industry. Going north again takes us along one of the most extensive sandy beaches in Britain past Balmedie, a coastline not unlike that of Jutland across the North Sea in its Sahara-like pattern of shifting sands, which have submerged Iron Age and medieval communities in their time. Cruden Bay lies to the north, where the oil pipeline comes ashore from the Forties field out in the North Sea. Peterhead was once Scotland's premier whaling port and is now an oil industry base, with some fishing still going on. To the north stands the St Fergus Gas Terminal, with gas pipes running north-east to the Brent and Frigg fields.

Another place of many shipwrecks – the reef of Rattray Briggs – is marked by the lighthouse at Rattray Head, after which the way turns north-west and then west along a picturesque and sometimes dramatic coastline with cliffs and caves, on pretty much the latitude of the northern shore of the Skagerrak across the North Sea. There are fishing villages along the coast and the fishing port of Fraserburgh: to its south inland a few kilometres stands Memsie Cairn and 10 km to its south-east the Berrybrae stone circle, within sight of the sea – both are monuments from the Bronze Age. Rosehearty was a seaport from the time of the Viking raids, once important for its fishing but no longer on a commercial scale. Banff was a Hanse town in the twelfth century and later on a fishing port, till the harbour silted up in the nineteenth century (to be dredged again in the late twentieth century). Portsoy to the west was likewise a busy port at one time, that now has restored seventeenth- and eighteenth-century warehouses at its harbour.

We are travelling west now along the southern shore of the Moray Firth, past Portknockie which goes back to the Iron Age and has the remains of a seventh-century Pictish fort, and past more fishing and ex-fishing (and smuggling) places, both villages and larger towns. Buckie's local community runs a Fishing Heritage Museum, and there's a tourism project called The Drifter that aims to interest visitors in the old fishing way of life. The Spey flows north into the firth at Spey Bay, where salmon fishing goes on and there is a restored ice-house built for the storage of the catch. Kingston and Garmouth to the west across from Spey Bay were shipbuilding communities in the age of wooden ships, using logs floated down the Spey from the inland forests. Lossiemouth is the port of Elgin (some 8 km inland) while Burghead at the eastern end of Burghead Bay was once a great port for the shipment of grain – there was an Iron Age fort on the end of its promontory. Findhorn, also once a port and now a place for sailing at the other end of the bay, is the third settlement more or less on its site: its predecessor was wrecked by floods in 1701 and the one before that was buried beneath the sands in the course of violent storms in the seventeenth century. The same thing happened at Culbin to the west, which became 'The Scottish Sahara' until forests grew up on it.

To Culloden Moor

To the south of Findhorn is the large tidal basin of Findhorn Bay with the town of Forres to the south-west of that – between them stands the mysterious Sueno's Stone, 7 m high, carved with warriors and headless corpses in evident commemoration of some ancient conflict of date unknown. Nearby is the Witches Stone where unfortunate women were judicially murdered in the seventeenth century. Nairn, to the south-west of Culbin Forest, was a fishing port that has turned to oil, with a harbour for pleasure boats. To the west again, on a northerly promontory beyond Whiteness Head, stands Fort George, one of the best examples of an eighteenth-century artillery fortress in Europe, built after the defeat of the 1745 uprising. South-west of there, a couple of kilometres inland from the Moray Firth, is the site of the Battle of Culloden – the last battle on British soil – which put an end to Stuart hopes in Scotland, and England, in 1746. The Duke of Cumberland defeated Prince Charles Edward on what was then open moorland but is now rather more forested. Just to the south of the site of Culloden stand some monuments far remoter from the duke and the prince and their troubles than we are: the Clava Cairns, monuments of the first farmers in this part of the world. A wooden house going back to some 3700 BC predated by perhaps a thousand years the building of a ring cairn over its site. As well as low ring cairns with open spaces in the middle there are passage graves where an earth mound once went right over the whole interior of the structure, reached by an entrance passage. The mounds and cairns had kerb stones around them and, in some cases, circles of standing stones, too.

Inverness at the end of the firth got its first stone castle in the twelfth century AD and the city's clock tower is the last remaining part of a fort built by Cromwell's forces in the course of their operations in Scotland. The River Ness reaches the sea through Inverness and connects via the Caledonian Canal to Loch Ness at the eastern end of the Great Glen. To the east of Inverness, on the Beauly Firth that continues the Moray Firth inland, the 180 m high hill called Craig Phadrig has a 'vitrified fort' of the Iron Age: one of several such, where something like a fire in a chimney took place on a scale to melt stone. It is supposed to have been the stronghold of the Pictish king Brude who was visited by St Columba in 565.

North-east to John o' Groats

North of the Beauly and Moray Firths is an area known as The Black Isle, which is actually a peninsula between these firths and Cromarty Firth. The people of the little fishing village of Avoch on the Black Isle's southern shore claim descent from Spaniards wrecked here in the aftermath of the Armada débâcle. Cromarty itself is just inside the mouth of its firth, facing north with a bay to its west in a manner reminiscent of the situation of Harwich at the mouth of the Orwell and Stour in East Anglia. The natural harbour formed by the first section of the firth was a naval anchorage in both World Wars of the twentieth century, centred on Invergordon, with gun emplacements guarding the mouth of the firth on the headlands of North and South Sutor. Dingwall at the eastern end of the firth was a Viking settlement; at the western end on the north bank, Nigg Ferry is the scene of oil platform construction. The next firth to the north, opening beyond the low promontory of Tarbat Ness with its lighthouse, is Dornoch Firth. On its southern shore at Tain are the remains of a chapel founded by St Duthus in around AD 1000 and the cathedral where his own remains became the focus of a pilgrimage in the fourteenth century. Further west at Edderton stands a 3 m tall Pictish stone in memory of a fight with Vikings and, nearby, some Bronze Age burial places. Dornoch is at the northern end of its firth's mouth, with a cathedral started in 1224 and the tower of its old castle still standing.

We are on the final north-eastern run of coast along the North Sea before the land turns west at the top of mainland Scotland. Near Brora there stand two Iron Age brochs, those tower-like homesteads built from a few centuries BC until about AD 100, with hollow double walls and living space inside: the one about 5 km north of the village is nearly 10 m across. A little further north, the Wolf Stone marks the spot where Scotland's last wild wolf was shot around 1700. Further along the coast again, the natural bastion of the Ord of Caithness rises to well over 200 m. Past more fishing villages and castles, with the occasional Iron Age broch and Bronze Age standing stone, we come to Wick on the river of the same name, which is probably linked linguistically to the Vikings who had a settlement here. Beyond Noss Head and Sinclair's Bay, lowish cliffs run to Duncansby Head, with its lighthouse to signal the entrance of the treacherous Pentland Firth. Here red sandstone cliffs are pounded by the waves into arches, chasms, stacks.

John o' Groats on Duncansby Head is Britain's most northerly mainland habitation, though the unpeopled Dunnet Head to the west is the absolutely most northerly mainland spot. John o' Groats got its name, only a bit garbled, from a Dutchman commissioned by James IV in 1496 to run a ferry service to Orkney, newly acquired from the Norwegians: his name was Jan de Groot. South of Dunnet Head, Castletown and its harbour were at the centre of the nineteenth-century production and export of flagstones, and so was Thurso to the west, Britain's most northerly mainland town. It is from Scrabster, just around Thurso Bay, that the boats go to Stromness on Orkney today (and Bergen on the coast of Norway, too, among other places). Orkney, and the Shetland Islands to their north-east, take us back out into the North Sea, in the direction of Norway where we began.

Map 14 From Aberdeen to the Shetland Islands

Chapter 16

Journey's end: unending saga

T he great body of water that constitutes the North Sea narrows almost to the point of closure in the east where it meets the Baltic, and again in the south where it meets the Channel. Only along its northern edge is there open water to other seas and oceans, and even here a string of islands extends halfway across the opening.

Orkney

The most southerly parts of the Orkney Islands reach to within 15 km or so of the British mainland, but the ferry from Scrabster goes to Stromness on the main island, or 'Mainland', of Orkney – past the island of Hoy and the 130 m tall stack called The Old Man of Hoy. (The sea cliff of St John's Head nearby is 300 m high.) Behind Hoy and in the midst, as it were, of Hoy, Mainland and South Ronaldsay is Scapa Flow, from where the British Grand Fleet sailed in 1916 to the sea battle of Jutland and where, in 1919, the German High Seas Fleet of seventy-four ships scuttled itself in protest at the Versailles Peace. Here, too, the *Royal Oak* was sunk in 1939 by a German submarine coming in through Holm Sound between Mainland and South Ronaldsay, which was thereafter sealed by the Churchill Barriers. The Churchill Causeway on top now links South Ronaldsay to the eastern part of Mainland Orkney. South Ronaldsay is archaeologically interesting for the megalithic tomb at Isbister, one of many neolithic monuments among the islands that make up Orkney. Hoy, incidentally, has its Martello towers, guarding Longhope Sound: like their counterparts in southern

England, they are of the era of the Napoleonic Wars and were built in this case in defence of a Baltic convoy assembly point. The island of Flotta that limits Scapa Flow on its south side is the terminal for an oil pipeline from the Piper field out in the North Sea to the east.

Stromness, where the boats come in to Mainland Orkney, is a very atmospheric one-street town – but it's a long street, with ample shops and with houses on its sea side that as often as not have little jetties of their own. Mainland has a rich archaeological heritage, including: the stone-built late neolithic village of Skara Brae, which ended up engulfed by sand in about 2500 BC; the Unstan chambered tomb, also of neolithic times; the even more impressive tomb of Maeshowe, with Viking graffiti scribbled on its stones thousands of years after its construction; the henges with standing stones called the Ring of Brodgar and the Stones of Stenness. All these neolithic monuments are ranged around the southern end of the Loch of Stenness. (There are other such groupings among the rest of the islands, possibly representing tribal or clan divisions in the remote era of the first farmers.) Mainland also has its Broch of Gurness of Pictish and then Viking occupation, its cathedral of the twelfth century at Kirkwall (the islands' capital), and its monument to Lord Kitchener, drowned on HMS *Hampshire* when she was sunk by a German mine in 1916.

Rousay to the north of Mainland has a megalithic tomb 30 m long, in which the bones of some twenty-five people were discovered who lived about five thousand years ago. There are the remains of a neolithic village here too, as well as a Viking ship burial and a Norwegian cemetery. Westray has a large Viking burial place and Papa Westray has neolithic houses at Knap of Howar, belonging to farming folk of about 3500 BC who also hunted and collected shellfish. Low-lying Sanday has the chambered tomb of Quoyness from about 3000 BC. North Ronaldsay is the most northerly of the Orkney Islands, with an Iron Age broch.

Shetland

Between Orkney and the Shetland Islands lies Fair Isle, 40 km south of Shetland Mainland from which it is possible to go by air and sea to reach it. (Shetland itself is reached from Aberdeen.) The complex patterns of the famous Fair Isle knitwear have been attributed, probably unfairly as far as the Fair Isle folk are concerned, to survivors of the Armada. Mainland

Shetland's southernmost tip is the site of Jarlshof, with human occupation from neolithic to Viking times: the mound of an Iron Age broch with seven bays stands besides the remains of Norse longhouses of the ninth century AD. (The Jarlshof name is curious for being an invention of Sir Walter Scott's in the nineteenth century.) On the little St Ninian's Isle, west off the Mainland promontory north of Jarlshof, a treasure in silver was found that dates to about AD 800 and so must have been buried to keep it safe from Viking raids. The island of Mousa on the eastern side of the promontory has a magnificent broch, 13 m high, the tallest building to have survived from pre-Roman times in Britain.

The capital of Shetland is Lerwick, settled by Dutch people in the seventeenth century and a prosperous fishing port from then on. On the last Tuesday of January each year a 9 m long replica of a Viking boat has been traditionally hauled through the streets and burned for the fire festival of Up-Helly-Aa, an eighteenth-century reworking of an old Norse feast. To the north of Lerwick, there are neolithic settlements and a burial site. At the top of this main island of Shetland, Yell Sound leads into Sullom Voe, and its great oil pipeline terminal, receiving oil from the fields out in the North Sea to the north-east. Yell is the second largest of the Shetland Islands, with rolling peat hills like all the rest except for Unst, the most northerly, which has the densest population of Shetland ponies. Fishing holds up as a major economic factor in the Shetlands economy.

Shetland lies about 180 km from the northern coast of mainland Scotland: at less than the same distance again to the north-east of Shetland is the East Shetlands Basin where the North Sea's northernmost oilfields – including Ninian, Brent and Statfjord – are located. These oilfields, on the border of territorial waters between Britain and Norway, may be seen as continuing an imaginary line across from, say, Duncansby Head in Scotland to Sognefjord in Norway that closes the North Sea on the northern edge of its rhomboid. Aptly enough, both the Northern Isles and the southern Norwegian coast, with the modernity of the oil industry in common between them, are places also of great human antiquity with archaeology going back to the Stone Age, soon after the end of the last glaciation and the formation of the North Sea.

All the countries around the North Sea have a common history, with constant interchange between them from the earliest times – as this book and its tour of the North Sea coasts are intended to demonstrate. That interchange will intensify in the context of modern communications and interdependent economies. All save one – Norway – are member countries of the European Union, and Norway has made its accommodations. Of the eight countries around the North Sea (maybe there will be officially nine one day with a truly independent Scotland), half of them already share a common currency. Will the North Sea, which has had so many names in the past, become in the not-so-distant future *Mare Europaeum*, the European Sea?

Meanwhile, North Sea oil and gas will not last for very much longer, fish will continue to decline and recovery – if and when it comes – will be slow; global warming and pollution will continue to modify the North Sea scene and perhaps, in the end, seismic catastrophe or a return to the ice age will alter it altogether. Short of such drastic changes, technology will bring us better ships under navigation by ever more sophisticated means, carrying goods and people as economics and fashion dictate. Like the archaeological and historical study of the rest of the globe, our North Sea Saga emphasises above all else the progress of technology. Arts, religions, social organisations come and go and they are all ultimately subject to the promptings and con-straints of technology as the basis for social subsistence: it is only in the technological sphere that a clear line of development from lesser to ever greater capacity is indisputably evident. The progression of boats is as vivid an example as any other – from paddled dugouts and skin-clad umiaks to bigger plank-sided vessels with oars and sails to huge wooden ships with elaborate sailing arrays to steamers and oil-fired leviathans of steel. Who knows where it will end? It has certainly been a very short and rapid course so far: only ten thousand years ago people were paddling around the creeks of the postglacial world in log boats, with nothing in sight like the North Sea whose history and geography we have been exploring in this book.

So long as the North Sea lasts as a body of navigable water, perhaps enlarged by global warning in the short run, and so long as human life is maintained around it in some form, this sea will go on as both barrier and highway in human affairs: more of a highway than a barrier while techno-logical progress continues, more of a barrier if it falters. The North Sea remains north-west Europe's home waters, and its seaway in and out and to and from everywhere else. It seems unlikely that air transport will ever wholly overtake carriage by sea for the world's bulkiest goods. The North Sea is no longer northern Europe's self-contained nexus of international relations (it started to lose that status a long time ago) but unless and until it ices over again or civilisation collapses around its margins, it will continue to be the busy scene of commercial – not least tourist – interchange in one of the world's historically most thriving and progressive zones.

Further reading

Bahn, P.G., *The Atlas of World Archaeology* (London: Time-Life Books, 2001).

Bang-Andersen, A., Greenhill, B. and Grude, E.H., Eds. *The North Sea* (Oslo: Norwegian University Press, 1985).

Boklund-Lagopoulon, K. *et al.*, *The North Sea World: Studies in the Cultural History of North-west Europe in the Middle Ages* (London: Four Courts Press, 2001).

Cunliffe, B., Ed., *The Oxford Illustrated Prehistory of Europe* (Oxford: Oxford University Press, 1994).

Cunliffe, B. *et al.*, *The Penguin Atlas of British and Irish History* (London: Penguin Books Ltd, 2001).

Ekman, M., *Destination Viking: the Western Viking Route* (Gotland: North Sea Viking Legacy, 2001).

Friel, I., *The Good Ship: Ships, Shipbuilding and Technology in England 1200–1520* (Baltimore: Johns Hopkins University Press, 1995).

Grimson, G., *North Sea Coasts of England* (London: Hale, 1976).

Hardisty, J., *The British Seas* (London: Routledge, 1990).

Heywood, J., *Dark Age Naval Power* (London: Routledge, 1991).

Hunter, J. and Ralston, I., Eds., *The Archaeology of Britain* (London: Routledge, 1999).

Hutchinson, G., *Mediaeval Ships and Shipping* (Leicester: Leicester University Press, 1994).

Kirby, D., Hinkkanen, M.-L. and Scammell, G., *The Baltic and the North Seas* (London: Routledge, 2000).

Lamb, H., *Historic Storms of the North Sea* (Cambridge, UK: Cambridge University Press, 1991).

Lewis, A. and Runyon, T., *European Naval and Maritime History* (Bloomington: Indiana University Press, 1985).

Macinnes, A. *et al.*, *Ships, Guns and Bibles in the North Sea and Baltic States, 1350–1700* (Tickwell Press, 2000).

Magnusson M., *Vikings!* (London: The Bodley Head, 1980).

Mollat du Jardin, M., *Europe and the Sea* (Oxford: Blackwell, 1993).

Morrison, D. and Fergusson, C., *The North Sea in Perspective* (Wood Mackenzie and Co., 1979).

Roger, N.A.M., *The Safeguard of the Sea* (New York and London: W.W. Norton and Co., 1997).

Pryor, F., *Britain BC: Life in Britain and Ireland before the Romans* (London: Harper Collins, 2003).

Shennan, I. and Andrews, J., *Holocene Land-Ocean Interaction and Environmental Change around the North Sea* (London: Geological Society Publishing House, 2000).

de Souza, P., *Seafaring and Civilization* (London: Profile Books, 2001).

Wilson, D., *The Northern World: the History and Heritage of Northern Europe AD 400–1100* (London: Thames and Hudson, 1980).

Woodman, R., *The History of the Ship* (London: Conway Maritime Press, 1997).

Index

The Index includes the Introduction and Chapters 1–16. Maps and illustrations are indicated in *italics* after their page numbers eg North Sea, 8 *map*. The filing order is word-by-word and numbers are filed as if spelled out.